S0-AFQ-463

THE DEATH TRAIN

CHRISTIAN BERNADAC

THE DEATH TRAIN

FERNI PUBLISHING HOUSE

Translated from the French
by
S. Van Vliet White

THIS EDITION
IS RESERVED FOR
FRIENDS OF HISTORY

© by France-Empire, Paris 1970
© by Ferni Publishing House, Geneva 1978

TO THE "TRAVELERS" OF TRAIN 7909

TO YVON CHOTARD

Neither the bull nor the fig tree knows you,
Neither the horses nor the ants of your hearth.
Neither the child knows you, nor the slow dusk,
Because you are dead today and forever dead.

The soft back of the stone does not know you,
Nor does the black satin where you are torn.
The muted souvenir is gone from others' knowing,
Because you are dead today and forever dead.

The autumn will come with its grail-flowers,
Its graping of fog, and mountains shouldered together,
But no one will look to seek you in your eyes,
Because you are dead today and forever dead.

Because you are dead today and forever dead.
Like all the dead on and in the earth,
Like all the dead forgotten, to be forgotten
In a littered mound of dogs obliterated.

                                        Federico Garcia Lorca

A mask of dry blood covered his face. He had to keep rubbing his right eye to get the lids apart. His fingers slowly explored the deep wound on his temple. For a dazed few moments, he wondered what could have caused it.... Then sounds and images began to flow back into memory. He tried to speak:

"It was a bottle...a bottle just came flying at me...."

But no word took shape—no sound.

He wanted to scream. His throat swelled. Then a dry croak. A whistle of air. Nothing. His hands hesitated, moving over his lips, questioning the bruised, cracked, bursting lips. Grotesque lips, gigantic lips. Little by little the sweat started—again the sweat—dissolving the dried blood on his cheeks.

He was lying on his left side.

Cries, like wisps of fog, came to him from far away. The train stood still, the car was silent. His hand slid over his naked chest, rested on the ground found a knee, another hand, one...like fire, withdrew, shrank back, sought safety on his chest again. Fear made him tremble. His skin was soaked in sweat, and then suddenly became icy cold. In less than a second he went all the way from thirst, from hunger, contractions, itchings, and the tom-tom beat at the back of the skull, to an inner thunder that possessed him and tore him, but refused to explode. It would only explode for the weak, the mad, who didn't want to die.

The will blocked off the reflexes. His whole body, muscles, nerves, dimmed before his eyes. He was only an eye. A million facets on each globe. The pupils fractured the light. The eyes bloodshot and excited. For the first time since he had left, his eyes probed into the shadows, this dark haze that replaced the poor air of the cattle car, and now he could see the floor and now he could see the cadavers, tangled bodies. A floor of bodies. A bed of bodies, on which he slowly awoke.

André Gonzalès has lifted up his head. Half conscious, half unconscious, he becomes aware of this mattress of piled bodies. He is horrified. He'll have to step on them.... His fingers curl around a big hitching ring bolted to the metal wall. His arm strains as it tears at his chest, at his hips. His feet look for a place to stand against the iron wall. They slide and stop still between two naked legs. André Gonzalès is crying, crouched in the angle of the walls. He is suffocating. The sheet metal sides burn his skin. Suddenly he runs, lifting his knees high, and collapses against the sliding door. He drinks the air, breathes through the crack, teeth against metal. The air is turgid and thick. His mouth is agape.

His nostrils block with the stink of emptied intestines, bile and vomit, stinking, fetid, suffocating vapors.

Breathe. Relax. Breathe. Pray again. Don't look down. Breathe and drink. Drink something to dissolve the plaques hardening the tongue and coating the palate, deforming the lips.

André Gonzalès stood up, found his footing on the floor of slime, and unbuttoned his pants.

Drink!

The urine which he swallowed seemed cool and sweet. He had kneeled on a heavy-set back.

Don't faint. Don't sleep. If you lie down you'll die. Die at eighteen. André, you were eighteen years old yesterday. And the others. All the others who are under you.

How old were they? No. Don't think about that. Don't think about them. No!

He was astonished to have heard the final 'No.' He could talk! To make certain, he repeats the word, No! No! No!

Don't think about them. Just get out....

He was wearing short pants and rope sandals, he remembered. He was climbing from rock to rock with his classmates of the Saint-Udo school in Ax-les-Thermes. The instructor reached out his hand to help him leap over the final foothold. Too late. He splashed into the melted snow of the Ariège. The icy water shipped against his long, somewhat skinny adolescent body. These scenes, and others from his childhood crowded behind his eyes, gave back life and roused him out of his apathy. Now he was praying with that somewhat fearful fervor that the Brothers of the Christian Schools of Saint-Aubin at Toulouse had inculcated. He was crossing the fields, drinking from the rushing rivulets, bypassing the troops of horses and sheep coming down from the pastures of Puymorens and Andorra. The smell of cut hay, the sound of cow bells, and pervading it all, the strange perfume of sulfur and camomille which mounts from the basin of the Ladres and from the eighty-three alkaline springs of Ax. It was all mixed up and confused, and it flowed over onto the plane trees of the boulevard of Strasbourg, where he had been arrested, his pockets stuffed with political leaflets. That was on April 21, 1944.

He wept now, more anguished, more intense than the first tears, washing away everything, even the remembered face of his mother. His fist struck against the sliding door:

"Help! Water!"

An answering croak, almost inaudible, but nearby. He wanted to howl with joy. His heart pumped and stopped. He asked over and over:

"Is there someone there? Is there someone there?"

A dark shadow cut the slender beam of light from a split in the shuttered opening, forward and to the left. André Gonzalès clenched his teeth. He must avoid a shock, no matter what it cost. He thought: "Maybe he's

the bastard who knocked me out with a bottle." He
stepped back, crushing dead flesh with his feet, the
compressed chest cavities gave out a final rough whistle
of air.

"You're there. You're alive. I saw you. Say something."

He flattened himself in the corner, to the right, ready to
leap if he was attacked, ignoring the foul liquid in which
his hands groped.

"Say something!"

He could make out a form coming nearer; a disjointed
doll, reaching for balance. Three more steps. Two. The
shape collapsed and crumbled. A dull thud, the flat of a
shovel on sand.

Carefully, André Gonzalès took the man's head between
his hands. It was a boy, young like him. Maybe he was
eighteen years old too. His eyes looked up, two little
points of light in a face incredibly swollen and discolored,
running with sores.

"Water!"

"Poor kid, I don't have anything. You have to breathe.
Come on. We're going to the door. There's a split. Me, I
drank my own urine. Later on, you'll see...."

They crawl on hands and knees to the center of the
car.

"That's it. Go slow. Breathe deep. Fill up your lungs."

He turned toward André and gasped:

"Thanks. That's better. I've got a pal back there, where
I was.... He's not dead. Anyhow, a while back, when
I moved, he moved too, and I felt his fingers on
my leg."

"We'll both go over there, but first another breath of
oxygen."

Five minutes later the only three survivors of the metal
car stood together near the sliding door. The two
boys from the far corner drank their urine, like André
Gonzalès. The last to come to life was the most
talkative.

"They closed us up in here to kill us off. They're going
to ride us around until we all croak. In Compiègne they
packed one hundred of us into a single car. Here there
are only three of us left alive, and in the other cattle cars,
maybe they're all cooked already. They did it on purpose.

They wanted us to start fights. There's no air in here. That's on purpose too. I'm telling you: this train is the death train. Not one of us will get out of here alive. You see? *"The Death Train."*

FIRST PART

WAITING

1

Compiègne Royallieu

"It is at Compiègne that we will wipe out the 'shame of Compiègne.'"

Die Schande, the shame: Hitler was talking about the capitulation of Germany on November 11, 1918, to end the First World War. In the same railway car of the same Great European Express, General Huntziger, chief of the French delegation, gingerly lowered his ass onto the edge of the armchair where Foch had sat twenty-two years before. Meanwhile, in the center of the city, General Buckler's flame-throwers were attacking those buildings which the bombardments had left standing. Hadn't Hitler said a hundred times, "Compiègne shall be destroyed"?

Hitler was accompanied by Goering, Keitel, Raeder, Hess and Von Ribbentrop. He issued a final order before climbing back into his armored Mercedes: that the copper steps of the railway carriage should be sawed up and the pieces distributed as souvenirs to the soldiers who had avenged the German honor in the clearing and in this historic train; the commemorative monuments and the one hundred twelve flagstones of the Armistice were to be dispatched to Berlin as quickly as possible.

The choice of the city of Compiègne as the frontier station for the "levy"[1] and as the selection point for major deportations, should also be classified as part of the program of psychological warfare.

The little village of Royallieu (Royal Place), lying to the south of Compiègne, owes its name to Queen Adélaïde who, in 1153, on the plateau, built her great royal residence, which was destroyed by the English in the Fifteenth Century.

In 1914, the Ministry of War hastily decided to build, at Royallieu, a model training center for young recruits. The barracks and the camp remained practically unchanged until 1941[2]. In June of that year, Royallieu became a concentration camp, under the Security Service of the German Army (S.D.), with headquarters at 74, avenue Foch, Paris.

1. The Vichy government undertook to arrange for the repatriation of a French prisoner of war in exchange for each Frenchman who volunteered to go and work in Germany.
2. "During the First World War, the barracks of Royallieu housed the 54th Infantry Regiment and a military hospital. Except for the period from 1922 to 1925, when it was occupied by some Indochinese and Madagascan units, the barrack buildings were used, from 1919 to 1939 by a balloon corps and a battalion of the 67th I.R. During the 'phony war,' the barracks were transformed into a secondary evacuation hospital No. 7, the HOE 2 No. 7. As soon as they had taken over the city on June 9, 1940, the Germans interned all the British and French military personnel they had captured in the vast sixteen-hectare quadrilateral, called *Frontstalag 170 KN 654*, under the authority of Kommandant Solf. When the Nazis invaded Russia on June 22, 1941, the German camp command panicked. They had sent the prisoners out to work in local farms and offices, now they did their best to get them under lock and key. They succeeded in finding only about half of the prisoners; the other half had prudently returned to their homes."

The above is an excerpt from *Compiègne 1939-1945*, by André Poirmeur. (Imprimerie Telliez, Compiègne, 1968.) Available from the author: 62, rue de Paris, 60-Compiègne.

This book, by André Poirmeur, was the first study published on Compiègne and Royallieu during the Second World War. It is not a monograph, but a genuine and indispensable historical work for all who want to understand the concentration camp phenomenon.

The engineer corps and the prisoners assigned to weatherproof this square with sides about four hundred meters long, do not appear to have strained their imaginations. The work had a makeshift allure which lasted until the Liberation. The walls were raised on two sides and capped with iron and porcelain; on the other two sides, a wire fence was masked behind wooden planks to a height of three meters; fifteen watchtowers, which were nothing more than raised platforms with roofs; twenty sentry boxes; chicanes barred the roads and streets surrounding the camp. So much for the outside.

The inner security, (barbed wire and entanglement), delimited a forbidden zone eight meters wide, patrolled by watchmen and police dogs. Almost fifty-four thousand prisoners[1] poured through the twenty-four major barracks set in a horse-shoe around the impressive central courtyard[2].

If we are able to forget about the lists of deportees and hostages, Compiègne was, generally speaking, an almost happy interlude between the "prison you have just come from" and the "concentration camp where you are just going."

Organized completely on military lines: showers, medical visit, registration, search, confiscation of forbidden objects, mess tin, blanket, finger-prints, identity questioning, second medical visit, roll call, assignment to the barrack room, welcoming speech by the senior officer.... Hope revives.

1. Deportees to Germany 49,860
   Shot, massacred, disappeared 2,300
   Sick who died 300
   Victims of bombardments................... 75
   Transferred to other prisons and into the TODT
      organization 600
   Escaped 120
   Liberated 430
   Hospitalized at the liberation of the camp 100
   TOTAL................................. 53,785
                        (Inquiry by André Poirmeur)

2. The barracks measured 60 by 15 meters, and the courtyard, 230 by 160 meters.

"They wouldn't waste so much time and paper on us if we were going to leave tomorrow."

"And then we can play football."

"And then, there's the library."

"And then, lectures, chapel, packages, canteen...."

"And then, if you arrange things right, you can get a letter passed to the outside...."

"We're not so badly off here, in spite of Jaeger...."

Eric Jaeger, "the dog man," was the horror of Royallieu. There always has to be one. Sergeant major, a loudmouth, proud of the vacuum he created around himself. Tiny, his sharp glance frequently dimmed by alcohol. His only friends were Prado and Klodo, two enormous, faithful dogs, who were said, in June 1944, to have "eaten" at least fifteen prisoners...which turned out to have been the fact.

But the true master of Royallieu was an elegant captain, with a slightly feminine walk—peccary gloves, ivory cigarette holder with a golden band. The old-timers described him to the new arrivals as an agreeable pen-pusher without any particular character.

"He's got a cushy job. Besides, you won't be seeing much of him."

The Hauptsturmführer Illers, Captain Doctor Illers, was the eyes and ears of the S.D.[1] in the camp. His Paris office on the Boulevard Haussmann was the center for all the documents, files, card indexes, and he prepared four copies of the lists of departures for the concentration camps[2]. The final destination of the convoy was imparted, by word of mouth, only to the chief of transport. Nine times out of ten he was an S.D. officer. Illers, although an S.D. himself, and being only answerable to avenue Foch, in theory, accepted the "recommendations" dealing with this or that matter of registration. In the last analysis, it was up to him, after having consulted a "synthesis" of the matter, to inscribe, opposite each name on the list "to go," the indication of the category in which the con-

1. *Sicherheitsdienst:* Security Service of the German Army.
2. Prepared for: Convoy Chief; Commander of the camp of destination; Compiègne archives; and R.S.H.A. Oranienburg (Central Security Service of the Reich).

demned person is definitively classed. All of the prisoners wondered about the crosses following their names on the roll-call sheets...this code was never deciphered at Compiègne. All sorts of rumors circulated about it. Actually, it was rarely respected, except perhaps, in the case of the first convoys.[1]

1.   One cross: category 0. The prisoners have no rights at all, neither letters, nor packages.

Two crosses: category 1. One package per month. No correspondence.

Three crosses: category 2. Two packages, one letter per month.

Four crosses: category 3. Three packages, one visit, two letters per month.

One-cross and two-cross categories were assigned to work in mines and outdoor camps; the others to work camps.

The day following the Allied landing of June 6, the various police and security services of the Reich—in agreement for once—considered that the impressive number of prisoners they held in France, should, under no circumstances, be added to the fighting strength of the Allied Invasion Forces or that of the Resistance, but on the contrary, had to participate in the German war effort in the concentration camps.[1]

In this month of June, 1944, all the regions of France were represented at Compiègne, and there were even, curiously enough, "strays" of nineteen different nationalities. Naturally, most of them were Resistance Fighters, but also, there were several hundred hostages, people rounded up by chance, and common law criminals.

On June 18, the camp was emptied: 2,145 prisoners were embarked for Dachau. Those who were forgotten;

1. See Annexes: Arrivals at the camp at Compiègne in May and June 1944. Most of the deportees of July 2 reached Royallieu by these transports (Annex I).
 — Convoys leaving Compiègne (Annex II).
 — Number of convoys leaving France (Annex III).

those who were sick in the infirmary; those who were held in "reserve"; those who had committed serious offenses while waiting for judgment or a transfer; the useful ones, employed in administration or the kitchen; the favored ones, with soft jobs; the "pigeons"...who once again had escaped the long trip and were sure that they had seen the final convoy leave for Germany. The day passed. Sure tips glided through the barbed wire entanglements, brought in by the outside labor force, enough to trouble the most optimistic.

"They've requisitioned the trains from Paris-Bestiaux."

"That means another departure."

"In spite of the landing?"

"Yes, in spite of the landing."

"What about the bombardments?"

"In spite of the bombardments."

"In spite of the Resistance?"

"Yes, in spite of the Resistance."

"Ssshhh, quiet."

The sound of a whistle.

"Here comes the Dean, to bugger the boys in prison blues."

Whistle.

"Evacuate!"

"Evacuate! Evacuate! That's plumber's talk. Compiègne is a tank, all right. When the water level gets too low— Zouppp—the siphon-convoy goes to work."

"Then it's the Dean who pulls the chain."

"Shithouse Blues...."

Monsieur le Doyen, waxed *moustaches élégantes*, black beret, smartly tilted over the right ear, had opted for "loyal" collaboration. The Germans leaned heavily on the narrow shoulders of this captain of the French cavalry. They even slightly amended the internal regulations of the camp, for his benefit: "All the prisoners, without exception, must give a military salute to all officers, non-commissioned officers, and German soldiers"...to which Commandant Pelzer had added; "and the prisoners would be well-advised also to salute Monsieur le Doyen." Despite dozens of attempts, it had been impossible to get Captain D...to alter his views. Conscientious, mincing, sickly, he loved stylized commands and his silver whistle.

He was spineless and probably megalomaniac. He recited the welcoming speech to new arrivals in a colorless voice: Germany forever. Discipline. Work. Family. Fatherland.

The barracks chief translated this message in practical terms: "If you want to stay out of trouble, don't try to be too smart."

Dazed and bewildered, exhausted by prison life and the physical danger of travel over France's disrupted railway system, they arrive, they find each other again, they regroup, they settle in, and they hope.

"Where do you come from?"

"What's happening?"

Within a few hours of gleaning the news from the new arrivals, the old-timers could construct a general picture of how things were going throughout the territory.

Two groups were always the stars of this performance, without wanting to be: The *Tullistes*, and the *Eyssistes*.

One hundred thirty-six hostages, rounded up at Tulle, wretched, horror-stricken and anguished, they shuffled over the flinty gravel of Royallieu and kept asking, what final screening would condemn them or perhaps—why not?—would save them. On June 9, 1944, the day before the crime of Oradour-sur-Glane, and following upon the courageous, but premature attack by the patriotic front (F.T.P.) against the German garrison of Tulle, General Lammerding's S.S. troops organized the repression. They chose one hundred twenty "examples" from among the five thousand men of the locality for the first reprisal.

"The Maquis killed forty of our men in that attack. For each one of our dead, three terrorists will be hung."

Out of the one hundred twenty, ninety-nine were strung up from balconies and lamp-posts. More discussions, "national interests," friendships, ass-licking, sellouts, "As for me Sir, I have always served Germany well," silences, bargainings, prayers, submission, tears, falsified lists, heroism, scorn, "Long live Hitler," "bastards," "assassins,"—all contributed to making the next choices. Selection followed selection. Finally, three hundred eleven remained.

"You are going to be deported!"

Departure. Canvas-covered trucks. Unloading onto the sawdust of the stable of the former 21st Light Infantry of Limoges.

"Get up along the wall."

They could see the machine guns.

"We're going to be shot."

"Vive Hitler!"

"Me not Maquis. Me not terrorist."

"I'm a volunteer for the German Army."

"Me ready go Germany."

A prisoner calls for silence.

"They're going to execute us...all volunteers for Germany, please raise hands."

Some hands go up:

"Me."

"Vive Hitler!"

"Quitters, cowards, yellow-bellies! You should be shouting 'Vive la France!'"

A dozen men have fainted.

The militia: Another selection. One hundred sixty-two Tullistes liberated: one hundred forty-nine remained. They were given permission to lie down on the straw and soon they were joined by the prisoners from the Centrale de Limoges. At dawn they were all roused from cramped sleep, shoved into moving truck vans and driven off. They parked between the high walls in the courtyard of a commandeered building at Poitiers, and got caught in the flack of a British bombardment that was aimed at the station, and all the while held in check by the machine guns of the guards: now there were one hundred thirty-six. This sad remnant momentarily breathed again when they came to Compiègne.

"What will they do to us tomorrow?"

The adventure of the *Eyssistes* was different, and to emphasize the difference, the administration isolated them in a camp within the camp. They were "old cons," shaved heads, wooden shoes, rough prison clothes.

"They were ordinary prisoners, criminals, pimps, black market manipulators, double-dealing collaborators...."

It only took two days for the news to spread around Compiègne, and Compiègne reacted by taking up a collection of tobacco and food to send to the "heroes" of the prison of Eysses. The prisoners of Eysses were transmogrified into the men of Eysses, and each was pleased to acknowledge that they merited their new renown.

In October 1943, the massive buildings of the prison of Eysses, just outside of Villeneuve-sur-Lot, received several hundred political prisoners from the south zone, and among them, one hundred fifty prisoners from the Centrale de Nîmes. This nucleus of Resistants—Communists and Gaullists—became the founders and animators of the battalion of Eysses. It was a unique collective. It had its elected representatives, its parallel police, its military command, its study and relaxation circles, its radio station, its handwritten newspapers, its outside informers, its liaison agents, its weapons, but especially its own soul. These men learned to know each other, love, respect and help each other. They sought to be, and they succeeded in being, a unit. It was together, and always together, that they succeed in breaking their way out of the prison, escaped their pursuers, and formed an inspirational resistance force (Maquis), with one thousand two hundred fifty men and women under arms.

The liaison agent in charge of setting up an operation of armed support from the outside was blocked from completing the deal. The chief of the commando groups of Toulouse, who was supposed to turn over a large supply of munitions, learned that the confidential agent of the prisoners was a Communist, and refused to honor the promises that had been made by Serge Ravanel, the national leader of these commando groups. Now the prisoners could only count on themselves. On February 19, 1944, taking advantage of the visit of a representative of the collaborationist Vichy government, the Eysses collective went into battle. The battle lasted for twenty-five hours, twenty-five hours of heroic struggle against a vastly superior force. Twenty guns and fifty grenades against a militia force which, on February 21, numbered—three thousand men.

"If you surrender, none of you will be harmed."

That very evening, Joseph Darnand made plans for immediate repression. He selected fifty men as representative of the movement....An improvised "court martial" condemned twelve of them to death. They were executed by a firing squad of mobile guards. Thereafter, the one thousand two hundred prisoners and the thirty-six hostages "held over" were taken to Compiègne, the first group without delay, the others after a stay at Blois. These were the "thirty-six" that we found at Royallieu toward the end of June 1944. The rest of the battalion had already been sent to Dachau.

2

June 30

Maybe there were one hundred of them waiting for the canteen to open. One hundred hungry men.

"Has the Spaniard come by?"

"I haven't seen him."

The Spaniard went to all the markets in the region and collected the spoiled food—he was the only "fresh vegetable" supplier in Royallieu.

When Maurice Baltet slipped behind the counter, a brutal "No more carrots," shut him up.

"Maybe you have a nail file?"

"Oh, that, yes."

Maurice Baltet goes back to the courtyard:

"Some people do physical exercise to keep in shape.[1] I think they'd be better off saving their strength. There's no certain news about the Allied advance, however— Bourgoin, from Troyes, is using his wedding ring as a pendulum over the map of France we drew for him. It registers—an advance of troops."

In a tiny room of Building 8, Monseigneur Théas, the Bishop of Mountauban, celebrated mass for a dozen old

1. From an unpublished manuscript, May 1970.

campaigners. The day before, he had asked permission to officiate in the camp chapel, and had been refused. The German administration preferred not to know anything about these "confidential ceremonies," even when the Bishop chose, as the subject of his first official sermon in Compiègne—*Liberty*.

"Because it comes from God, the life of man is sacred, and requires to be respected by all. God created us free. Liberty is a gift of God. Hence it is sacred and must be respected by all."[1]

Two men knelt to pray on the cement, near the campaigners. The oldest, just turned fifty-three, was a garage mechanic from Lyons, Henri Chant. And Henri Chant was a Jew. He had been converted long before his arrest, and now he asked Mgr. Théas to baptize him. A few minutes before this prudent "private mass," he whispered to him:

"You'll be baptized this afternoon and will receive your first communion tomorrow. I should also tell you that a departure to Germany is planned for Sunday, and you'll be on the list."

And that day, the garagist from Lyons prayed as he had never prayed before. Next to him was a famous prisoner, known throughout the camp, the "young bridegroom,"

---

1.   The camp's nominal commander was a lieutenant colonel of the Wehrmacht, seriously wounded in 1918. One day, at one of these endless roll calls, he came to see us and said to Mgr. Théas:

"My Lord Bishop, I regret for you to see you here, but on the other hand, I am happy to meet someone from Montauban. I was seriously wounded in 1918, when I was a young officer. I stayed there a long time and was very well cared for. I didn't go back to Germany until 1919. Perhaps you were at Montauban at that time?"

"Non, Monsieur le Colonel, at that time I was also a young officer, in the occupation in Germany."

The Colonel was somewhat embarrassed. He said:

"Why, my dear Bishop, don't the French show more friendship for us?"

"What do you expect, Colonel? Friendship cannot be commanded."

(Unpublished manuscript, Raymond Cremel, March 1970.)

Marc Gervais; in a unique ceremony, he did indeed marry
Odile Acker in Royallieu.

"Marc Gervais[1] was born on February 10, 1921, at
Nangis (Seine-et-Marne). He chose a military career
and was preparing for Saint-Cyr in 1940. He didn't
hesitate in becoming active in the Resistance, and
especially in the A.S. After the suppression of the
line of demarcation and the dissolution of the army,
he tried to contact the Free French Forces. He was
arrested in Spain in 1943 and handed over to the
Germans by the Spanish militia, and then transferred
to Fort du Hâ in Bordeaux. Liberated in June 1943,
thanks to the intervention of his family and the steps
they were in a position to take, he returned to Paris,
where he resumed his activities in the Resistance network. On April 26, 1944, he fell into the hands of the
Gestapo for the second time.

"We had been engaged since June 19, 1940. The date
of our marriage was set for May 6, 1944. Marc was
originally imprisoned in Fresnes.

"On May 17, he was transferred to Compiègne. We
were informed of this by an anonymous telephone call,
and two days later, the information was confirmed by a
short note written by Marc himself, dated May 17. 'We're
leaving Fresnes today—destination unknown. Probably
Compiègne.' I immediately left for Compiègne with
Philippe Gervais, Marc's older brother. We knew that
convoys left Royallieu regularly. Several of our friends,
deportees, had already gone over the road, three or four
kilometers, which separated the camp from the station at
Compiègne. At dawn, on Saturday, May 20, my brother-
in-law and I were already waiting at the crossing of the
bridge over the Oise. Like ourselves, other families were
waiting for the passage of the convoy. It arrived very
soon. Walking slowly, the column of deportees passed,
surrounded and insulted by soldiers armed with machine
guns. Among all these sad faces, we looked for that of

1.   Unpublished manuscript of Odile Acker (later Madame
Boissonnat) and Philippe Gervais. Marc Gervais left for Dachau
on July 2, 1944. He died at the Vaihingen camp on April 2,
1945.

The camp of Royallieu, at Compiègne (drawing by Jacques Goth while a prisoner at the camp). This camp served as a transit constituting "an almost happy interlude" between the prison you had just left and the prison you would be going to. Most of the major convoys were made up there.
Center of Contemporary Jewish Documentation

Marc. We didn't see him. Then we decided to walk
toward the camp.

"When we arrived, there was already a straggling line
of families of prisoners waiting along the road to hand
over packages. There was a long wait, agitated by the
flight of bombers crossing the sky. German soldiers
threatened the silent line of visitors. When our turn came,
I was surprised to see that the interpreter was a Frenchman, Commander Avisse, whom I had known a year
before at the military hospital at Val-de-Grâce, where I
was the librarian. What was he doing at Compiègne? I
didn't have any idea. He recognized me, went into an
office, closed the door, and then came back a bit later to
say that our package was accepted. What was he doing
at Compiègne? Did he play a role in the events which
followed? We'll never know.

"Now that we felt sure that Marc really was in the
camp, my brother-in-law and I decided that I would stay
in Compiègne for a few days in order to request visiting
rights. So, I went back to the camp the next day and
asked Commander Avisse for his advice. After hours of
waiting, he presented me to a German non-commissioned officer, whose name I have forgotten. I got no
satisfaction out of that vague and very abrupt interview. I
went to the camp several times a day, asking to see my
fiancé. I was always refused. We did exchange letters,
however. Some greedy guardians were willing to act as
secret mailmen. In this way, I got a letter on May 23, and
another on May 24. The next day, when I had just met
with another refusal and was on my way back to
Compiègne, planning to return to Paris, discouraged by
all my failures, I was stopped by a German soldier
following me on a bicycle. He asked for my identity card,
took it and told me that I was prohibited from leaving
Compiègne, and that I must return to the camp that same
afternoon, at 3 o'clock. I did so. Two German soldiers,
armed with machine guns, led me into a small room.

"Seated behind a table, covered with a military cloth,
was the non-commissioned officer to whom Commander
Avisse had presented me three days earlier. He was
playing with a pair of handcuffs. Spread out on the table
in front of him was my identity card, and a small, gray

dossier. He questioned me for what seemed to be a frightfully long time. There were long silences, disturbed only by the restlessness of the police dogs enclosed nearby. The Officer left the room and returned with two guards. He explained something to them in German and pointed to me. Then he turned to me and said, 'You should get married. Are your papers in order? Go to Paris and get them and come to the gate of the camp on Saturday, May 27, at 10 o'clock with the mayor and the parish priest. If you wish to, you will be able to get married.' He handed my identity card back to me and made a sign to the guards to let me leave.

"On Saturday, May 27, at 10 a.m., the deputy mayor of Compiègne, Maître Bourquin, Canon Delvigne, the arch-priest of Compiègne, mama and I, stood before the gates of the camp. They opened for us. We were led into a barrack by an escort of six armed soldiers.

"Soon Marc appeared, between two guards with machine guns, and behind him, two other prison comrades accompanied by two more guards. The comrades were to serve as witnesses, but since they didn't have any identity papers, they couldn't sign. Finally mother and Canon Delvigne served as witnesses. The marriage took place. While we completed signing the registers of civil status and the Church register, all the officers of the camp came up. They marched past, congratulated us, wished us all happiness, and the Kommandant of the camp kissed my hand.

"We had permission to spend one hour together, Marc and I, within sight of the guards. We sat down together on a little wooden bench, with the two guards standing behind us. Whenever we moved at all, we felt the muzzle of the machine guns on our backs. But that didn't keep us from exchanging letters, news, messages, money and a metal saw.

"At the end of one hour, they made us leave the barrack. We were stopped in front of the first enclosure of barbed wire, but we couldn't resign ourselves to separating.

"The guard aimed their machine guns. Someone said, 'Look, they're going to shoot.' We looked up at the watchtowers. It was true. They were all ready to shoot, and the barrels of the weapons were aimed at us. His last words to me were, 'Never despair, that would be a sin against the Holy Ghost. Never despair. Never.'"

* * *

Edouard Aubert walked along the barbed wire that separated camp C from camp A:

"Here,[1] among the group of prisoners walking around in camp A, I thought that I had recognized an old friend from Lyons, a friend, a brother, a fellow-militant with whom I had worked in the C.G.T. (General Confederation of Workers—Textile Union of Lyons) from 1936 to 1939, and later on in the underground Resistance, when we found ourselves together again in 1941, after my escape from Stalag 11 A. Anyhow, of course, since my latest arrest, I didn't know what had happened to him. But was this really my friend? I had to be certain. I cupped my hands into a megaphone (after making sure that there were no security guards around, for such acts were forbidden and punished) I shouted, 'Pierre,' and then his name, 'Lachaize—Lachaize!' The man didn't answer. He continued to walk around and talk with the others. Probably I had made a mistake.

"But just the same, I found out it was Pierre. And he had heard. What had happened was that he was arrested under a false name and trained himself never to get caught by answering to his true name, so as not to disclose his identity. This is one of the elementary rules of clandestine warfare. He had heard, and even more, without betraying himself, he had seen where the call was coming from. How fantastic to find him here. The only question was, how to communicate. Apparently it was impossible. The Germans, the Kapos, never let anybody pass from camp A to camp C, or vice versa... except, sometimes, for some forced labor job....One time Lachaize succeeded in getting himself selected for a transport of bedsteads...and he came to camp C.

"I can't go into all the tricks we used to get together, with a bit of luck thrown in, and to exchange a few

1. Unpublished manuscript of Edouard Aubert, May 1970.

words despite the surveillance. It was through him that we had real news about the camp, and what was taking place, and also about the situation in general. It was also through him that we learned that a convoy was being prepared, and that we were able to get across some information as to our identities and our state of mind to the leaders of the underground National Front in camp A, so as to help in the establishment of liaisons.... The struggle continued...."

This Clandestine National Front, so perfectly organized that it could transmit coded messages to London, that it could camouflage a personality, that it could collect and distribute, before a convoy, in just a few hours, fifty or sixty kilos of metal saws, spikes, drills and knives, never succeeded in establishing unity and forging a true underground force. Its leaders held irreconcilable views on the Resistance; the lives they had led kept them worlds apart.

"There was a little sailing ship...."

In an angle of the football field, Father de La Perraudière led the choral group of Compiègne.

2:00 p.m.

"Attention!"
Siren.
"Attention!"
Whistle.
"General roll call! General roll call!"
The Dean carefully draws on his white gloves.

"We had just finished our meager noon meal,[1] and we were already getting the order to assemble, barrack by barrack. In the ranks the word passed from group to group: we're going to take part in the roll call for the next departure. Dejection swept over us. Nobody joked any longer. Anxiety and anguish hung over the camp.

"We were lined up in columns now and were marched into camp A, where the prisoners were already standing in compact groups. As soon as we got there, ranks were

---

1.   Unpublished manuscript of Henri Liotier, May 1970.

broken and a dense crowd gathered around the empty table set up in the center of the terrain.

"That table, where it was—the whole scene—there was something threatening about it. An officer, all smiles, followed by half a dozen secretaries, came and sat down. Then the circle was broken up by a squad of troops, and everybody was pushed to the right of this central table. The roll call began. The silence of the grave fell on our group where everyone waited fearfully to hear his name snapped out. One by one, as if whipped forward by the voice which had called them, the men filed in front of the table and, one by one, added to the group that was taking form to the left. The last letters of the alphabet had just been called out and I was still in the group to the right. Luck was running with me, and already, egoistically, secretly, I felt a stab of joy. I took a deep breath.

"It was only a momentary reprieve. The S.S. was just relaxing for a quarter of an hour, and then the roll call began again. The pangs I had felt before came back again. I listened. The danger point had passed. None of the men of Riom had been called. The cramps in my stomach eased. It's better now. That was a narrow escape. Then the S.S. officer reached out his hand and picked up a second list. As soon as the first names were called I realized that this time we were all in for it. All the men of Riom were sucked in by the table, and then I was drawn into the vortex also. I followed the others, like an automaton, toward the officer who, with a casual gesture of his hand, indicated the group to the left, which absorbed me in silence.

Father de La Perraudière was the third priest called up.

"Some of the prisoners didn't answer to the roll call.[1] The German repeated the name again only once, and then passed on to the next. I didn't understand, at that time: it was a very simple means of avoiding transport. The list was longer than it had to be. The officer only needed to go on calling names until he had the requisite number. I learned later on that those who hadn't answered weren't bothered. The only thing was...someone else

1. Unpublished manuscript of Père de La Perraudière, May 1970.

went in their place. I was on the list, and I answered 'present.' And still, I had only arrived five days ago. I was with a group of about fifty from the prison of Tours. That didn't seem to have any particular importance. Many of my comrades from Tours, a good hundred, were to be part of the convoy."

A new alphabetical list. The Dean required standing at attention.

"Almost all the prisoners there refused.[1] The Dean then demanded that we show the respect due to his rank. Somebody shouted out, 'Shut your damn trap,' and that ended the discussion.

But the Dean insisted that we come to attention.

"Then a hobo,[2] a real force of nature who had come from the Saint-Michel prison, pushed aside the stupefied crowd and hurled at the Dean the word that made Cambronne famous: 'S-H-I-T.'"

Claude Mathieu was crying, in the ranks of those who were retained.

"He looked at me without a word,[3] and tears flowed down his cheeks. I looked down, feeling shame, but hoping, out of egoism, or an instinct of self-preservation, that I would not hear my name...'Habermacher Maurice'....'Present.' I experienced a great interior shock, but at the same time, a great satisfaction and consolation. Then I dared to look my friend, Claude, straight in the eyes. We hugged each other and both wept."

Paul Weil, Alphonse Kienzler, Edgar Amigas had followed each other for two years, from prison to prison, from ordeal to ordeal.

"Weil Paul." "Present."

"Kienzler Alphonse." "Present."

Perhaps Edgar Amigas is the only man in this crowd who hopes to hear his own name.

"During the first weeks after my arrest in September 1942,[4] had the luck of meeting, in prison, some idealistic

1. Unpublished manuscript of Maurice Voutey. April 1970.
2. Unpublished manuscript of Georges Bixel. June 1970.
3. Unpublished manuscript of Maurice Habermacher. June 1970.
4. Unpublished manuscript of Alphonse Kienzler. March 1970.

comrades, full of fire, who had joined the Resistance, like myself. I can't keep from remembering fervently my friend, Edgar Amigas, from Toulon. He studied in Grenoble. I had the great good fortune, for two years, to learn with him the meaning of true friendship. We were scarcely ever separated during this period, and we were together when we gave the knock-out blow to the guards of Clermont-Ferrand when we attempted to escape. This drove the guards and police completely mad with rage, and they beat us both almost to death with rawhide clubs and blackjacks. We were together in that. We were together in hunger, in cold, in despair, and in exaltation whenever favorable military news reached us. And finally, together we took part in the mutiny of Eysses. I saw him at Compiègne for the last time.

"For some unknown reason, the name of Edgar Amigas was not on the list for departure. He did everything he could to join us. He tried to pass for someone else. He begged, but it was no good. We were terribly saddened to find our little team so abruptly diminished by the loss of one of the best of us. I shall never forget the suffering of our friend. Despite all the risks of deportation, he would have preferred to stay with us, so as not to break the link of friendship that we had forged under the cruelest of ordeals. Paul Weil and I tried to console ourselves with the thought that he might have a greater chance of surviving because of the approach of the Allies...."[1]

4:45 p.m.

A non-commissioned officer stapled the alphabetical lists together. The Dean called for silence.

"The roll call is...."

"Shit! Filthy cunt!..."

"The roll call is...."

"Bastard! Whore! We'll get you!..."

"The roll call is terminated. Tomorrow afternoon, you will be taken over to camp C."

1. Edgar Amigas left Compiègne in the convoy which followed that of July 2, and died in deportation.

"We don't want to be put in with the criminals. We are Resistants."

"Shove it. Let the Dean talk."

The Dean was livid. His two guards, machine guns in hand, couldn't keep from smiling.

"Now you will go and get your baggage in order. Your things will be taken by cart to the station, and you will find them when you arrive at your destination. For the voyage, it is forbidden that you take with you anything in addition to a haversack containing food—less than a kilo, and for those who possess one personally, and I stress 'personally,' a blanket."

We all returned to our barracks. Anguish. Questions.

"Now it is time for us to say goodbye to those who stay behind,[1] to give them our final words for the family, in the event that they are freed. Alas, how few of them will remember their promises. The sad egotism of joy that makes us forget the rest.

"I am already imagining that ultimate instant, when I shall be seeing my wife, and perhaps—who knows—also my children, along the way which leads to the station. God, I hope that they can be kept from knowing. I hope that they do not come. Not to say this last wordless goodbye, not to bear the sight of someone we might never see again....But isn't this a proof of egotism? Wouldn't it be better, on the contrary, to see them, to hide our own anxiety, to show them, by our confident attitude, that we continue to be strong? Yes, that is the best. I prepare myself for it, as so many others must have done before me."

5:15 p.m.

Henri Chant, the garagist, found Mgr.Théas in building 8. "I baptized him,[2] and confirmed him. On July 1 he

---

1. Marcel Guérin, memorial booklet on the "Death Convoy." Imprimerie du Semeur, Bourges (Cher), October 1949.
2. Unpublished manuscript of Pierre-Marie Théas, formerly Bishop of Mountauban, later of Tarbes and Lourdes. March 1970.

partook of his first communion. The next day he left for
Dachau, on the Death Train. Although the baptism had
been performed in secret, it became known, and I was
denounced to the Germans. I was severely molested for
having committed such an offense. Before the departure,
I distributed, to those who wished them, medals and
rosaries which Abbé Rodhain, the almoner of the prisons,
had sent to me. Nearly all the hands reached out toward
me. Without knowing the fate of those who were
leaving, all the hearts were in the grip of anguish. Later
facts came to prove that this immense moral suffering
was, alas, justified."

The National Front of the underground resistance did
not succeed in re-grouping. Its members, dispersed in
various blocks, issued contradictory orders. Some of
them, as Gaullists, didn't want to have anything to do
with the Communists. Some Communists refused to
establish contact with the Gaullists. Sometimes, however, meetings of Frenchmen as different and as opposed
as Georges Villiers, Edouard Aubert, and Joseph Helluy
sealed an alliance leading to a unique and particularly
effective action.

Dr. Joseph Helluy, assisted by Maréchal, a school
teacher, managed to collect such an impressive number
of saws, files, chisels, gouges, shears, that he decided to
entrust a batch of tools to some thirty internees. These
"responsables" were to get into different sections of the
train and enforce the conditions for escape.

"A comrade[1] who was remaining in the camp came to
see me and said, 'Order of the Resistance.' You must
contact X of Nancy (Dr. Helluy) who will have a kit of
pocket tools. A group of about twenty comrades of the
Resistance will mill around you and make sure that you
get in the same part of the train. During the first night of
the trip, you must saw through a wall board and escape."

"By some miracle,[2] in the noise and chaos, I came

1. Unpublished manuscript of Georges Villiers. April 1970.
(Translator's note: In France the word "comrade" is freely used
for any "in-group" member, left, right or nonpolitical. It does not
imply that the person so designated is a communist.)
2. Unpublished manuscript of Edouard Aubert. May 1970.

across Georges Villiers. I can't remember how it happened...or which of the two of us recognized the other
first...besides, that doesn't matter. But on the other
hand, I do remember very well my instinctive reaction of
hostility and mistrust...my stupor also...Georges Villiers,
here! I've seen everything! This big industrialist of
Lyons, whom I knew as one of the guiding spirits of the
employers' association, this man with whom I had
clashed before the war as a militant union leader of the
C.G.T. I think we had even been on an arbitration panel
together. He spoke for the bosses. I spoke for the
workers. It was some time after 1936, as part of the
procedure for settling labor disputes.

"But that wasn't at the base of my feelings....It was
that I knew—that we knew—that he had carried on the
functions of the mayor of Lyons...and that exactly at the
time when the Resistants of the southern zone were
being tracked down and arrested, and exactly at the time
when I was arrested myself in Lyons by the Vichy police,
packed off to the Saint-Paul prison, and then condemned
with other comrades, also accused of being terrorists, to
hard labor, by a 'special tribunal' sitting in the Palais de
Justice of Lyons...."

Edouard Aubert and Georges Villiers exchanged their
histories and the reasons for their Resistance.

Aubert continues: "Yes, that's how it was. For a time,
the differences in class, like the grievances, became
blurred, disappeared. We talked it out frankly, and I didn't
try to hide what I had felt about him....Of course, it is
impossible for me to reconstruct this tense conversation word for word. We were lying side by side....
But I'll never forget one thing he said: 'My poor
Monsieur Aubert, who would ever have guessed that
we would come together again under these circumstances?'"

Edouard Aubert and Georges Villiers traveled in the
same boxcar. They had decided on that. But Georges
Villiers had to keep his appointment with Dr. Helluy.

Gabriel Rykner, Pierre Bernard, André Page, Pierre
Roux and Mario Nikis were grouped around Claude
Lamirault, the chief of the Jade-Fitzroy network.

"You'll be wanting some files, saws...."

Lamirault was amply supplied by the clandestine committee:

"Who wants them? Here's how we'll go about it...."

Dr. Solladié and his father-in-law, Dr. Bent, couldn't believe their eyes.

"A package, and what a package. It must weigh at least forty-five pounds."

"Who brought it?"

"Alice Landau. She came from Montauban. It took her five days."

All the clients and friends of the two doctors had prepared the package. Forty pounds of foie gras, and sausages...five liters of white wine.

"Let's get together with all the friends of Tarn-et-Garonne...."

"And Mgr. Théas?"

"Of course. But you can't invite a bishop just like that."

"I'll hunt up a stool somewhere...."

And Mgr. Théas installed himself upon the stool.

Here were the friends from Tarn-et-Garonne, and there the Marseillais, further on those from Toulouse and Ariège, with Dubié, the famous chief cook in their midst. The Normans were perhaps the most spoiled of all, thanks to two gigantic packages received by Francis Fagot: butter, cakes, boiled salt pork, rabbit, chocolate, sugar, vieux marc liqueur.

"This is a last meal to end all last meals...."

"Oh, shut up and eat."

Seated on his bed, Robert Schmidt closed the prayer book in which he had just written his last will. He turned toward his friend, Roger Rouillon:[1]

"I want to ask one very important, final favor of you. I'm certain that I'm not coming back from there, so will you please take this little book, and when you get back, give it to my family."

"But look here! it could just as well be me...."

"No. I know that I'm going to die."

Robert Schmidt was right: he died in the Death Train, on July 2.

Albert Charpentier, and dozens of other prisoners, tore

1.   Unpublished manuscript of Roger Rouillon. May 1970.

a heel off a shoe to hide a letter that they hoped to throw out during the voyage.

A fat little man offered to trade his signet ring for a knife.

René Bandel looked around for a piece of oiled paper.

"What are you going to do with that?"

"Didn't you ever read the prison colony stories from Cayenne?"

"Yeah!"

"Well then, I've got a plan in mind."

"A plan?"

"I wrap the knife up in oiled paper and hoopla, it's a suppository...."

"Good night!"

3

July 1

Kruchen, the German chief of depot—tiny, steel-rimmed glasses, delicate moustache—made a second check on the two sections of train 7909. On the wooden clipboard that he held in his hand were fastened telegrams sent by the two Paris services which, working closely together, organized the convoys of deportees: H.V.D. and T.K.[1] Muller, the deputy station chief, licked the point of his pencil and initialed the copy-sheets to be sent to Alfred Carpentier, French station chief of Compiègne, Raoul Merlin, a deputy station chief, and Alfred Pâques, switching-track chief.

It was Raoul Merlin who was responsible for assembling the 7909, as well as most of the other deportee convoys.

---

1. H.V.D.—Hauptverkehrsdirektion (General Transport Authority). T.K.—Transportkommandantur. The telegrams were addressed to Ü.B.F. Compiègne (Überwachungsbahnhof, German checking station on occupied territory) at least four days before a departure.

On June 28, the Paris-Bestiaux station sent to the marshaling yard of Compiègne some fifty standard freight cars: 40 men, 8 horses. They had been rounded up from all over... almost every model in circulation was represented: old trains from *France-Midi*, fifteen square meters, German, Belgian, Italian freight cars, and even, somewhat out of keeping among these old, wooden crates, a metal car.[1] The special cars, coming generally from the Gare du Nord, would only arrive the next day: eight freight cars with observation boxes[2], three passenger carriages with lateral doors for each compartment, and finally, a flat car.

It wasn't always easy to organize the convoy, and then place it on tracks IV and VI adjacent to the warehouse. The German railway employees at the station were painstaking and obedient to orders (even in July 1944). They checked the condition of the material scrupulously and regularly rejected all vehicles revealing the least flaw, and particularly those with loose planks.[3] Those they refused were shipped back to Paris.

The deportation platform (once used for outgoing travelers: Soissons and Villers-Cotterêts) couldn't accommodate convoys of more than twenty cars because the switches were too close to the terminal buffers. Hence train 7909 would be divided.

1.   These freight cars of welded sheet metal with a rounded roof were constructed in 1930 in the workshops in northern France.
2.   Certain covered cars (10% of the total in 1944) had a raised box in which a man could find place. Originally these boxes were occupied by brakemen. When pneumatic brakes were introduced on freight trains (after 1926) these boxes became useless. Nevertheless, they were retained on a large number of cars. Some were still to be found between 1950 and 1958.
3.   Derville and Lemaître, station inspectors, asserted to Raoul Merlin that, on several occasions, they had unscrewed and removed the nuts from certain bolts fixing the floorboards in vehicles intended for the convoys of deportees. (Derville Report, March 1966.)

9:00 a.m.—Compiègne. Camp of Royallieu.

The kitchen detail unloads a truck of green beans:
"The Red Cross is good at these things: one thousand eight hundred kilos....What they lack in quality, they make up in quantity. They'll get their bellies full at noon."
"How many will be leaving?"
"I don't know. Nobody knows. More than two thousand."[1]

9:40 a.m.-Compiègne Station.

Alfred Pâques, switching-track chief, dispatched the two sections of 7909 onto tracks IV and VI.
All of the French staff of the Compiègne Station felt that 7909 would be the last train of deportees. The most fantastic rumors were coming in with the freight trains. "The tracks will be bombed." "They are completely emptying the whole camp." "The Resistance is going to attack while they're getting on the train."
Muller and Kruchen made a final check before turning over the 7909 to the two S.D. officers[2] who were expected at 3:00 p.m.
Track VI.
"Van with tailbrake."
"Flat car."
"Escort car."
The two men advanced slowly along the paving stones of the platform.
"Fifteen freight cars with observation boxes on numbers 5, 10, and 15."
"Perfect. Officers' carriage."
They return along the line.
Track IV.
"Cars from 16 to 32."

1. Annex IV gives the list of those who left, the list of those who died in transit, and a report on the staff of the convoy. With its 2,166 deportees, the Death Train was the largest convoy ever to leave Compiègne.
2. *Sicherheitsdienst:* Security Service of the German Army.

"Observation boxes on 20, 25, and 30. Escort car between 25 and 26."

And that accounted for the thirty-seven elements, each one in place. And this peculiar arrangement of the departure platform—or rather the two departure platforms—explains why it was impossible the next day for the deportees to recognize exactly their position in the convoy as a whole. Those who climbed on the last wagon on track IV or the first on track VI would be in the middle of the train after the two sections were coupled.

10:00 a.m.—Compiègne. Camp of Royallieu.

The prisoner-doctors, assigned to the infirmary, and held over for the next departure, in liaison with the underground Resistance committee, "manufactured non-transportables" as fast as they could get away with it.

"The infirmary[1] was as stuffed as an egg with everybody we could possibly camouflage. So many fake patients for the Secret Army, so many for the Communist Party, so many for the other Gaullist organizations. But a few places were still available. Jacquet[2] received 8 cc of Propidon in the buttock. His fever went up to 40° and he developed a suppurative inflammation (phlegmon)...so that he was barely available for the final convoy to Buchenwald.

"Turruel, the national secretary of the miners' union developed a 'colonial' dysentery.[3] An A.S. (Secret Army) commander had diphtheria, carefully applied by the

1.   Unpublished manuscript of Dr. Paul Weil. February 1970.
2.   Raymond Jacquet, mayor of La Tour-du-Pin: "Dr. Paul Weil gave me an injection of 8 cc of Propidon, a vaccin which induces fever, in my left buttock, which made me so ill that when the S.S. inspectors came to chose the men for departure, they had the impression that I only had a few more hours to live. This injection cost me an infernal, great abscess on the bone and I had to be operated on in the camp infirmary. Thus it was only by the convoy of the month of August that I left for Germany." Unpublished manuscript. April 1970.
3.   Colonial diseases had, for the Germans, the prestige and mystery of the unknown tropics (Paul Weil's note).

Departure of a prisoners' convoy from the camp of Compiègne. The deportees, lined up five by five in a column, walked the four kilometers to get to the station. They were surrounded by guards, gun in hand.
Center of Contemporary Jewish Documentation

doctor with a silver nitrate crayon. The positive bacterial swab was supplied by the patient in the neighboring bed who, by luck, just happened to have a real diphtheria. I next chose an old gentleman whom I respected, but he refused out of a high sense of group responsibility. Nor did the system work for Dr. Fuchs. I gave him the same Propidon treatment that I had administered to Raymond Jacquet, but the German nurse suspected something wrong about the fever, and so he was shipped off with a shot of Propidon in the buttock."

And in the same way, and at the same time, they embarked a score of men with jaws fractured by the Gestapo, broken ribs, buttocks flayed raw, one man with both legs in a plaster cast, one on a stretcher, and Jean Hoyoux. Jean Hoyoux of the 'miraculous cure.' His adventure is a story in itself.

"My name is Hoyoux, Jean;[1] born in Paris (13th arrondissement), August 13, 1917. I am of Belgian nationality. I rejoined the Belgian forces of Great Britain when I left Liège on February 13, 1942. That was the day I was liberated from the Saint-Léonard prison where I had been held for sabotage and enemy propaganda. I was in solitary confinement for three months, but I withstood it well enough, and they freed me for lack of proof. I knew that my freedom was temporary at best, so I lost no time in getting in touch with my service. My chiefs decided to send me to England immediately, by what we then considered the normal passage: France, Spain, Portugal, Gibraltar. I had a lot of trouble on this long-way-around, but a lot of luck too, and so I reached England in July 1942, where I immediately enlisted in the special services, as an information agent, and for action.

"After intensive training, I was parachuted into France in the outskirts of Niort on August 23, 1943. My special mission was to gather the information needed for the destruction of the V-1 launching pads. I passed this information on to London by radio.[2] Everything went

1. Unpublished manuscript of Jean Hoyoux. April 1970.
2. Lamirault had also forwarded information on this subject to London. At Compiègne, on the verandah where official German

well until Shrove Tuesday, 1944. An agent, a Frenchman who worked for the Gestapo, succeeded in infiltrating the Delbo-Phénix network which had been helping me in my mission. He contacted me in a store in Niort. His name was Georges Ledanseur. Although the deputy chief of the network introduced him to me, I didn't trust him from the first. We talked of one thing and another. At the end of half an hour I was sure that the man in front of me was a German agent. He sensed it. He felt that he was discovered and he drew his revolver and shot at me, to the utter stupefaction of his guide, who didn't understand what was going on and tried to intervene. He was shot through the neck.

"The other balls got to me: one of them tore through my scalp, one was planted in my left forearm, one in the left lung, one grazed the right tibia for a length of ten centimeters; the final ball, aimed straight at my heart, was deflected by my wallet and passed through the lining of my jacket. (At least, this is what I deduced later on when I noted two bullet holes on the left side of my jacket)...the ball intended for my heart must have been badly crimped.

"Don't get the idea that I let my attacker simply empty his gun into me without moving. I noticed, from the time he came in, that he kept his right hand plunged in his pocket. It made me conclude that he was armed, but since I had been taught in England that it was impossible to shoot from inside a pocket, I kept telling myself that if he drew his gun, I'd have plenty of time to neutralize him. Unfortunately, my British instructors had failed to mention that, in one case, you could shoot from the

papers were displayed, he came across a poster which boasted about the efficiency of the new "total arm." But Lamirault had sent off the description of these strange concrete rails without knowing what they were to be used for. His barrack mate, Pierre Bernard, briefed him. "I explained the operation of teleguided rockets (actually, these were still only V-1's), which I had described in 1930 in *Monde*. Lamirault exulted. Now he understood the part played by these concrete crescents which he had bombarded in the north, just on the chance that they were a worthwhile target." (Unpublished manuscript of Pierre Bernard. May 1970.)

pocket—with a revolver. And Ledanseur had that sort of weapon.

"With the very first show, I jumped on him, without even being aware that I had been seriously wounded. A pitiless death struggle began. My weapons were anything I could get my hands on: paper cutters, vases, flower pots, chairs. There was real carnage in the little office of my friend Gibaud, located behind the store. I shouted, 'Gibaud, there's a revolver in the bedroom, hurry. Run up and get it.' I was about finished...with a final burst of strength, I leaped on Ledanseur and he staggered. Gibaud came back down. Ledanseur ran to the door and opened it. Gibaud handed me the revolver. I shot. Ledanseur dropped. Then the blackness closed in. I just had the time to cry, 'Gibaud, finish him off,' and then I fainted.

"But Gibaud didn't have the guts to finish the job. He dragged him into the cellar and closed the door. I was secretly transported to the hospital at Niort. In the meantime, Ledanseur had unscrewed the ventilator in the cellar and had dragged himself to the Kommandantur. The Germans immediately cordoned off the city.

"I was given blood transfusions day and night at the hospital of Niort, under the supervision of Dr. Laffitte and the care of a Sister. I remained in a coma....The Germans knew I was wounded and were searching all the clinics and hospitals. The Resistance of Niort decided to evacuate me. A very determined group 'borrowed' a German truck being repaired in the Citroën garage. They dressed themselves in Wehrmacht uniforms and while the hospital was actually being searched by the Germans, these incredibly brave comrades placed me on two planks and carried me out under the very nose of the Gestapo. The first stop was Saint-Liguaire where Dr. Boyer gave me an injection to ease the pain. And then, from cellar to attic, from attic to barn, until we reached a farm hidden in the forest of Hermitain. There Drs. Suire and Allard, without anaesthetic, and with a bottle of cheap brandy as a disinfectant, extracted the bullet from my lung with a scalpel and forceps.

"It was terribly cold, but I never sweated so much in my life.

"Dr. Allard contacted my service in Paris. London set up the 'operation Lysander' to bring me back by plane.... Everything was ready, except me. In the light of my condition, Dr. Allard refused to have me moved.

"This heroism cost the French Resistance eighteen dead, and many deportations.[1] It couldn't be helped. What had to happen did happen. It took the Gestapo only a few days to find us. They encircled the farm (six autobusses of the Brivin company, full of soldiers). The leader of the detail forced the farmers to walk in front. I didn't have the courage to open fire.

"It would be useless to describe the treatment I suffered, in spite of my wounds. When I got into my cell in the prison of Pierre-Levée at Poitiers, I realized that I was black and blue from head to foot, with all the torture I had undergone. Nobody could believe it anymore. I can hardly believe it myself. I prayed that they'd shoot me....They changed the guard at midnight, and the German nightwatchman took the handcuffs off my wrists and ankles. He often brought me a little bread. He used to say, 'I have a son who is a prisoner of the Russians. Maybe he'll find somebody over there, like me, to ease his suffering.'

"Then, one fine day, I learned that I had been called to Paris....The Gestapo of Poitiers were furious to think that I could slip out of their hands. They wouldn't allow me to walk, but kicked me along the ground as far as the station.

"The day after I arrived at Fresnes, I was taken before General Falkenhausen. He received me very cordially, asked me to sit down. He looked me over carefully for a few minutes, and took in my physical condition. 'It was them. It's not me.' He asked me if I was hungry. I answered that I hadn't eaten for four days and four nights. He gave instructions and his orderly set four ham and cheese sandwiches and a beer before me. After this feast the general told me that they had been looking for me since 1942, that I was considered a good soldier, and

1. Drs. Laffitte, Suire, Allard, and Boyard (see *Doctors of Mercy*); Messrs. Gibaud, Pinaud, Barbotin, Martau, Souchard, Ferrand, Michaud *dit* Petit Louis, etc.

that I would not be shot, but deported. He concluded, 'That's the best that I can do for you.' He held out his hand to me and wished me good luck.

"When I arrived at Compiègne I was still very weak and my wounds had re-opened....I was coddled in the infirmary, but was far from recovered when I was selected for the train of July 2."

Noon—Compiègne. Camp de Royallieu.

"Ah, kidney beans like that. They haven't made any like that since 1914."

"It's a change from chickpeas."

"One more ladle, colonel. There's a bit left."

2:00 p.m.—Compiègne. Camp de Royallieu.

Chief warrant officer Peter Feld, with an evident lack of enthusiasm, clicked his heels. Two officers of the Security Service of the German Army installed themselves in the waiting room of the Kommandant of Royallieu.

"Lieutenant Colonel Posseckel telephoned me. He will be here in a few minutes. He had a luncheon in town."

The two officers didn't reply. The warrant officer, a former school teacher, had been in Compiègne since June 1942. It was the first time that he had seen the two S.D.s assigned to organize the departure of July 2, and to accompany the deportees as far as the Frontier Station of Novéant.[1]

---

1. Questioned by an investigation commission on July 12, 1948, Peter Feld limited himself to saying: "I'm very sorry that I can't give you the names of these officers....The Compiègne Camp Commandant, Lieutenant Colonel Posseckel, was opposed to massive train embarkments of the prisoners. The two S.D.s then stated to the said Commandant that the transport was organized on their responsibility, and that the orders were issued by the German High Command in Paris."

Lieutenant Colonel Posseckel died in 1946; Warrant Officer Peter Feld in 1950.

2:15 p.m.—Compiègne. Camp de Royallieu

"Assembly."

Siren. Whistle. Roll call. Roll call.

The barracks chiefs checked the bundles.

"You'll find everything on arrival. Keep the minimum on you. For that matter, you will be searched very very thoroughly. If you want some good advice, wear several shirts and sweaters, and an overcoat...."

First alphabetical list.

"Put your baggage here."

"Bowls here."

"Knives over there. Just keep your mugs."

A big, easy-going non-com, seated on the back of a chair, said:

"Will the sick and disabled identify themselves. They will be taken to the station in a car...the car will be drawn by a horse, but it's a car just the same.

The Dean passed, with his head hunched between his shoulders.

"Hey, Dimwit, lose something?"

The Dean walked a little faster, and turned behind the barracks.

Standing in single file. The clinking of cups and spoons.

"Start off. Toward the gate of camp C now."

3:10 p.m.—Compiègne Station.

The two S.D. officers, accompanied by station chief Muller, went onto the freight platform while a score of men on detail from Royallieu came with two wagonloads of straw, and deposited a bale in front of each freight car. German soldiers climbed up on ladders and closed off two of the car apertures by nailing boards over them, the other openings were sealed with a tangle of barbed wire.

The work detail rolled up a barrier of empty barrels. Armed sentries between the tracks. The freight sector of the station is now out of bounds.

3:45 p.m.—Compiègne. Camp de Royallieu.

German police came,[1] and without waiting, started the search. Taken by surprise, the first ranks gave up their knives and identity papers, which the police took, without any formalities. But those who came next had the time to get organized, and each one found an ingenious way of hiding his personal objects. The police weren't even amazed at the fact that they couldn't find anything more, after they had processed the first few. And nevertheless it wasn't for lack of vigor or system. During this time the column sweated under a sun of lead."

"I wasn't subjected to a thorough search.[2] The soldier in charge of this job discovered a calendar in my coat pocket with a picture of the Cathedral of Amiens on the cover. He looked at it for a few moments and then handed it back to me, and said, 'beautiful cathedral!' and left things at that."

In front of gate C there were a dozen men who had been less lucky. They were stripped and searched.

5:00 p.m.—Compiègne Station.

In the tiny office of the train agents, Cyriaque Frizon examined the service list for July 2. Martial Dorgny, the mechanic, burst out laughing.

"Ah, yes, old pal, you're on the list too, just like me."

"Is that supposed to be funny? That makes seven Sundays in a row. And there's no train on Sunday to get back from Reims before night. And who else?"

"The fireman. It's Robert Coville."

The three men were friends. Frizon was the oldest: fifty years, solid muscles, a bit of a moustache under a fine nose, cap always perched on the top of his head. Dorgny: forty-three years old, wide chin, heavy brows, hair plastered down behind, square features, starting to put on a belly, the very opposite of Coville: little and dry.

1. Unpublished manuscript of Henri Liotier: already cited.
2. Unpublished manuscript of Pierre Dhenain. April 1970.

The crew of the 7909 was formed. The three men separated with a joke:

"I hope the food baskets are full."

"We're having rabbit tonight. I'll save the skin for you."

7:00 p.m.—Compiègne. Camp de Royallieu.

The two swinging barbed wire gates of the entry of camp C closed behind the "departing guests" who were crammed into two hangars:

"On the inside,[1] not the least bunk or bed, only a few armfuls of straw scattered over the flooring to furnish the 'people pen.'"

"Between the two buildings, armed sentinels. Jaeger, 'the dog man,' loosened his beasts, Prado and Klodo.

"Dr. Solladié, pushed by the crowd into the second building, decided to try to get out to join his father-in-law, Dr. Bent, in the first group.

"'You're crazy. Jaeger and his dogs are out there.'

"'Who speaks German?'

"'Me.'

"'Translate for me, "Please excuse me. My father-in-law is sick. I want to be with him."'

"'But he's crazy! Are you going to try to tell all that to Jaeger? He's crazy.'

"'Why not try?'

"'O.K., O.K., this is how you say it....'

"Solladié repeated the phrase, half opened the door, slipped and fell into the arms of Jaeger.

"'...Oh!'

"'Now what?'

"'Excuse me! I can't remember my sentence...but you speak French. My father-in-law....'

"Jaeger grabbed Solladié by the scruff of the neck, and pushed him toward the first door:

"'Is that it?'

"'*Euh!* I don't think so.'

"Second door. 'Is that it?'

1. Unpublished manuscript of Henri Liotier. Already cited.

"Solladié recognizes a face from Montauban.

" '*Oui!* That's it.'

"Jaeger, magnanimous: 'Get in.' "

Others preferred to try to sneak out...running behind the guards' backs.

"We jammed up to the windows[1] to call out to comrades who weren't with us, but with whom we wanted to be. There was an open door opposite my barrack. A comrade ran toward a friend from whom he didn't want to be separated. I too, had someone I wanted to join, but a sentinel shouted and threatened to shoot. Tough! But when the sentinel turned his back, I leaped out of the window, followed by two other comrades. Opposite, all the prisoners who were crowded at the door, separated and made a passage for us. Everybody cheered this new victory. But I lost myself in the crowd as quickly as I could, with my heart beating heavily. Friends united again, with only such a very short time to feel the joy of friendship. Several of us moved together, stood shoulder to shoulder as if to face up to any challenge. Standing like that, we felt so strong. Nothing could happen. We would win."

Dr. Paul Weil in this transit enclosure, recognized Professor Chaumerliac:

"I had been arrested in his laboratory,[2] and now he was paying for the splendid welcome he had extended to those forced back from Strasbourg, particularly to Professor Waitz, who was already in Auschwitz. I found Francis Rohmer, the neurologist, and Professor Vlès. Apart from the admiration I had for his scientific work, and for his honesty and courage in the Resistance, I felt a special closeness for him, because my fiancée had been his secretary. I hadn't any news of her since the executions at Eysses where she had been told that I was killed. He and I talked together for a long time. Professor Vlès no longer thought that he would be a professor with the Museum one day, although it was the position that he had hoped for after the Liberation. Was this a premonition of his early death?

1. Unpublished manuscript of Col. René Puyo (already cited).
2. Unpublished manuscript of Dr. Paul Weil (already cited).

"A magistrate come up to us. He was Presiding Judge Théron, arrested for his role in the Resistance. I engaged in a diatribe against his fellow-magistrates, who were too indulgent toward the occupying forces. Then this great gentleman assumed the difficult defense of certain of his colleagues, although his own recent attitude had given the lie to their submission. He was to die on the following day. I don't believe that there are any men that I admire more than I admired him."

11:00 p.m.—Compiègne. Camp de Royallieu.

Near René Prungnaud an old prisoner murmured:
"Now we cease to be men."
The men from Niort grouped around Henri Lambert, the Mayor of Sainte-Pezenne.
"Those who find some place to lie down[1] are stumbled on by those who are forced to move at night for needs imposed by nature. For it must be added that many prisoners suffered from dysentery, so that in the course of the night, there was a continual coming and going to try to reach the toilets, composed of two or three big carbide cans, opened at one end, and placed in the lateral corridor of the building.
"Even this corridor was occupied by prisoners, crowded, or lying side by side, up to the very edges of the containers. So crowded that those who had the luck, in all that darkness, to be able to get close to the receptacles were sometimes confused by the darkness, and evacuated on the floor, walked in it, and on the way back, involuntarily wiped their feet on comrades lying near them on the ground.
"Others were too weak to hold back, and let everything go into their trousers, or even lost control where they were standing, in a horror of embarrassment. Then came the violent anger of the neighbor, who found himself caught in the total degradation, and, moving in the darkness, plunged his hand into the shit, or rolled over

1.   Brochure by Henri Lambert: *Compiègne-Dachau par le Train de la Mort.* Niort, Imprimerie du Progrès, 1951.

onto the place sullied by some miserable creature whose guts had betrayed him."

The fat little guy still hadn't succeeded in swapping his signet ring for a knife. He kept on trying.

* * *

A young man is singing in the night.[1]

> *We fight for France,*
> *For her freedom with honor.*
> *We fight with our hearts and all of our courage.*
> *The freedom of France will be won by Resistance.*
>
> *France will be free,*
> *A free France for Frenchmen,*
> *We'll stay true to France,*
> *And to the Resistance.*

"I can only remember a few words of this song, but it started up again and again during the night; this and the *Marseillaise*. They were sung over the objections of those who were afraid of reprisals."

* * *

"None of us slept in my corner[2]...we were plotting ways and means of escape. Volunteers were selected and hiding places chosen to conceal the equipment from last-minute searches the next day. Conversations on what passed yesterday continued. Some read the Bible, others prayed. One of my comrades who had been a porter in the *Negresco* at Nice, recited Victor Hugo's verses to us...I was strangely sad, in my heart of hearts, to be only twenty years old."

"With the help of Pierre Germaine[3] of Point-Sainte-

1. Unpublished manuscript of Henri Cluzel. August 1970.
2. Unpublished manuscript of Jean-Baptiste Perreolaz, May 1970.
3. Unpublished manuscript of Maurice Baltet, already cited.

Marie, we loosened the rod of a casement bolt to pry up one of the floor boards, if we got the chance, and attempt to escape."

Victor Michaut distributed "prison knives" to the men of Eysses, that had been made out of the covers of tin cans.

The friends of Marcel Gaillard told fortunes with cards:

"Le Quennec offered to lay out the grand spread.[1] There were four men, Clerc, Trabichet, Titin and Le Quennec—the nine of diamonds and the nine of spades were side by side. Fortune-tellers say that this is the certain sign of violent death within a short time...all four men died on the next day."

Around Father de La Perraudière, a sort of optimism prevailed:

"...but naturally[2] with a shadow of melancholy when we thought about this departure toward the unknown which we always had refused to believe was possible for us. The Father gave us confidence by telling us that this day of the feast of the Visitation of the Virgin Mary to her cousin, Elizabeth, was a beautiful day to leave."

1. Unpublished manuscript of Marcel Gaillard. June 1970.
2. Unpublished manuscript of Marcel Moreau. April 1970.

SECOND PART

THE CRIME OF JULY 2

1

Point of Departure

5:00 a.m.—Compiègne. Camp de Royallieu.

"On your feet! Assembly! Roll call!"
The Marseillaise. Song of departure.

"Shut up. The car put at the disposition of the tired gentlemen is about to advance." *(sic)*

Canon Goutaudier, the curé of Mailly, Paul Fontaine, French consul at Liège, assisted by Chivalier and Vidali, climbed into the invalids' cart. About a dozen of the older men joined them.

"98, 99, 100."

Every formation of one hundred men was separated from the following by five steps. The first 'exchanges' among friends and relatives take place. André Page gets caught in the act, and a gun butt in his ribs corrects him.

Two field police recount the square. Now there are 114 men. Laughter. Exasperation. Temper. Shouts. Another recount. Dividing up. More exchanges. They would have had to have a police guard behind every man.

5:15 a.m.—Compiègne Station.

Two trucks loaded with soldiers arrive at the freight platform. The eight sentinels who had kept a night-long watch over the train 7909, rested their guns against the terminal buffer of track VI.

The soldiers of the second truck were already installing two machine guns on the flatcar.

5:15 a.m.—Compiègne. Downtown.

On the first floor up of No. 62, rue de Paris, Yvette Forré was preparing breakfast for her husband. He worked for the P.T.T., and started his morning shift at six o'clock in the telephone exchange. Yvette Forré had passed part of the night in prayer. All of the convoys from Royallieu passed under her window, and she prayed for all of them.

It was the Germans, themselves, who had notified all the residents of the rue de Paris the night before of what the transfer schedule would be, to see to it that all shutters and windows would be closed. They wished to avoid a repetition of the "regrettable incidents" of the previous year, 1943. Hundreds of Frenchmen became renters of these apartments for a few hours so that they could catch a last glimpse of a relative, a friend, a Resistance comrade. Some people, like the proprietors of the *Café de la Victoire*, made a good business out of it by renting their upper windows at a high price.

Yvette Forré kissed her husband goodbye and closed the door to the hallway. While she cleared the table in the dining room, she kept on thinking of the men, perhaps of the women and children who would soon be flocking into the deserted street. She drew up a chair and stared fixedly at the painted flowers of the wallpaper. She placed her hands on the table and her eyes caught sight of the bronze dog with his ears cocked, which had ornamented the buffet for years. A German shepherd dog! What an irony. In less than an hour, in Royallieu, dogs like these baring their fangs and gashing at leg after leg. And suddenly, raising her head, she noted this picture of the Holy Family, bought in 1935 at Porte de l'Etoile, from the bookseller, Madame Dumont. It was a big picture, a good meter in height, which seemed to be resting on the ears of the bronze dog. Yvette Forré smiled: on that day she didn't have enough money and Madame Dumont kept insisting that she take it with her anyhow:

"But yes, but yes! If it gives pleasure, never hesitate. You'll come back to pay me tomorrow."

She remembered the voice, "Mais si, mais si...." she strung out her words like beads on a rosary.

And the next day she had gone back to pay Madame Dumont.

Yvette Forré lifted the painting off its hook on the wall. She had the impression that all the wallpaper flowers that weren't behind the Holy Family had suddenly faded. She leaned the big picture against a chair and went to the kitchen to find a dustcloth.

Lallich, the painter, had composed a scene...very Italian in inspiration, very Saint-Sulpician, Joseph in a smock, kneels at the feet of Mary, who lovingly cuddles an innocent, plump and haloed Jesus.

This picture had become more than a pious symbol for her during these dreadful days of the occupation. It had even, perhaps, lost that sacred quality she had seen in it the day she bought it. Ever since men, women and children had been locked up, deported, it had become the symbol for her of the "family that ought to be." As long ago as June 22, 1941, when she saw the first prisoners of Compiègne file past—Soviet citizens arrested the day after the invasion of Russia—she had imagined them broken, separated and miserable, and she had wept in her kitchen. Today, on this July Sunday, she herself, Yvette Forré, thirty-six years old, housewife, timid, wife of a model employee, could do something for these uprooted beings who were going to be packed into wooden boxes. She would hang the picture at the window of her bedroom. The picture, and a banner—no, the picture and two banners. On the first, she'd write, in tall letters, "Peace on earth to men of good will," and on the second, "Love one another."

"Now we'll see what happens."

5:15 a.m.—The Town of Soissons.

Like every other morning, Paul Legros grumbled over
his big bowl of burned barley, "coffee."
   "Always the same dishwater."
And then, like every other morning, he opened his
pocket knife and cut into his three hundred grams of
rationed bread. He strapped his sack over his shoulder,
looked out at the plum trees in the garden, put on his
cap, lowered his head and walked quickly to the Soissons station. He was the switchman in cabin No. 2.

5:30 a.m.—Compiègne Station.

A diminutive non-com checked the electrical connections for the rail searchlights: guards' van and flatcar,
cars reserved for the escort and observation posts were
provided with batteries and swivel-lights. The only fixed
installations were the six lamps placed under the floor
boards of the freight flatcar and the escort cars. They
were controlled from the front passenger car, and the
beams lit the underside ot the rolling stock.
   It drizzled. An impalpable rain. An invisible mist.
The non-com ordered an unarmed detail to load the
bales of hay into the freight cars. The soldiers were
satisfied to finish the job by sweeping the trailing hay off
the platform of track IV. This left track VI with a little
extra hay underfoot, not much of a comfort, but something just the same.

5:55 a.m.—Soissons Station.

Paul Legros respectfully greeted his boss, Boquillon,
the station chief.
   "All O.K.?"
   "O.K. Monsieur Boquillon."
   "Here's the order sheet. Give Bailly his."
Lucien Bailly came into the office:
   "Hi, Bailly. How goes it?"
   "O.K. Monsieur Boquillon."

Without speaking, the two switchmen crossed tracks Nos. 1 and 2 and separated in the clearing.

"We forgot to ask Boquillon if the tracks and buildings workers had finished repairing the cabins."

"We'll see."

On the morning of the arrival, "Iron Resistance" had dynamited Lucien Bailly's cabin No. 1 and set fire to Paul Legros' No. 2. The repair gang, under guard of the German police, took thirty-six hours to change two bolts, to solder three cables, and restore the station to service.

6:00 a.m.—The Reims Station.

Paul-Emile Renard, the general secretary of the Reims Station, was filing the dispatches that the telegraph office orderly had just delivered to him. The telephone rang.

"It's me!"

Renard recognized the voice. He smiled. The little messenger boy had done his work well. Before depositing the telegrams on the desk of Richter, the German station chief, he had distributed the carbon copies to the leaders of the "Iron Resistance."

"Hello."

"Yes."

"Have you seen the 7909."

"I've seen it."

"My 'connection' from Compiègne told me that it would be the last train of deportees to leave from there...but what you don't know is that Falala[1] is on the

1. Head station master: "Following the bombardment of the Reims Station installation by English planes, on May 1, 1944, at 6:13 p.m., a German troop train which had been delayed there since 3:57 p.m. because of a mechanical breakdown was hit by bombs. In the course of an investigation by the German Surveillance Service on May 3, the office of the head station master was searched by the German police. They confiscated certain letters as evidence, and took him to prison. On the 25th, the Hauptverkehrsdirektion (General Transport Management) informed the S.N.C.F. (National Society of French Railways) that it was forced to appoint someone to replace him, in spite of

list to leave, Falala, and also a doctor from Reims,
Bettinger. Hell, that means about thirty from around
here."

Paul-Emile Renard stood up and went over to the
window. Before him lay the station, still partially wrecked
by the bombardment of May. Scorched walls, gutted
installations, twisted rails. Only one track remained intact.

He took his decision: the 7909, the last train from
Compiègne, would never reach Germany.

"Who?"

"Who can pull the trick?"

There are very few on the service list for Sunday. Not
him, too young.... Here we are: Roger Ollinger. Ollinger,
a strapping, good-natured guy, thirty-five years old, six
feet tall. And to make it easier, Ollinger already has some
explosives hidden in his laundry. Ollinger would be
taking over his shift at electric switching post No. 2. He's
the one who should switch the 7909 toward Reims.
Ollinger would get there at 7:00 a.m.

"That will do, but who will I get to take his place?"

6:00 a.m.—Compiègne. Downtown.

Yvette Forré opened the shutters and hung the "Holy
Family" on the handrail in front of the window. She had
given up the idea of the banners ("How could I attach
them?") She had nailed two big pieces of cardboard
onto the frame. She thought, "from a distance they'll take
it for a head with ears."

The street was deserted.

Yvette Forré closed the window and drew the muslin
curtains.

the intercession of the General Management in his favor." (*La
S.N.C.F. pendant la guerre.* Paul Durand. P.U.F. 1968.)

At the last minute the name of the head station master was
deleted from the list. He left in the following convoy.

6:00 a.m.—Compiègne. Camp de Royallieu.

"Forward.... March!"

The first of the three columns stands at the gate of the transit camp.

"They gave each of us[1] a hunk of bread and sausage meat rolled up in paper. The quantity of food made me guess that the trip was going to be a long one. I'm a butcher by trade and I could see that the sausage meat was already contaminated. I told the men around me to be careful, or it would poison them. Claude Mathieu and I threw it away. It was immediately picked up by others.

"Dozens of other hungry prisoners, especially the young ones, like Jean Martinez, who was only eighteen, gulped down the sausage in three mouthfuls.

"March!"

Five by five, dragging their feet, they left.

The guardians grumbled. When there were only sixty of them, it was impossible for them to keep the men in

1. Unpublished manuscript of Maurice Habermacher, already cited.

line on the way to the station. They planned to have three trips there and back; although the return trip would be by truck, that still made three times four equals twelve. Twelve kilometers on foot. What a Sunday!

The bells began ringing.

"Two women on the sidewalk[1] watched while France marched away. One of them said to the other, pointing to me 'Look, that one's laughing.' "

"We hadn't gone[2] more than one hundred meters when one of my comrades was almost killed by being beaten by a rifle butt. I never knew why. The guard couldn't have been more than eighteen. Before leaving the camp we had been warned, through an interpreter, 'You are not permitted to exchange one single word with the population on the way to the station, and you are ordered to stay well within the ranks of the convoy, for the trip will be as good as you make it.' "

"Because I raised my head[3] to look at a window which had opened, a sentry bashed my head violently and knocked off my béret. I had to scramble to get back in line, kicked along by this *posten*.' "

The group around Henri Billot whistled *La Madelon,* and the one around André Page: *J'irai revoir ma Normandie.*

"Some of the men dared sing out loud,[4] in spite of the threats of the soldiers. Catcalls and slogans started up all over. I recognized the famous, 'they'll get the fat, but not the skin!' Our last, pathetic defiance.... It was already hot and the prisoners were wearing as many items of clothing as possible. They didn't believe that their possessions would be returned on their arrival. I was wearing an imitation suede jacket, with a sleeveless pullover and a warm knitted sweater with a high rolled collar underneath. My equipment was completed by a heavy wool blanket which I carried on my shoulders."

1. Unpublished manuscript of Georges Bixel, already cited.
2. Unpublished manuscript of René Puyo. February 1970.
3. Unpublished manuscript of Noël René Bidault. June 1970.
4. Unpublished manuscript of Pierre Dhenain. April 1970.

"Tears on the cheeks of this woman,[1] huddled over her two kids. Maybe he was going past, her husband, their father. An old man is bent over his cane.... We crossed the Oise River. Fishermen stopped and watched us go by with that meditative withdrawal deep within themselves, like the peasants in Millet's *Angelus*. Millet's grandson could have felt this. He was in the convoy."

"While we were crossing the bridge[2] over the Oise, I kept staring at the water of the river. I heard the policeman walking close to me yell, 'You dirty pig, don't get any bright ideas about jumping into the water.' And he threatened me with his gun. Now and then, along the march, a few hands fluttered behind windows. Pity and worry, but also, sometimes, a fierce determination could be seen on the faces signalling a last goodbye.

"Someone had opened the window[3] and hung a big picture outside, 'The Holy Family,' and a courageous inscription, 'peace on earth to men of good will.' This picture, this inscription, comforted me profoundly. Confidence came back and I vowed to myself, as I walked, that if I ever got out of it, I would come back to this street in Compiègne and thank the person who had given me this hope."

"I saw 'The Holy Family'[4] and thought of my own family. The guards sneered at it as they walked by."

"'Peace on earth...'[5] an extraordinary message. It echoed in the ranks close to mine like an evident sign of hope, and even of imminent aid. At least we knew that we were not alone in Compiègne. Some unknown heart had beat for us."

"I have a strange,[6] clinging memory of our walk to the

1. Unpublished manuscript of René Prungnaud. April 1970.
2. Albert Canac (*Revue du Tarn,* December 1961).
3. Unpublished manuscript of Jean Migeat. May 1970.
   Migeat returned to Compiègne in 1966. He followed the rue de Paris until he recognized the house and the window. He went in. Twenty-two years later, he thanked Madame Forré for her brave gesture.
4. Unpublished manuscript of Jean Lartigues. February 1970.
5. Unpublished manuscript of Jean-Baptiste Perreolaz, already cited.
6. Unpublished manuscript of Pierre Ropiquet. March 1970.

station. My first memory is of the fear that gripped me. I
was twenty years old. Really only a kid. I kept looking
around for my old friends from Niort. I swapped places
and shifted around in the ranks and finally caught up
with them. Alongside André Tesson....I felt safe. That
was the day that I discovered the statue of Jeanne d'Arc.
It seemed to me that I had just finished my history
lessons. But what I'll never forget is that, from a tiny attic
window, somebody threw a little bouquet of flowers on
the column of marching men, and a voice cried out,
'Courage, my boys.'"

The accordeonist, André Verchuren, walked beside
Jean Migeat.

"André, André, I embrace you."

André Verchuren had just enough time to catch sight
of his mother in the shadow of the carriage entryway.

6:00 a.m.—Compiègne Depot.

Coville, the stoker, hammer in hand, took the first
dancing steps around the 230 D for his inspection. The
230 D was the granddaughter of the Atlantic locomotive.
Compact, in spite of its length and finish, restrained, in
spite of an exuberance of jacks, rods, arms, and tubing at
the level of the axles and the bogie. She was the best
little runner among the heavy trains making frequent
stops.

Throttles, flywheel, guide rod, valve, a little grease in
the blow-off cups...the engine comes alive. Already, up
above, squeezed onto the little sheet metal bridge,
linking it to the tender, Riedel, a depot stocker, loads the
hearth. The first dust glides into the ignition pit. In the
silence of this hangar, coated with thick soot, the 230 D
begins to warm up. The blue needle of the pressure
gauge rises.

Riedel asks, from the cabin, "It's still for 9 a.m.?"

"You never know with them."

"We'll probably leave well before that, as soon as
they're all loaded on."

7:05 a.m.—Reims Station.

Paul-Emile Renard pushed the swinging door of switch station No. 2. Roger Ollinger was leafing through a magazine.

"You've seen the 7909?...It's a train of deportees."

"That's what I came to see you about. This train is the last. The very last train of deportees. We've all talked about it together,[1] we all agree: this convoy must not reach Germany. Can you imagine what a blow we'd be striking. What a knock-out! What a victory!"

"And you want me to...."

"Yes. It's too late to organize an armed attack. And anyhow, it must be guarded like all hell. A lot of us would get killed. Do you still have the plastic bombs?"

"Two or three little bundles. I even have one with a clockwork system. The latest model—très chic."

"You're ready. You'll do it?"

"What a question. You'll have to get somebody to replace me here. I have to get to Saint-Brice."

"Are you walking."

"I've got a bike."

"Good. I'll put one of our boys here to take your place. I'll keep you posted about the movement of the train."

"The best place would be behind the glass-works...there's a slope where nobody ever goes."

"It's a kilometer from here. That's enough."

"A little more, perhaps a kilometer and a half, but further along there are the little kitchen gardens. And there'd be too many people...on a Sunday."

"How much time do you need?"

"Let's say an hour. The train is set for between 10:30 and noon. Send me someone at 9 o'clock."

Renard holds out his hand.

"Thanks, thanks Roger. Good luck."

"Shit, Paul-Emile, just say shit for luck!"

"Shit!"

---

1. Iron Resistance in liaison with Free French Forces.

7:20 a.m.—Compiègne Station (The Sheet Metal Car).

"That's all. Don't move. Don't talk," and the interpreter walked off. ·

The block of one hundred men, grouped in front of the only metal car of the convoy relaxed from "attention," and stretched. From the last row, a voice, a big poker face, brown blanket around his shoulders: "Oh! aren't we the chancy bastards. A brand-new freight car."

In the first row, André Gonzalès has his head held down, staring at the footboard.

"Hey, kid...."

No answer.

"Hey, yes, you."

"What do you want?"

The prisoner who had spoken to him was three places over to the right.

"Change with me.... Hell, too late. They're coming."

The interpreter, with a soldier on each side, slipped between the car and the first line of soldiers.

"I believe that you have already been warned...."

He had no German accent. He was hardly more than thirty. White skin. Little nose.

"You know the price schedule. For one escape attempt there will be two hundred of you in there, instead of one hundred, and you'll be naked.... For one successful escape, ten shot; for two escapes, the whole carload. This is the regulation. It will be carried out. Those of you who have knives or metal objects, drop them on the ground. There will be no punishment. If later on I find a knife, the guilty man and the two men nearest him will be shot. Now I shall walk to the rear. Drop your knives on the ground. I shall not be looking."

The interpreter and the two soldiers moved around the group.

"No knives? Nothing has fallen? We shall see in a short time."

His voice was calm and gentle.

"Climb aboard."

When his turn came, André Gonzalès climbed in. He heard the man behind him say, "They must be mad. We'll never make it. A hundred of us in there...."

André Gonzalès squeezed into the right rear corner.
Dark. Heavy. Musty. The men coming in were black
silhouettes against the square of light framed by the
door. The walls were warm. Words. Dozens of words. All
the same.

"This is it."

"Keep going."

"Watch out. No room. It's the subway. We're packed.
Sardine tin."

"It's hot."

"Take off your sweater."

"Don't shove."

The interpreter's voice cut through the noise.

"Very good. Push in a bit more."

Two soldiers use their rifle butts to open a meter-wide
breach in the center of the wagon. The interpreter
climbed in and took off his cap.

"Final warning. I am going to have my cap passed
around. Put in it any money you may have hidden, knives
and any object which could be used for escape."

Gonzalès thought that this officer had surely been
educated, at least partly, in France.

The cap passed from hand to hand, over heads, and
came back empty to its owner.

"Very well. Now we shall search you."

He spoke to the two soldiers accompanying him, in
German, and they opened a little further space with their
rifles, but without violence.

The interpreter moved forward, stooped down, and
picked a knife up from the floor....

"You there.... Get him outside."

The man he pointed to—forty years old, dark-skinned,
average height, dark blue sweater—was lifted off his feet
by the two soldiers.

"But, it's not mine. It's not me...."

...They threw him down, between the tracks, on the
cinders. The soldiers rushed him. A dozen blows of the
gun butts...on his skull...on his face. He only cried out
twice.

During the "session" the interpreter disappeared.

The guards ordered two prisoners to get out and load
the wounded man back on the car.

The sliding metal door clacked shut.

Night.

Five, six beams of light, blinding, tiny, came through the cracks of the boarded-up window shafts and the sliding doors, spreading out in a rippling fan over the heads of the men.

"But we can't see anything in here."

"Better open the window-shafts."

"Squeezed in like this, we'll never live through it."

Eyes become accustomed to the darkness.

"The guy they beat up is going to croak. Blood's pissing out."

"We need a doctor. Isn't there a doctor in here?"

"Believe me, he's going to lose all his blood. My pants are soaked with it already."

"Lay him down."

"There's no room."

"If I ever get my hands on those bastards."

A low-pitched, powerful voice calls for silence.

"Let me through, please. I'll take care of him."

André Gonzalès closed his eyes: behind them was the smile of his mother, a river, a white rabbit.

7:30 a.m.—Compiègne Station (The Weil Car).[1]

When we left the camp we determined not to be separated: Kienzler, Rohmer, Professor Vlès and myself. When we reached the station, catastrophe. The group was separated for the two sections of the train, and Kienzler and I were together, along with some other comrades from Eysses, but our two friends were forced into the adjoining car. Ours had a domed roof, which meant that it must contain about twenty-five per cent more air, but there must have been a hundred prisoners in each car. A little harangue by a German on the price to be paid by the rest of us, if one of us tries to escape. I was standing toward the back, but since I was the tallest, I was the one they searched. I've always had that kind of relative bad luck. He found a small box of emergency

---

1.   Unpublished manuscript of Dr. Paul Weil, already cited.

medicines, cursed me out, but didn't take them, and smiled....

There was a little barrel of water and an empty tub next to the door. Michaut, Kienzler, Dartout and I took charge of the herd shut up in the car. It was a spontaneous reflex arising from the training at Eysses....The key words—everybody seated, close together. This way, chests will be at about the same level, and air divided up equally. Clothes on the floor and not hung up, so as not to interfere with air circulation. That was the hardest order of all, because there were fastidious ones who were still worried about the creases in their coats. One distribution of water every two hours, a half glass; double ration for the oldest and the youngest. All bowel evacuation must be thrown out of the window.

The heat was unbearable. A former soldier didn't want to sit down, and received my fist in his face. Only Fuchs sat higher than the rest, astride the barrel. His buttock was still sore from the Propidon injection. He couldn't sit on the floor, and so he kept guard over the water.

7:30 a.m.—Compiègne Station (The Rohmer Car).[1]

According to what we could guess, the little car with the flat roof was meant for us. "That's great," the man next to me said, "we'll be only fifty. It's smaller than the others. They can't expect to get a hundred of us in there." He was deluding himself.

As arranged with Rollot, I rushed forward at the first order, leaped into the wagon and helped him climb on, then together, before the S.S. had a chance to stop us, we hoisted Professor Vlès, whose movements were very restricted by the heavy blanket around his neck, which

1. Francis Rohmer, *"De l'Université aux camps de concentration"* in *Témoignages strasbourgeois.* Publication of the Faculty of Letters of the University of Strasbourg, 1947. Les Belles Lettres. Paris.

Francis Rohmer, Chief of the Neurological Clinic of the Faculty of Medicine of Strasbourg, born February 20, 1915, at Colmar. Arrested March 8, 1944, at the hospital of Clermont-Ferrand.

had slipped down. But Armand lost his balance, tripped on the track bed, and his haversack fell to the ground. He tried to pick it up. A big brute took advantage of the situation, beat him up with the rifle butt and cursed him. It was difficult to pull him on board.

Fifty of us filled the car, but we had to crush together hastily because a second group of fifty had to get in. It was unbearable. The sliding door closed, but not for long.

A non-commissioned officer came in with two field police and started the usual little speech, prepared for the occasion, with a sugary voice. Square head, shaved neck, steel-rimmed glasses, he made me think of a drawing by Hansi. But this wasn't the moment to smile. "All those who have knives...." No reply. Suddenly he starts to shout: "I know you have them." He grabbed the nearest man, searched him, beat him with the butt of his revolver. He struck at random, and finally he victoriously waved a nail which he had found in a pocket.

Gripped with fear, a prisoner handed a knife to him, another a file... we could hear a few heavy objects fall to the floor that the prisoners tried to get rid of. The search was over.

The S.S. gave us a last bit of advice: "At the least attempt to escape, the sentries will shoot. If there is a successful escape we will chose a certain number of you at random, and they will be shot immediately. Get that?" We all got it. What a pleasure trip this was going to be! He left, belching out curses. He left with his attendant escort, who seemed very pleased with everything. He slid the door closed, hammered it into place, and padlocked it. The walls echoed. Our coffin was sealed....

There were a hundred of us locked into this freight car, smaller than the others, and for how long? One day, two days, more? The predictions were around three days. Where are we going? Dachau? Buchenwald? Auschwitz? Struthof? What will happen on the way, and when we get there? A refinement of cruelty to prolong the uncertainty. But what was certain was that we didn't have any water. There was a barrel, but it was empty!

...and soon we wouldn't have any air. There were two window shafts opposite each other, about seventy-five by fifty centimeters, strung over with barbed wire. The air didn't circulate. The men in the middle of the car were already complaining and we would have to do something quickly to take care of the situation. We couldn't all stand, and we couldn't all sit. Our eyes grew accustomed to the almost total obscurity. We decided to set up a system of rotation. Fifteen men would stand up, while the others sat, each one fitted into the other, like pieces of a puzzle, back against chest. Professor Vlès was behind me. Rollot was between my legs. Confidence revived, and the morale was good. We joked about ourselves, sardines in a can, horses laid end to end. Some of us hummed a tune, waiting for the departure. The great departure.

7:30 a.m.—Compiègne Station (The Sirvent Car).[1]

I was separated from my friends, those who had been with me since Limoges, who had followed the same hard road, step by step. I was in the ranks with Pascal de Lucas, a very young schoolteacher from Nice, only twenty-one years old, who shared my cell. In spite of the tortures inflicted in the interrogatories, his memories of his youth on the Côte d'Azur, and his dreams in the Maquis brought light into our darkest moments and colored the gray monotony of prison. He was sadly affected by this departure at dawn. He sought blindly for comrades who had been dragged off into the other cars. This was the morning of his death.

A cattle van swallowed us up. We were piled in and immediately paralyzed in a coagulated mass of a hundred men, where there wouldn't have been space for forty.

1. Unpublished manuscript of Louis-Eugène Sirvent, March 1970. Born at Allauch, Bouches-du-Rhône, October 30, 1908. He was the chief private secretary of the departmental administrator when he was mobilized in 1939. When he was demobilized he was named secretary general of the administration of Allier at Moulins. He organized underground communications....Arrested for the first time in 1942, and released, he became an intelligence agent (Jade-Fitzroy, A.S.). Again arrested by the Gestapo, May 29, 1944.

The door slid shut, leaving us half-stunned in the semi-dark.... Our tormentor took over his load of living-dead. Suddenly we were face to face with the unimaginable, the insuperable. Now we had to hold firm for the days that were coming. But we had been told that transports to Germany took four, six, sometimes eight, ten days. Hold firm, or die. But how?

The door clashed open. A big, swarthy officer with a paper in his hand, called out in French: "Who wrote this card?" We were blinded by the daylight. Nobody replied. The question was asked again, with threats this time. Then a young man in the rear answered: "I did."

An S.S. plowed through the mass like a bull, bellowing. He charged the boy. All I could see was his powerful back, his neck enormous under his cap, and his terrible, flailing fists. He pulled the Frenchman out of the car and hurled him down on the platform. Again the door rolled shut. The soldiers on the outside joined in the game. They crushed him with their boots. We heard him howl, then his voice faded, then silence. This time when the door opened, they threw him, bleeding, onto our heads. The Frenchman had written on a postal card: "I am leaving for Germany. Long live the Resistance." In the darkness of the freight car we managed to make a little space for him to lie down and die in peace.

7:30 a.m.—Compiègne Station (The Puyo Car).[1]

As I got into the car, the field police who was standing at the footboard to count us, noticed a little green ribbon

1.   Unpublished manuscript of Col. René Puyo, already cited.
    "I was a second lieutenant in the artillery in 1939. My tour of duty started in Alsace, then Belgium (Namur), Dunkerque, England, and back to Caen to terminate that brief and catastrophic campaign trapped near Grenoble, where I was saved from internment by the Armistice. Like many of the other young men, I had dreamed of victory. Try to imagine my feelings then. But the Army of the Armistice restored some hope and faith. We trained at the 24th R.A. of Toulouse. In addition, often during the long nights, I joined a few comrades in concealing weapons. Then came the occupation of the Free Zone by the German Army. I

A photograph of Dr. Illers, taken after the war. He had been the listening post of the S.D. (Security service of the Reich) at Royallieu. His service was the center for all the files and indexes, and it prepared, in quadruplicate, the lists of departure for the camps. He was the one who, after having examined each case, decided upon the category in which the condemned prisoner was definitively classified.

A.F.P.

in the buttonhole of my jacket. "What's that?" he demanded, and struck me a ringing blow. I climbed up as quickly as I could to escape his fist. He pulled me down, and asked again, "What's that?" I answered, "Croix de guerre." He tore the ribbon off and I got away with a resounding blow from the butt of his gun, which I could have done very well without.

7:40 a.m.—Compiègne Station (The Habermacher Car).[1]

I found myself close to the door, with Claude Mathieu, and a group composed of patriots.... The rest of the car was full of common-law criminals. It began to get hot.

was expecting something else, alas. On December 19, 1942, I became a member of the group that developed into the Pommies Commando. After I had assumed responsibility in the Toulouse area, I became Commando Chief in the Ariège where I had two large companies under my command, one centered in Saint-Girons and the other in Foix-Pamiers."

René Puyo was denounced to the Germans and arrested. Saint-Michel de Toulouse, then Compiègne.

1. Unpublished manuscript of Maurice Habermacher, already cited.

The escapes, often incredibly extravagant, of Maurice Habermacher, could provide material for a book all by itself. Taken as a war prisoner to Germany, he escaped from Cologne on September 4, 1940. It took him nearly two months to get to the Jura mountains on foot. He decided to join the F.F.L. Captured while he was crossing the Swiss frontier, he escaped the next day from the Gestapo building in Besançon. Then, in the region of Briey, he contacted the Resistance and was assigned to welcome and shelter Russian prisoners employed in the mines. He was arrested while traveling on a truck... filled with weapons. He was deported to Tilsit in eastern Prussia.

Two days after his arrival he was assigned to a work detail, loading a train with equipment to be sent to the Atlantic Wall. He hid in a cement mixer. The train left. Ten days of travel under Allied bombardment....At Brest he crawled out of the cement mixer, and contacted the Breton Resistance who told him that the only way still open to get to England was across the Spanish frontier. He passed back and forth across the border, since his Barcelona contact assigned him to set up liaison with the Pyrenean Maquis. On June 4, 1944, he was picked up by a

We stripped to the waist. One of us proposed that we sit in rows, each between the legs of the man behind, and not move any more. That left about thirty who still had to stand, for lack of space. We agreed to take shifts, and that's when the first incident broke out. Some small-timer had managed to hang on to his knife during the search, and took it upon himself to use it now to cut a piece off his hunk of bread. One of the "toughs" who saw what was going on lost no time in alerting the Germans on the platform, probably hoping for a reward.

The doors were unsealed, and opened. We were immediately evacuated from the car, which was searched from top to bottom. Our clothing was thrown on the platform. For a final dirty trick, they took away the container of water and the slop bucket....

We got back in and tried to organize ourselves as best we could. The removal of our clothes had given us a bit more room. But still, we couldn't all sit at the same time. It got hotter and hotter. The 'tough' who had denounced his neighbor with the knife, started to pester us, the Resistants. The rest of that element joined in. They blamed us for causing the loss of the barrel of water, and even for their deportation to Germany. They told us that they had been perfectly comfortable in the French prisons, and they asked nothing better than to stay with Maréchal Pétain and keep out of trouble....

Noise and tension both built up. We swung two pairs of trousers suspended under an open light shaft and got a bit of fresh air. We agreed not to urinate. A "tough" who was standing up, got the perverted inspiration to squirt all over the seated men. Others promptly imitated him. To be honest, they could hardly do anything else, since there wasn't an unoccupied square foot of space. Those who had eaten the sausage meat began to have stomach cramps, and writhed about. Their bowels moved, it was inevitable, and everybody was in the shit. That, and the growing heat made it impossible to breathe. A fight—the first one—broke out. The blows

German patrol, was tortured, was transported. His last effort at escape, in the Paris subway, failed and he was taken to Compiègne.

were violent and blood flowed. The wounded men called for help.

The Germans slid the door back again, one with a machine gun ready to fire into the heap. I crouched instinctively, and closed my eyes. No, they didn't shoot, but several of them climbed into the car and conscientiously laid about them with the butts of their guns. But the briefly opened door had let in fresh air, and it calmed us down.

And still, the train didn't start. It got hotter and hotter. The most weakened ones broke down and began to cry for water. We told them to be quiet, because the Germans might shoot from the outside.

7:50 a.m.—Compiègne. Camp de Royallieu.

The third column marked time:

"Houde was on one side of me[1] and a junior air force non-commissioned officer on the other. An S.D. officer noticed him, came over, and I remember his words. 'A nice mess for a French Army non-com. What did you do?' He answered, 'Me...nothing...,' and then the latent resentment broke out. 'Shut up, you bandit...you'll see what it costs to be a Gaullist.'

"The escort took its place, helmeted, machine guns under their arms, grenades hanging from their belts and in their boots, along the whole length of the last segment. A moment of waiting. Two deferments of departure had been received. Two men left the column and returned to camp A. The human flood stirred slowly.... Here was the rue de Paris, the quai de Narlay. I was on the lookout. Would I catch sight of someone I knew?...

"I caught sight of the corner of the bridge, and over there...yes, it was her. She was there, my wife. I recognized her. What a change since my arrest. Take courage! I shifted over from the left side, where I was, to the right where I could see her better. She was not alone. Two of her sisters were with her. I thought of my

1.   Marcel Guérin, already cited.

baby son whom she was nursing. I stiffened up so that I
would not betray my emotion. Now, now I was close to
her, if it can be put that way, since we were at least
fifteen yards apart, and between us there was still the
escort and that big Feldwebel of the Kommandantur of
Compiègne, who took part in my arrest. A few farewell
gestures, a wave of the hand, but not a word. My throat
contracted. It was already ended. I turned around often,
but I couldn't see her any more. Then I relaxed and
breathed more deeply. The hardest moment, the one I
had been most afraid of, was passed."

7:55 a.m.—Compiègne (Freight Car with Eighty).

The second column was packed away. The final squad
was counted, and then counted again. There were only
eighty. Long discussion among the guards, and then:
"On board!"
This car would never be "complete." It was large—
relatively—for eighty travelers.
"I obeyed the command as soon as it was issued.[1]
"I didn't wait for the guards to give me a 'gentle' push.
The first to enter, I rushed to a window shaft laced over
with barbed wire, and I obstinately refused to leave my
place throughout the whole voyage. The others said,
'Hey, little guy, get away from there.' But me, the little
guy—I remembered what a Spaniard had told me when I
met him in Compiègne, and I wouldn't move over an
inch. This Spaniard had given me good advice: 'You're
young and quick. You get into the car first, and don't
move away from the airshaft.' Perhaps I owe my life to
my selfishness there."
"I was the last to get into the car[2] where I found some
of my comrades from Le Mans whom I had known in the

1. Unpublished manuscript of Jean Martinez. April 1970. He
had been arrested on May 22, 1944, denounced by the Gestapo
of Cahors.
2. Unpublished manuscript of Jean-Yves Chapalain, deputy of
Sarthe, former mayor of Le Mans, County Councillor, March
1970.

military prison: Soyer, the Jardins, father and son, Sable and Colas. Since there was no space left for the last one to get in, I had to install myself on the slop-bucket, and I rode almost all the way to Dachau on this improvised seat."

"This car had an observation box.[1] It was occupied by a German. The Friends of the Resistance had succeeded in staying grouped together in the front, right corner. Emile Moderc had his leg in a plaster cast. It had been fractured just before his arrest, while we were scaling a wall. Maurice Perrot had his head shaved. He had dyed his hair blond to avoid recognition. In prison and at Compiègne his hair had started to grow, and it was black at the roots. Because we all made fun of him, he had had his head shaved so close, that he was going to be one step ahead of us when we got to Dachau. Petit had printed tri-color flags. Guerzoni had been captured in the Maquis near Semur-en-Auxois. Petitot was a natural born rebel. He had gotten into a fight with a German in a streetcar. The German had tried to arrest him, and he jumped from the moving car. He was chased by a pack of German soldiers, and his luck gave out. He could have outrun all of them. He was a track champion, but he ran into a closed alley."

8:35 a.m.—Soissons Station.

On platform No. 1—wearing blue-gray uniforms with the Red Cross insignia, Countess Olivier de La Rochefoucauld, Madame de Pennart, and three nurses were filling tin buckets with water. The Red Cross of Soissons

1. Unpublished manuscript of Maurice Voutey, April 1970. "I was nineteen years old. I was a student-teacher. I had joined the Resistance in 1942, right after the execution of four of my highschool comrades, shot on March 7. At first I was a member of the F.P.J. (Popular National Front of Youth), and after the formation of the F.U.J.P. (United Front), I was in charge of that organization for Dijon. By the Spring of 1944, I had become Departmental leader. I didn't really have any time to get into this work because I was captured by the Gestapo right after my nomination."

had been discreetly alerted the evening before, by Boquillon, the station master.

Madame de Pennart trembled. She was crying silently,
staring at the deserted platform No. 2. There, between
the two switch posts...on June 18...two weeks ago to
the day, she had caught sight of her husband at the
window shaft of a car filled with deportees. Track 1,
track 2, the platform, the armed guards, the freight cars,
the signals, the shouts, the train left, and she hadn't been
able to cross over to him, only fifteen meters away....

"Good morning, ladies. They'll be getting here between
nine or nine-thirty."

8:45 a.m.—Compiègne Station.

Accompanied by a sentry, Alfred Pâques stood some
fifty meters in front of the first section of 7909 to direct
the coupling manoeuvre. The switching cabin brought
track No. VI in line and rang the depot. Alfred Pâques
signaled with his arm.

Martial Dorgny, at the controls of 230 D turned toward
Coville. The stoker opened the exhaust. A whirlwind of
white steam enveloped the locomotive. Softly, with the
palm of his hand, Dorgny advanced the regulator. The
one hundred twenty tons of the locomotive and tender
started to vibrate, the unbraked wheels frictioned on the
rails. The gigantic tangle of iron, water and coal groaned
forward, hawking steam.

"Hey, what about me. Are you forgetting me?"

Rieder, two hands on the guide rail, swung on board.

"This is no fun for me, but I'm part of the trip. I've
become the look-out for planes, bombardments, machine-
gunnings. Muller, himself, assigned me. And listen to
this, there isn't just one 'Bahnhof' with us, there are
two."[1]

---

1. Generally, each convoy was accompanied by one of the
German station staff from the place of departure. French railway
workers called them "Bahnhof" (Paul Durand has published in
the French University Press a masterly study of the French
railway system, S.N.C.F., during the war).

"There must be something peculiar about this load."

Dorgny shifted the control and the bogie moved past the switch intersection.

Pâques waved a greeting at the mechanic: "Hello."

The sentry followed the locomotive.

Dorgny pulled on the cord of the whistle and slowed down.

Twenty meters further on a German trackman shook the rolled flag free of its black leather container.

Throttle valve closed. Brake engaged. A burst of steam. The flag held downward. Contact. The buffers screech back, absorbing the shock. The locomotive pushes the section on track IV back by less than a meter.

The switching cabin covered the red and blocked the position on the outward track.

The station chief, Carpentier, went back into his office. Merlin was seated near the window.

"Did you see...?"

"Not much. I thought I saw Marcel Guérin...."

The two men spoke at the same time.

"If only that could be the last!..."

8:50 a.m.—Compiègne Station (The Guérin-Canac Car).

"Ouf!...That's it.[1] Here we are, and I'm lucky to have my friends around me. There's no room to move, and the arguments are starting already. At this moment I remembered the lettering on the freightcar.... 'Forty men or eight horses.' Obviously, the French Army had been very generous to its soldiers!...Silence!..."

"In my group[2] there was a comrade in work blues who

1.   Marcel Guérin, already cited, was an intelligence agent in the British and Belgian networks. Arrested May 3, 1944, following denunciation.
2.   Albert Canac, *"Récit d'un rescapé—Le Convoi de la Mort du 2 juillet 1944"* (in *Revue du Tarn,* No. 24, third series, December 1961, Imprimerie coopérative du Sud-Ouest, Albi). Albert Canac, boarding school headmaster of the military academy of Andelys (commander of a group of army children). The school was forced to evacuate, first to Béziers, and then in February 1944, to Tulle where he was arrested on June 9 at dawn, along with all

insisted on getting in with us, although the sentinels kept pushing him back, probably thinking he was a railway worker. The poor man didn't understand a thing. He withdrew a bit and then came forward again. The Germans changed their minds and stuffed him in with us, definitively.... 'The bastards, we're all going to conk out here.' But a doctor cut him short: 'Don't talk. Move as little as possible.' We promised to take his advice."

"I hid the rod of the casement bolt in a blanket,[1] after having bent it into a horse-shoe shape, and then I covered everything with some rye straw that littered the floor of the car. Later, when they conducted the search, I cheerfully handed up the nail file I had bought at the canteen in Royallieu."

8:15 a.m.—Compiègne Station.

Frizon, the conductor, followed a guard and crossed the last barrier in the freight depot. His "guide" pointed out the flatcar with the mounted machine guns.

"No, the tail van. Work."

"Not to move."

The soldiers on the flatcar laughed and gesticulated. The convoy interpreter came running up.

"Climb up onto the flatcar."

"I can't. I've got my job to do."

"What job?"

"If the train stops, I have to put a detonator signal on the track a kilometer back."

"Well then, it's all the same if you leave from the flatcar or the van. Get on up."

"Regulations forbid it...."

"I'm the regulations. Get on up!"

the other men of Tulle, and "retained" as hostage. Out of twenty professors and monitors picked up in the school of Tulle, one was hung, two set free, and fifteen deported.

According to a dependable witness from Tarn, the man in blue was Jean Bories of Tessonnières, who died in deportation (note by Albert Canac).

1.   Unpublished manuscript of Maurice Baltet, already cited.

He spoke in German to the soldiers and one of them held out a hand.

"Your limousine awaits. Get on up."

Frizon put his basket down on the floor of the flatcar.

"There we are!"

9:05 a.m.—Compiègne Station.

Muller shook hands with the S.D. officer. Pâques, with expert control, placed the 230 D on track IV. From where they stood, neither the officer nor Muller could see the locomotive and the section manoeuvre on track VI. Forty guards were installed in the observation boxes and escort carriages. The cordon of sentries broke formation. The men were to return to Paris by truck.

Whistle!

The section on track IV doubled past the part of the train standing still, went one hundred meters beyond the switch and backed up to couple with its other half. Muller closed the door of the S.D., gave a military salute (he was a captain). Dorgny turned the wheel of the throttle valve, 9:15 a.m., July 2, 1944, the 7909 got under way.

2

The First Kilometers

The Rohmer Car.[1]

The train rolled slowly. "What? No springs," Nikis joked. Less than half an hour since we left Compiègne—our legs were asleep, we ached all over. The huddled position was intolerable. The sun broke through the clouds and the heat intensified. Some got up to take off their jackets and when they tried to sit down again, the line had slid over, and they were forced to remain standing. Cattish comments revealed the tension. Those who were standing wanted to sit, and those who were sitting wanted to stand. Faces reddened and sweat poured down the temples. Professor Vlès, seated behind me, was very calm, and nevertheless, he felt imminent catastrophe in the air, and he wanted to avoid it. "Take command of the car," he told me, "I'm feeling too old." And what about me? Wasn't I too young? If only we were all from the same prison, where we knew each other, even without seeing each other. But for our little group of the Clermont-Ferrand military prison, called the

1. Francis Rohmer, already cited.

"92," the others were unknown, and in addition, in the car, we weren't all political prisoners. A certain number were criminal convicts, and there was nothing about their looks to reassure us.

I took over. I tried to get them to understand what could happen. I gave them a bit of advice: strict discipline was indispensable. The small amount of water in the flasks had to be reserved for the sick.

My little speechifying seemed to work. The arguments stopped. Calm was restored. The train rolled slowly along tracks that had been torn up by repeated bombardments.

The Habermacher-La Perraudière Car.[1]

The train moved. But for lack of openings, the air barely circulated while the heat continued to increase. We were suffocating. Some wanted to drink, others wanted us to save the water. I saw that there would soon be a fight about it. I raised my voice and proposed that a leader be appointed for the car, and that he would decide, in case of disagreement. As almost always in such cases, they said, "Good idea. You take charge of it yourself!"

This was the time when I realized that I was practically surrounded by strangers. At one end of the car, a dozen or more comrades spoke Spanish or Catalan. There was a great difference in ages. I needed helpers, but the only two men I knew were really boys, barely twenty years old. They wouldn't have the authority. Who could I get to help me? I asked them to appoint a man for each end of the car to take charge of the distribution of water, for it was true that we'd had nothing to drink since the night before. A few had quarter-liter mugs and they were passed forward. We'll only give one-quarter per man this time. When the distribution was finished, one of the comrades in charge of it whispered to me, "One hundred seventeen were passed out." They were cheating already....

1. Unpublished manuscript of Father de la Perraudière, already cited. See also, *Witches of the Sky.*

After a very long stop, the train started rolling again. It went slowly and stopped often. This early July heat built up terribly. Some of the men started to take off their clothing. But an old watchmaker from Paris stayed completely buttoned up in all of his clothing. "I want to die decently dressed." I still didn't believe what was in store for us, and I exclaimed, "Look here, now. There's no question of dying!"

The heat had become unbearable. I realized that I had to save my strength, and I sat down as best I could between two comrades. A bad move, without doubt. Maybe the air was more mephitic at this level. Whatever it was, I found myself sinking into exhaustion. As I lost consciousness, I fell back against the comrade behind me. He tried roughly to prop me back up. No matter what he did, I couldn't hold myself upright.

How long can a journey that's endless last? Its very sluggishness seeped into the soul with the despair of a man condemned forever. More heat. We're bathed in sweat. We suffocate. Yes we're going to die here. But at the end of how much time? Oh, God, at the end of how much suffering?

The Car of Eighty.

"Their threats[1] echoed in our minds—an escape attempt: ten shot—an escape: twenty shot.... Was it because I was sitting there that I felt I had to talk. There was no doubt about it. Sitting upright on the slop bucket gave me the appearance of dominating the situation. I talked it over with Vigouroux, the police commissioner of Tarbes, and together, we tried to convince our comrades. We reached an agreement: no escapes during the convoy, which would certainly result in the threatened reprisals. In contrast, when we get to our destination, those who wanted to try their luck would be free to act, and we would help them.

1. Unpublished manuscript of Jean-Yves Chapalain, already cited.

"Very soon some of us started to crack up: 'I'm suffocating,' 'I'm thirsty.' I can never forget the young Jardin who couldn't stand any longer, he doubled over on his knees and his nose and ears began to bleed, the first signs of asphyxia. Several comrades succeeded in raising him up to the height of the window shaft so that he could breathe a bit of fresh air. He revived slowly but was very pale and weak during the whole trip."

"To my utter amazement,[1] as soon as we got going, some of the comrades pulled out what they had succeeded in hiding from the guards, in spite of the search: knives, forks, and even one good metal saw. That started up talk about evasion. Unfortunately, the older ones didn't agree, and they kept us from trying, on the theory that we young ones would be able to jump better than they could, without breaking a leg. And they were afraid of the reprisals with which we had been threatened."

The Puyo Car.[2]

We had taken our jackets and shirts off a long time ago. We weren't hungry, because we couldn't breathe. It was impossible to sit. Everybody wanted to get his mouth close to a crack. Anger welled up, it was impossible to satisfy everybody. There were young and old among us. The young were losing control of themselves and were ready to fight in order to survive. With enormous difficulty, we succeeded in getting a car leader appointed, Captain Folliot. I knew him, he had been captain in the regiment where I was a second lieutenant. He died before the night was over, totally spent by the efforts he had made to save the rest of us.

He told us: "If we want to remain men, and try to survive, each of us must think first of his neighbor; economize our strength, and don't move at all, or as little as possible. When the temperature drops, we'll be able to breathe more easily. Above all, remain calm, and leave

1.   Unpublished manuscript of Jean Martinez, already cited.
2.   Unpublished manuscript of Col. René Puyo, already cited.

space for those who suffer." He called upon me to take charge in my corner.

It was already too late for us to prepare calmly, for the care of those overcome by asphyxiation or madness. In spite of the courageous stand of a few men, we were going to be overwhelmed, quickly, by a flood let loose by delirium, and not by egotism. In Captain Folliot's corner, some of the men had started tearing at each other, with wild, animal howls accompanying their flailing. Captain Folliot and other comrades had to hold them back by force.

By this time some of the men were completely naked. We were all sweaty and dirty. No trace of personality was left that had distinguished one man from another. Eyes were swollen, vision clouded, and our mouths were gasping open. What were we breathing? Vitiated air— there is no name for it. When we looked at each other, we looked into fiendish distortions, hallucinated features, which frightened us, blurred my madness, the madness coming upon us, the madness already upon us.

From the back of the car, a few seconds later, climbing somehow over the top of our heads—a comrade already maddened by advanced asphyxia. He wanted to live, and plunged for the crack two meters away. Poor kid, he fell against me and crashed into a comrade alongside. I tried to help him get up, and received a punishing clout from his fist that threw me down. I understood. He thrashed about for a couple of minutes while blood spurted from his nose, and his face turned purple.... How can I say that he breathed his last, when there was no air to breathe? Catastrophe loomed. Two more comrades fell into my arms, without any more air to breathe, bearing the same stigmata.

The Sirvent Car.[1]

Beyond any hope or reason, there were still some extraordinary human reactions. Order was established.

1. Unpublished manuscript by Louis-Eugène Sirvent, already cited.

Some stood, others sat, as instructed by a leader, a doctor appointed to give help from his corner. The sickest and the oldest could breathe, from time to time, at the grilled slits and board joints where a little air filtered through. We felt better. Some of us waved the blankets about a bit to keep the air in movement. Conversations resumed. I think someone even sang.

The Weil Car.

"Some of the men[1] were developing nerves. I suggested we play the popular game, 'You're Out!'"

"Every movement,[2] every elementary need posed a problem. We had to solve each as it came up. We had to be in agreement on what would be obligatory for everybody. The unit that had lived through Eysses together had accumulated a great deal of experience to back it up, and above all, it had the strength of its unity. This was a major asset, and often, even an example. It must be evident that the situation didn't encourage an exchange of philosophies, or of life histories. It wasn't a question of reciting our lives, but of saving them.

"As the years pass, I realize more and more how much we owed to our doctors. From the very start they had the necessary authority, and our men from Eysses supported them. In the middle of the car, I saw our dear old 'healer,' Dr. Fuchs, Stéphane to me, from prison yard 2, cell 23, who was, along with Henri Auzias, our representative at the central prison, the spokesman for the rights and the honor of the Resistants imprisoned. With him was Dr. Paul Weil, our 'Grand Popol,' from the Eysses infirmary, goodness made manifest. What did they tell us, these two, when, with a rheumatic jerking, the accursed train began to move? I can't remember their exact words, but they could be summed up as 'save your strength.' A simple tactic that amounted to staying in place, which turned out to be extremely difficult in practice.

1. Dr. Paul Weil.
2. Unpublished manuscript of Victor Michaut. July 1970.

"Wedged between the others, limbs ankylosed, breath coming in gasps, life draining out of each of us....Soon we had to take our clothes off. I wore my leather jacket for as long as I could. It was precious to me for many reasons. It was part of my 'insurrectional' outfit. I had recuperated it, with some fine, big infantry boots, in the prison depot when we were equipping ourselves for the battle of February 19, with the hope of being able to join up with the Maquis in the Dordogne region. The leather was solid, and I felt better protected. I took it off regretfully, my chest running with sweat. Body pressed against body—it wasn't all that simple, not even among men who respected each other. I can still hear the words of my comrade, Miguel Portolès, former mason, former fighter for the Spanish Republic, and a Resistance fighter for France. Two of his neighbors had been among the staunchest *combattants* of Eysses, and now they were grappling with each other in the car, nerves abraded to the point of fury. Our Spanish friend stopped them with the words: 'You are still not enough acquainted with suffering.'

"Miguel knew—a man in exile who sang the flamencos so beautifully when there was something to celebrate in the prison. He was the one who had had the courage, during the night of February 20, to tell us, just in time, that we would have to abandon a combat which had become hopeless, when the central prison was encircled by the militia and the Germans. And as for suffering, we were going to become acquainted with it!"

The Helluy-Aubert-Villiers Car.[1]

It had been decided that the most affected would take shifts at the ventilation shafts, but the effort to get to the openings was so great that they exhausted themselves beyond any benefit they derived, and we were forced to drop the arrangement, over their protests, after several painful trials. These poor creatures had to be satisfied with a dampened rag held to their foreheads, and

1. Unpublished manuscript of J.-B. Perreolaz, already cited.

a few fatherly words of comfort from the helpless doctors.

A general nervous tension seemed to invade us. The humid heat, the dripping walls of the car, the scant air burning our lungs, and the explosive mood of the men made it imperative for us to step in quickly and force-fully so that the dangerous situation would not degen-erate into a collective drama and total panic. We were "les Responsables," the elected leaders, and luckily, we were supported by our comrades. We had to subdue the most violent and use every means to enforce the regular rotation agreed upon. Everybody stripped to the skin. We were sliding around in the bread and sausage meat that they had distributed to us on departure.

The convoy advanced so slowly that it didn't allow any improvement in the circulation of air in the car. The monstrous sweating and almost total immobility forced upon us, created an extremely tense internal situation, at the edge of exploding into group hysteria; the slightest spark would have been enough to cause an explosion. Only a discipline respected by all, and maintained by no matter what means, imposed a relative calm that was very fragile, at best.

The first serious troubles broke out with the need to empty the container of excrement outside the car. Some men who couldn't wait, soiled themselves and the surrounding floor. Violence flared immediately, and the first blows were exchanged. Some refused to co-operate in the movement to and fro indispensable for evacuation. It is true that handling the relay under these conditions was extremely disagreeable, and difficult.

Personally, I remember being forced to resort to strong measures, to the extent that I could. One of my neighbors, whom I didn't even know, hadn't been willing, or able, to hold himself back during the long wait for the slop bucket, in permanent demand (an ordinary tin can). He had relieved himself on the floor. When the tin can finally reached me, I forced him to pick up his mess, and I didn't offer to help him.... The poor old fellow, at least much older than I was, snarled and wept, but did as he was told, and cursed me out.

Despite the stink prevailing in our car, this severe discipline maintained the order indispensable to prevent the outbreak of violence and the imposition of the "law of the jungle." However, I must say that the emptying of the tin-can slop bucket, the only possible method, presented unimaginable difficulties; even for the *blasé* operators we were in the way of becoming.

And always that implacable sun....

9:30 a.m.—The Town of Soissons.

Pierre Galand knocked at the door of Cady Obrier, his cousin. He was breathless, his face bathed in sweat, exhausted by the effort he had just expended.

"Pierre! What's wrong?"

"Hurry. Quick. I'll explain everything while we walk. You have to go to the station. I came on my bike from Compiègne."

Madame Obrier broke in:

"I don't understand at all. What is it?"

Pierre Galand looked at his wrist watch.

"We only have a few minutes. I'll explain. My brother, Louis, is in the train of deportees which will be coming through the station here, now. I knew Boursier from the camp at Royallieu; he is in charge of picking up garbage. He warned me yesterday evening that Louis would be put on the train this morning, at Compiègne. I left Champien during the night. I got a glimpse of Louis while they were leading him to the station, but there was a big roadblock.... He didn't see me."

"So then you got back on your bicycle."

"And here I am."

"Forty-five kilometers! You poor kid."

"Don't worry about me. You're a nurse. You could get onto the platform. You could speak to Louis."

"Wait just a minute...give me the time to slip on my uniform."

9:35 a.m.—Reims Station.

"Hello. Switch Post 2. Renard here. The 7909 is expected at Vic. It is scheduled for Reims at 11:40. Let's set the operation for 11:00. Over."

"Operation 11:00. Understood."

"Agreed. You can leave. I've found a replacement. Don't wait for him."

9:40 a.m.—Locomotive.

Rieder shouts into Dorgny's ear:

"Planes!"

The *Bahnhof* (German traveling S.D.) saw them too.

"Stop! Stop!"

"No worry. It's not for us. Look, they'll pass at least a kilometer away."

"Stop. You have to stop!"

"Have it your own way."

9:40 a.m.—Guérin-Canac Car.[1]

I could distinguish an intermittent, dull rolling noise from the west. The throbbing of airplanes tore through the air and the earth shook. The Allies hammered away relentlessly at the enemy positions. Bitterness yielded to hope and joy. It no longer mattered that we suffered, that bad luck had robbed us of our chance to fight. Even our death didn't matter now. The cause we fought for was going to triumph. During the alert, the convoy stopped at the verge of a forest. Our guards patrolled the tracks, but very ill at ease. Their laughter was sickly. I raised myself on tip-toe and was able to catch a glimpse of them through the grilled opening. My comrades asked me to listen because I was the one who understood German.

For the most part they were young, and all during the voyage they had been brutal beyond anything we had

1. Albert Canac, already cited.

ever known. They had their eyes fixed on the sky and stumbled along without watching their step. They kept watch on our cars with rifles and submachine guns trained on us. Just in case these "terrorists" attempted to escape. When the all-clear sounded the convoy moved again with desperate slowness. The tracks were blocked at several points, and stops were frequent.

9:40 a.m.—Tail Car.

"Make room for me."

"Shut up."

"I tell you to make room. I come from around here. We're going to pass by Vic-sur-Aisne. I'm going to give my paper to a station worker. They'll let my brother know. He works at the Soissons station. If only I could see him!"

Robert Legros, with a big, black beard and heavy moustache, shoulders his way through. He recognizes every bush and every building.

He rereads, perhaps for the hundredth time, the few words he had scribbled in camp C on a bit of packing paper. "To Legros, Paul—Soissons Station—Switching cabin:

"My very dear Paul,

"We didn't have any luck on April 3. I was caught in a roundup and so was Marie-Louise[1] who was sent to Fort de Romainville on June 28, and I to Compiègne on the 29th....Today, July 2, we're leaving for Germany. If you still can, write to Géo and tell him that everyone from Besse is here with me, and that Madame Vallor got caught with Marie-Louise.

"After eighty-one days of prison at Clermont, we were good and hungry....

"Love to everybody, and embrace them all for me.

"Your brother, who still has some damn tough moments to live through. Robert."

1.   Madame Robert Legros. The original of this message was given to me by Robert Legros's brother, Paul, to whom it was addressed. (December 1969.)

Paul Bion spoke for the first time since leaving Compiègne:

"Hey, you with the beard, since you know the guys at the next station, maybe you could ask them to write home for us."

"I haven't any paper, no pencil."

"I've got a pencil."

"...and paper? There's no more space on mine...."

Bion held out a sheet of tissue paper.

"I always keep some, just in case...."

"Hand it over!"

Legros slides down between Bion's legs, and writes: "Paul, if you can, send a word to these addresses, and tell them that their husbands are leaving for Germany, and that everything's all right, and that they hope to come home soon."[1]

Legros stood up painfully, "Two more curves, and we're there."

9:45 a.m.—Pernant.

The train slowed down, approaching the grade crossing. The police adjutant, Desmet, waited near the side gate.

"Those are deportees from Compiègne!"

A package fell at the feet of Yvette Belot, the gate keeper. She moved back a meter. Desmet saw an arm slide through the barbed-wire opening. A man cried out. In the observation box, a German shouted. Dozens of pieces of paper fluttered down. The gate keeper stepped back still further. Desmet warned: "Don't move. Above all, don't move. They'll shoot. We'll take care of it later."

Later... Desmet and the gate keeper picked up eighty-six "letters" and a packet of paper money. The brigade police spent the afternoon dispatching the letters and the parcels from widely dispersed post offices.[2]

1. There followed the addresses of Madame Courtine, Montaigut-le-Blanc (Puy-de-Dôme) and of Madame Bion, Compains (Puy-de-Dôme).
2. The packet had been thrown from the airshaft of the Verchuren-Bernard car. Elzear Girard was the one who "had the

9:50 a.m.—Soissons Station.

Madame Obrier and Pierre Galand were turned back at the main entrance.

"Don't bother us. The train hasn't come in yet."

All the entries to the station were guarded by the German police. The nurse held out her Red Cross card at each sentry post. Finally one sentry agreed to go and see the detachment chief. Two minutes later, the reply came back:

"The authorized members of the Red Cross are already on the platform. Your name does not appear on the list. We regret."

Madame Obrier grabbed Pierre Galand by the arm:

"We may still have a chance. Nearly all the trains leaving Soissons stop at the grade crossing."

9:50 a.m.—Vic-sur-Aisne, Station.

"Hello, Soissons? Vic here. I want to speak to Paul Legros...."

"Can't be done...since the sabotage, the telephone has been cut off with all the switching posts."

"Can you go and get him?"

"Not possible. We're waiting for the 7909."

"That's just why...I have to tell him...." The railwayman who had found the letter thrown out by Robert Legros hesitated....What if the person at the other end of the line...."Who's speaking?"

"H...."

H...wasn't a reliable element.

"Oh well, never mind. I'll see him this evening."

10:05 a.m.—Soissons Station.

Lucien Bailly, who had put the 7909 on track VI,

idea of the packet....I took up a collection, about twenty men contributed. I used my shoelace to tie the bills up." Unpublished manuscript of Elzear Girard. August 1970.

recognized the black beard of Robert Legros at the air shaft.

No sentinels in front of this freight car.

"Lucien! Is my brother at the station?"

"At cabin 2. I'll get him. Here, catch this bottle."

Would Bailly take the risk of going the whole length of the train along the platform teeming with guards. No! That would be too dangerous. The train will be stationed from ten to fifteen minutes. He had time to go behind the north depot by the marshaling yard.

"Paul."

Paul Legros was standing by the the switch cabin.

"Paul. Hurry. Your brother...."

Throat knotted up. A gasp.

"My brother?"

"He's in the last car, opposite my cabin. Go through the marshaling yard. There's nobody. Hurry."

10:10 a.m.—Soissons Station.

"No ladies, I cannot allow it."

"But these men are thirsty. A little water. It will go very quickly. It's terribly hot."

"Those men have water."

"But...."

"Quite useless to argue."

The S.D. officer was already on track 1. The three Red Cross nurses went sadly back, carrying their full buckets.

Behind the whole string of cars, Frizon, the train foreman, was walking up and down the platform, stretching his legs. At each turn he walked a little further. In the pocket of his blue coveralls he had a piece of bread, some sugar and a half-liter of water.

He passed the escort car, lowering his head. Then two quick steps.

"Hey, hey you guys...."

A face smiled, a hand reached out of the shaft....

But it was a German who seized the bottle and broke it on the rear wheel.

"Verboten. You, get in with them. You, get in."

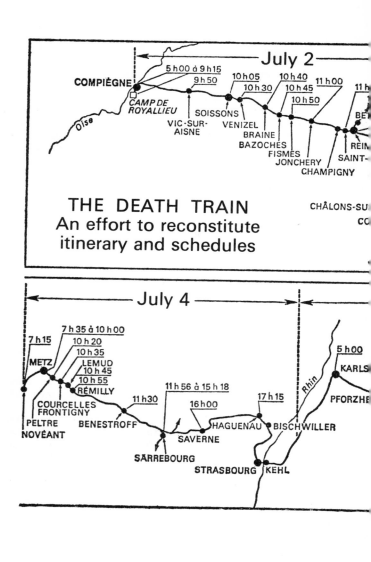

THE DEATH TRAIN
An effort to reconstitute
itinerary and schedules

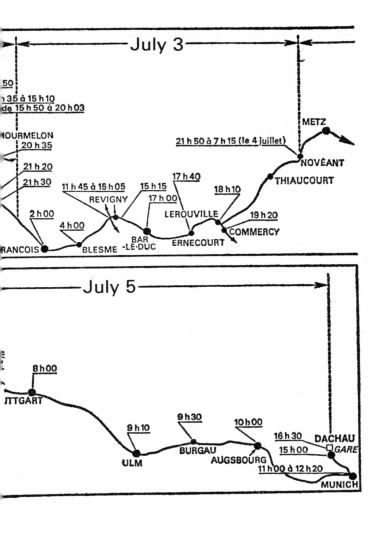

July 3

50
h 35 à 15 h 10
de 15 h 50 à 20 h 03

MOURMELON
20 h 35

21 h 20

21 h 30

METZ

21 h 50 à 7 h 15 (le 4 juillet)

NOVÉANT

THIAUCOURT

17 h 40

2 h 00

11 h 45 à 15 h 05   15 h 15

REVIGNY   17 h 00

18 h 10

4 h 00   LEROUVILLE

19 h 20

BAR   ERNECOURT   COMMERCY

RANCOIS   BLESME   -LE-DUC

July 5

8 h 00

UTTGART

9 h 10   9 h 30   10 h 00

16 h 30   DACHAU

BURGAU   15 h 00   GARE

ULM   AUGSBOURG

11 h 00 à 12 h 20

MUNICH

He shook him. One of the machine-gunners collared him:

"Go back. Start again. Go with them. I shut you in terrorist wagon."

They laughed.

Frizon closed his eyes.

10:12 a.m.—Soissons Station.

Karl Bender, the German station master, short, fat, scar on his left cheek, raised the signal flag.

"Let's go. All aboard."

10:14—Soissons Station.

Another fifty meters. Paul Legros came out on the paving stones of the north depot, cut across track IV. The train started. Two German soldiers leaped onto the footboard of the tail brake. Three meters. A soldier waved his submachine gun. Silhouettes at the airshafts....

"I didn't dare call out. They would have shot at me.[1] I was crushed. If I had only a few seconds more. I went back home, leaving my post. I was so overtensed, I could have caused an accident."

Coming out of the station, Paul Legros passed Louis Desongins.

"I've just picked up an aluminum plaque on the tracks. A prisoner must have.... What's the matter with you? You're white as a ghost."

"It's all right. Forget it. My brother was in the train, and I couldn't get to see him."

1. Unpublished manuscript of Paul Legros, December 1969. Robert Legros died February 15, 1945, in a Dachau prison work force.

10:17 a.m.—Soissons. Grade crossing.

Madame Obrier and Pierre Galand arrived in time at the barrier of the road to Reims. Whistling and steaming, the 7909 appeared behind the gate keeper's cottage.

"Let's get back. We're too close."

Calls of "Oh! Oh!" and suddenly, "Whee-oo, look here."

"It's Louis! It's him!"

"Here, Whee-oo."

Flatcar and tail van.

"I didn't see him. I couldn't see him."

"Me neither."

"But it was Louis. Nobody else makes a noise like that. Just Louis. That's the family call. That was his voice. His voice."[1]

The Rohmer Car.[2]

Nerves were raw and anguish mounted slowly. At the far end of the car a comrade felt sick and fainted. The men passed him, hand over hand, and lifted him to the air shaft. They fanned him with a rag. He came to and asked for water. Someone who had been carefully economizing his water flask, handed it on up. The sick man drank avidly, while the others watched with jealous eyes...all except the man who had just sacrificed the little water he had. A few minutes later, a second man fainted. The same process was repeated, and he recovered.

After that, we were forced to abandon the practice. It broke the façade of calm and provoked unrest. Arguments started up again, with more and more violence. Everybody started to blame the men near him for his cramped discomfort. But what Professor Vlès had been fearing happened, and the common-law prisoners started fighting. I heard shouts: "Dirty bastard...you took advantage when I wasn't looking. Fink...." They began to claw at

1. Three hours later, Louis Galand was dead.
2. Francis Rohmer, already cited.

each other. Nikis tried to intervene, to calm them down. He got close enough to receive a blow that sent him stumbling back over those seated behind him. They held him back, to keep him out of the fight. He tried to break loose, kicking wildly. It took some time to pacify him.

B..., who a few minutes before, had been humming a song, didn't have the strength to continue. He was suffocating and his face was distorted. Next to him L... seemed to be dozing, with his head on his chest.

We had just passed Soissons. The train kept going back and forth, shifting from one track to another (as a result of the bombardments, tracks frequently had to be bypassed). The heat never let up. It would be like that all day. Thirst was obsessive. To try to ease it, some of the men ate bits of their sausage meat, but it was peppered and only intensified their suffering. In spite of all our pleading, the guards refused us water. It was rare that the railway workers risked their own lives and succeeded in passing us a bottle.

Suddenly a terrifying cry of despair: "L... is dead. He looked as if he was asleep. I shook him to wake him up. He crumpled." The speaker kept staring at his dead friend. He couldn't accept the reality of this new grief. The eyes of the dead man were half open, his face was purple and a little saliva drooled from his lips. He must have been dead for some time, and nobody had noticed. And very soon, there was a second death. It was Nikis' neighbor, the man who had held him back during the first scrap. Suddenly he began to cry, flounder about and attacked one of his comrades. Blows were exchanged, and he fell back, exhausted. A few minutes later, he stopped breathing.

3

Sabotage

"Monsieur Renard, there's a call for you, in your office."

The secretary general of the Reims station grabbed the phone.

"Renard here. Hello."

"This is switch post No. 2. Set for 11 o'clock."

Olliger had succeeded. He had succeeded. The track would blow up at eleven. Paul-Emile Renard lit his first cigarette for the day.

"Want a cigarette, Jacquet?"

"Thanks."

Jacquet, the deputy station master had replaced Marcel Falala, after the latter's arrest, and was sitting at his desk.

"You appear in excellent spirits, for a Sunday."

"There's a reason. The track will be blasted at eleven o'clock at Saint-Brice."

"What?"

"Eleven o'clock. Saint-Brice, just before the passage of the 7909. It is the last train from Compiègne. It will never reach Germany."

"But, you're crazy!"
"I don't think so."
"You're crazy. You'll get us all shot. All of us."

10:50 a.m.—Fismes Station.
(The Metal Car. André Gonzalès.)

For an hour, they had supported the man who had
been beaten to death by the guards at the Compiègne
station. Then they let him fall. The air rattled out of his
dead lungs. In his corner, André Gonzalès prayed. A
string voice called for silence.
"Let us pray."
"Poor sucker."
"Let us pray. I am going to recite the prayer for the
dying."
André Gonzalès continued his private prayer.
Someone screamed: "I don't want to die." Then other
voices repeated it."
"We have to tear up the floor."
"Hail, Mary...."
"We're going to die."
In the darkness, slit by violent rays of light, a swelling
of tumult engulfed the right side of the car. Now, in turn,
the strong voice expired in a rattle.
"Stop. I beg you. Stop."
"You and your prayers."
André Gonzalès turned his back to the car, hunched
into the metal corner, with his arm protecting his head.
He couldn't understand it. He couldn't imagine it. He
could vaguely sense the swarm of men, and he heard
their howling.
"Don't move any more. Don't kill yourselves."
They killed each other.
Men armed with knives, forks, bits of metal, they
trampled on the prostrated forms beneath them. Hands
and feet pounding. Blows. Blood spurts.
"Help."
The car, like a great resonating drum, magnified the
screams and blows struck against the walls, the fear, the
madness, the delirium.

Near André—a father and son. At the start they had only thought of protecting each other, of loving each other. Now they were rolling about, arms and legs tangled, cursing each other. They pulled loose from each other. The wave surged apart. The shafts of light shone on two blades. Father and son turned.

"I'll show you."

"Shithead."

"I'm going to slice you up!"

They sliced.

The son leaped on his father's back. The knife....

In the demented frenzy, everyone could hear the "hah-hah-hah" of the son, panting with joy, as he struck.

"Then, what happened at my feet, so near to me,[1] was beyond all human believing. The son leaped upon the body of his father. Fear kept me back to the wall. All around, others were fighting, everywhere, choking each other, but all I could see was this one scene, right in front of me.... The son bent over his father. He was weeping, his knife, plunged into the body, tore at the flesh. The belly was opened. He was rabid. He plunged his two hands into the guts, pulled them out and wound them on his head and around his neck, intestines and all. I turned my back. I felt his madness reaching into me. This must surely be the end of my life. I could see my parents looking down at me. I wept. I prayed. I suffocated. I was thirsty. The metal burned. And that noise, the screams that wouldn't stop. Blows. I had to keep standing. If I sat down, if I stretched out, I'd be dead. At that moment a bottle broke over my head. My right temple split. There was a deep, wide gash. Blood poured over my face, a whole river of blood. I fell to my knees. Then blackness. The rattling of the dying blurred. No. I must stand up. Stunned, stupefied, I fell back down onto the dead bodies. I leaned on them. I could make out some dark bulks. The 'son' screamed, right against me. The others finally restrained him. One last effort. It is my death. Dear God! And I fainted."

---

1.   Testimony of André Gonzalès, April 1970.

10:50 a.m.—Fismes Station.

The station chief, Louis Chassard, held out his hand to Lucien Tangre:

"Manteau has let you know? You can never be sure. The bastards are sending through a train of deportees to test the repairs on the tracks. Maybe your son is with them...."

The Tangre family lived near the station. The Gestapo of Reims had come there on April 4 to arrest Georges Tangre, eighteen years old. Raymonde, his young sister, came to join her father on platform 1:

"Here comes the train. If only Georges isn't there...."

The escort guards took there places.

"They're crying for water, Monsieur Chassard, we've got to do something."

The station chief spoke to a policeman:

"Yes, you can give them water, but only water."

Chassard, Lucien and Raymonde Tangre filled some bottles.

"Quickly, they're going to start."

"...and Georges?"

Raymonde ran along the platform: Lucien Tangre distributed six bottles.

The signal flag waved.

"And then, so soon, the train started to move.[1] We were there, desolate, not believing our eyes. Suddenly, a name, we heard a name, mine: Raymonde, coming from one of the cars. It was Georges. Really Georges. We stood there on the platform, broken, destroyed. What could we have done against those soldiers who saluted me mockingly, and laughed to see me cry? I was sixteen years old.... I will never forget their faces. Believe me... never. And our poor father, standing beside me. I would have given everything, if only he wasn't there. His son, his 'Big Georges' was leaving him. We had only seen him for a few seconds... but I had heard his voice. My father said, 'Georges,' and then, 'my son'... and the train was gone."

1. Unpublished manuscript of Raymonde Tangre, August 1970.

"On July 2, 1944, more than 2,000 prisoners gathered at Compiègne were piled into the cattle cars of train No. 7909, one hundred men per car. The outside temperature was 34° C (nearly 94° F). The train was composed of twenty cars and the air vents were covered with barbed wire. I saw all these cars, standing still, and out of them came a murmur.... Through the openings, I could make out white faces.... The men cried out for water.... Coming closer to the apertures, we saw frightened faces, empty eyes shining with fever." Statement of Monsieur Viret, who lived very close to the railway at Saint-Brice.

Center of Contemporary Jewish Documentation

10:15 a.m.—Fismes Station.
(The Helluy-Aubert-Villiers Car.)[1]

It was when the train stopped at Fismes that we heard the frenetic screams, wails and pleas of our comrades locked in the car behind ours. We could hear everything, very clearly; cries for help, for air, for water, and muffled, but repeated banging on the walls. Then curses and continuous violent hammering. We didn't know then—of course, we couldn't have known—that our poor comrades were all dying of suffocation, locked into a hell that was driving them mad, that they were fighting each other in the effort to survive...and sometimes even killing each other.

Fismes was truly the entry of the Inferno.

We tried to calm them from our car, but it was no use. They had reached the point of no return. For them, the end was beginning.

11:00 a.m.—Jonchéry-sur-Vesle.
(The Guérin-Canac Car.)[2]

As we approached the little station of Jonchéry between Fismes and Reims, a comrade helped me get out a little note that I had hidden in my heel, intended for my family. I wrapped the note in my handkerchief with a little pebble I had picked up in Compiègne. I forced apart the barbed wire at the airshaft and managed to throw my message a few meters from the track. A station worker saw it, and picked it up. I felt better. They'd know that I was leaving, and that I wasn't dead.

11:05 a.m.—Saint-Brice.

Marcel Chenet stowed away his shovel and rake in the garden tool shed. It was too hot to break up the clods. Maybe, at the end of the afternoon, after the storm. He could feel it in the air...the heaviness, the humidity, the hot air, all spelled storm. It would burst around evening.

1. Unpublished manuscript of J.-B. Perreolaz, already cited.
2. Unpublished manuscript of Albert Charpentier, already cited.

Marcel Chenet walked along the tracks. It was the shortest way to reach his house. He had turned forty. He was in charge of cleaning the offices of the "Junkers" aeronautical construction firm at Courcy. He had a pass which permitted him to enter military areas. He had frequently slipped plans to the intelligence network.

Suddenly, at less than two hundred meters from him, there was a flash of lightning, a powerful explosion, a cloud of dust. He flattened himself down between the rails. The explosion really had come from the tracks, and not from the glass works, as he had first thought.

"They've blown up the track. I'm going to go see."

The rail was twisted, torn. At least two ties blown out...a pit dug. Spectacular, but not very serious.

He was at this point in his observations when he saw, behind his back, uniformed men running toward him, waving their arms extended by submachine guns.

"Hell!"

Marcel had only three hundred meters to cover to get back home safely, not far from the tracks. He ran at top speed.

11:15 a.m.—Saint-Brice.

"Open. German police."

Marcel Chenet opened the door.

"Your papers."

An adjutant took his entry pass for the German military areas. By this time four police were searching the house.

"Gut, gut" said the adjutant, satisfied. "Excuse us, Monsieur."

"What are you looking for?"

"It's who we're looking for...whoever sabotaged the railway."

The adjutant and soldiers left. The track was fifteen meters away. The 7909 crept forward. The locomotive stopped at the Saint-Charles grade crossing of the Champigny-Saint-Brice highway.

The adjutant stared at the train.

"May I go and see?" Chenet asked.

"Sure."

"Can I give them a little water?... It's so hot."

The adjutant stared at the train again, and the air shafts.

"All right, but do it fast."

Marcel took three bottles of beer and three bottles of water and headed toward the train. The escort jumped down from the footboards. The adjutant and Marcel Chenet stopped in front of the last car.

"Where are we?" and the deportee held out his hand for the bottles.

"At Saint-Brice near Reims."

"Let's go," said the adjutant, "and now goodbye, Monsieur."

"Thanks. Thanks for having let me....I mean thank you for them."

The two men shook hands.

Chenet returned by the rue de Bois-d'Amour, parallel to the railway.

11:15 a.m.—Saint-Brice (The Car of Eighty).

"With the consent of our sentry,[1] perched in the brake cabin, a man passed a bottle in to us. He had some difficulty because of the planks and barbed wire that barred the opening. We all drank a spoonful of water."

"My car had stopped opposite my father's garden.[2] He was employed as transport foreman for the Goulet-Turpin firm. A number of deportees had thrown bits of paper, scribbled in haste, on the roadbed. A few of the men among us had managed to hide a little paper and a pencil during the search. I scribbled a quick note for my father. Unfortunately, my father never found the note, and until June 1945 he thought I was lost."

1. Unpublished manuscript of André Tixier, June 1970.
2. Unpublished manuscript of Gilbert Delescot, May 1970.

11:20 a.m.—Saint-Brice.

A score of German soldiers from Reims circled the crater of the explosion, and about fifty others set out as sharp-shooters to cover the countryside.

Camille Démoulin was the first linesman found by the V.B. chief of the Reims station. Within five minutes they were joined by Jules Bardin and his crew, liable for home duty.[1]

"Are you in charge here?"

Jules Bardin didn't understand immediately, and the German drew his revolver.

"Are you in charge here?"

"Yes, I'm in charge."

"You are being held as a hostage. Step forward."

Jules Bardin laid down his shovel.

"We are going to walk along the track. I advise you to fully examine the condition of the rails. If anything goes wrong when we start moving the train again, you will be held responsible. You will be shot."

"I had two brothers killed in the war of '14, and I was wounded. I'm fifty-two years old...."

"That's war, Monsieur. Clean war, without terrorists."

And the German pressed the barrel of his revolver against the temple of the chief linesman.

"Just one false move. Just one word...."

11:20 a.m.—Reims Station.

The Red Cross welcome center, which occupied several barracks in the freight yards of Reims was now in an uproar. The railway workers had spoken of a de-railing or a bombardment... only one thing was sure: less than four kilometers away, men were dead and others, perhaps, dying.

"We must go there."

---

1. Linesmen liable for home duty were not permitted to leave their homes for shifts of twelve to twenty-four hours, and were assigned to take action in the case of accident over a given length of track.

"But everything is ready here to receive them."

"You heard what all the track workers were saying—even if they didn't agree on the cause of the accident—the prisoners are thirsty. They're literally dying of thirst. We have to go there."

"How?"

"On foot. With water jugs."

"Are you going to tell Mademoiselle Pierre, Madame Chatalain and Doctor Bouvier?"

"Not yet. When we have more information. The permanent service ought to be able to settle this problem."

Three nurses and four young first-aid workers left the freight yard for Saint-Brice.

11:20 a.m.—Saint-Brice (The Fully-Thomas Car).

Trouble started in this car, from the very beginning, at Compiègne.

"The first aboard[1] had made themselves relatively comfortable. They sat down, which forced the late-comers to stand up. This was the source of arguments, shouts, curses, scuffles and finally blows. Everybody wanted to lie or stay seated and justified this on the grounds of old age, ill health, faintness, or some physical disability. The two ends of the car formed hostile groups, each claiming that the other was less crowded. Once started, the discussions never stopped. The only solution would have been to count the men and to put fifty on each side, but this was impossible.

"Unfortunately, the majority in the car were common law criminals, out-and-out thugs and gangsters, opposing the intelligent minority of true Resistants. There was no possible way of reasoning with them, and even less of establishing any discipline, which was the only thing which could have saved us, or cut down our losses. With a little goodwill, it would have been possible for us to place ourselves properly and make the best possible use

1. Statement of Lieutenant Colonel Jean Thomas, E.R. This account was published in No. 156 (1954) of the *Bulletin des Anciens de Dachau.*

of what space there was available. Not even this could
be accomplished. Even before the convoy got in motion,
it was clear that the conditions in the car were going to be
extremely bad. With the shaking and the shuttling of the
train, everyone found a place, for better or worse....

"I had my back against the groove of the sliding door.
Barrois was between my legs, and used them as arm-
rests. The sun beat down on the tar-paper roof. Two of
the four ventilation shafts were open. The heat was
intense and the lack of air became suffocating...and the
immediate result was an inordinate thirst. We had a small
barrel of water and decided to make the first distribution
of a quarter-liter to each. One man, with a quarter-liter
mug, dipped into the barrel and filled all the containers
held out to him, mess tins, tin cans. The operation
proceeded slowly. The distributor counted out loud at
each ration: there was a careful check to make sure that
nobody came back for seconds. And just the same, he
counted out one hundred three servings of water. Nobody
was ever able to identify the three cheats.

"The water they drank made them want to drink
more...they had hardly finished the first quarter-liter
when they started to call for a second. It got hotter
and hotter in this rolling coffin, and we gasped for
air....

"The calls for water became more insistent and arguments intensified. And again, the lack of discipline
proved damaging. The shouting made them even thirstier.

"At last, some of the men standing near the barrel
plunged their own containers into it, and this unleashed
a tempest of howls. The men tried to justify themselves
by claiming that the Germans were not barbarians and
that they would fill the bucket again once it was empty.
Finally, to keep the peace and restore equality, we had to
make a second distribution. Once this was done, we just
continued to the third, until the water was gone. Now
there was no way at all to appease our thirst.

"The situation became tragic. One man, propped up
against the wall, collapsed and fainted. He was the first.
Then, one after the other, we began to lose control and
strength. It became extremely difficult to move at all. Our
limbs were paralyzed and already asphyxia began to do

its work. We were powerless to take care of our unconscious comrades."

Jacques Remaury's right arm had been torn open by a
bayonet on the platform at Compiègne. He was dismayed
to see that the wound was festering and that he would
be unable to defend himself.

"Was he going to need to defend himself by force?[1]
We saw some of the comrades go mad, suddenly hurl
themselves at each other, and beat each other to death.
One big, dark man who looked like a gypsy, stood up
with a bottle in his hand. Barcos saw him come forward
threateningly. One terrible blow of a fist felled him. I was
panicked and pressed myself flat against the sliding
panel of the door. There Mulez, Lavigne and I pulled the
bodies of our dead comrades over us. Protected in this
way, dreadful hours passed. We were trampled by the
other prisoners ad they fell over us.

"It was then that I tried to find help in prayer. From
time to time I heard some dull thuds—made by comrades
launching themselves head first against the walls of the
freight car.

"At one point I heard raucous crying followed by a
frightful howl. I looked out from between the corpses
hiding me and saw a bloody head with only one ear. A
fellow-prisoner had just sliced off the other ear. Mulez
was an atheist, and he said to me, 'I don't know how to
pray. You know how to pray. Say one for me. I think
we're goners.' I buried myself again behind the wall of
dead bodies. One of the dead bodies emptied its bowels
on me. 'My God!'"

"Some of the men hardly reacted at all anymore.[2] One

1. Statement of Jacques Remaury, May 1970. "I was arrested
by the border police at Bonac-sur-Lez (Ariège), on May 12,
1944. I was taken to Foix by the sinister Berkane. I was first
taken to Lauqué, and then to the civil prison at Foix were I was
held for about ten days. I left there with Puyo for the prison of
Saint-Michel at Toulouse, and then to Compiègne."
2. Statement of Dr. Georges Fully, General Secretary of the
Association of Former Prisoners of Dachau. This account, like

meter in front of me, a tall man with glasses was lying prone across the bodies of others.

" 'What's the matter? Can't you hold yourself up like everybody else?'

"He didn't try to answer. Between twisted lips, he kept repeating: 'Don't let me die. Don't let me die.'

"Then a cry struck panic in our hearts. 'My brother's dead. My brother's dead!' A Dutchman...he was cradling his brothers' blotched, purple head in his arms...asphyxiated. His eyes were wild, unfocussed. It was so dreadful that I didn't dare to look at him any longer. I felt that I would also go mad.

"The whole car had become an oven and none of us could breathe. Insanity swept over us like a scorching desert wind. I don't know what happened after that. All I remember is a murderous plunging of bodies...thrusting at each other, an infernal brawl, dull thuds, harsh screams...and blood.

"I looked at the tips of my paralyzed fingers, and watched them turn purple. My heart beat wildly and my lungs refused to dilate. I could no longer move at all.

"A body fell heavily across mine. A hoarse.... 'The dirty bastards.'

"I recognized one of my comrades. I tried to calm him. He was beyond hearing. He stumbled up and threw himself at a foaming, demonic figure who countered with a violent kick in the stomach. My friend crumpled and stiffened with a final gasp....

"Now the knives and chisels which had been hidden from the search came out...and the fighting was bloody. They sliced insanely at each other. As if in a nightmare, I saw throats cut, gaping wounds, gouged eyes...there are no words to describe a scene like that.

"There were only the few of us, cowering in a corner, who escaped the contagion of madness. The dementia spread inexorably, and still others pitched into this hell of killers and killed."

that of Lieutenant Colonel Thomas, was published in No. 156 (1954) of the *Bulletin des Anciens de Dachau*.

11:20 a.m.—Reims Station.

Paul-Emile Renard, the general secretary of the Reims station, joined the "saboteur" Ollinger in switching cabin No. 2.

"You're alone?"

"Yes."

"We're in a mess. The Gestapo gang of Reims are conducting a search in the station. They're going to question everybody who knew that the 7909 was a train of deportees. But that's not too bad. We're used to it. What's worse is that the bomb flubbed. A little virgin's fart...one twisted rail...."

"It's not possible."

"I saw a track man come back with the gauge to get repair material. Right after the explosion the German station chief, Richter, sent out a crew, and in an hour the train will be in the station."

Roger Ollinger opened the notebook for change of shift.

"I'm off at noon. I still have time...if I can find some plastic. But here, there's nothing but bars of 808. And that's not strong enough. If only I could find some P.2. That really blasts off."

"Stop kidding yourself. Since this scare, they're probably watching the whole stretch from here to the border. The whole Gestapo, Richter, everybody in sight, they're all hanging on to the telephone."

"There may be some way...for the plastic....I might be able to find that, but no detonator. Or maybe we can find a way to derail the locomotive. I'm going to talk it over with Betheny at the Reims shunting yard."

11:30 a.m. to 2:00 p.m.—Saint-Brice.

A tiny pond, a canal, two rows of poplar trees, two fields of beets, a gate keeper, a workers' town dominated by the red brick chimneys of the glass works of Saint-Brice, a few rabbit hutches, an empty lot, a public dump, some kitchen gardens, six "villas." Between 11:30 a.m. and 2:00 p.m., the 7909 would switch back and forth three times over this single kilometer. This shunting was incomprehensible because the track ahead was cut. A captain had come from Reims to direct the maneuver. He probably thought that the Resistance was waiting for a favorable moment to attack, now that the train was immobilized.

The Gestapo staff at Reims conducted searches at Champigny, Tinqueux, Thillois and the outskirts of Vesle. In the upper part of Saint-Brice two men were held under arrest.[1]

1. A number of sources gave me these facts, but I was unable to ascertain the names of the two inhabitants arrested. (August 1970.)

The Liotier Car.[1]

An hour ago, I took off my jacket. Now I'm bare to the waist. All my companions have done the same. If I can, I'm even going to take off my shoes and socks, because sweat is burning me under my feet and makes me suffer.

As if trying to breathe this humid air wasn't bad enough, a smell of urine made it even more terrible. We weren't able to move, and there was no slop pail, so we relieved ourselves where we were, like animals. Every now and then you could feel warm liquid flowing down your legs. Those who had dysentery had to void their bowels on the floor. We had to keep up our courage with all of this, because there was no other choice for any of us. In spite of this gross unpleasantness, the car stayed calm.

Of course, some of us started to complain about the heat, but on the whole, it was still bearable.

We all hoped that, when the train started to move, the air would be blown into the cracks. Then it would be renewed and the bad smells would be blown away. Unfortunately, the advance was so slow, and the stops so frequent, that the ventilation wasn't improved. The opening of the two airshafts was insufficient to provide a renewal of air. The outlook was pretty dim, and everybody realized it perfectly.

My feet started to slide around in the liquid mess, but it was impossible to sit down. As a matter of fact, it was about then that we noticed that the carbonic gas had begun to stagnate at floor level.

The situation had gotten beyond us. I was suffocating. The hot air burned my lungs, and my body ran with sweat. My skin was irritated and burned by the contact of the bodies all around me.

Blisters formed and burst, and the sweat that flowed over this raw skin made me cry out in pain, in spite of myself.

The recent calm gave way to a groundswell of disjointed noises. Some begged for air, some for water. An old man was sick. The nervous tension started to build

1. Henri Liotier, already cited.

up. I felt death in the air. We had agreed to alleviate the lack of oxygen by having each of us spend a minute at the airshaft to breathe the air from outside. We started the rotation, but inspite of the self-imposed discipline, the operation didn't go smoothly. Some claimed that a minute was too long. Others accused their neighbors of cheating. It took all the authority that a few of us could muster to keep the procession from degenerating into a fist fight. A leaden sun burned the walls of the car. We were in open country. But what was happening? Those close to the shafts called out, "Water...Water."

These words echoed back and forth, the length of the convoy. We looked at each other, questioningly. Anxiety took hold of us. Every man tried to get to the openings to find out what motivated the screams. Our train had stopped just beside a little pond. Peasants were working in the fields around it.

They heard our cries, they saw our gestures, and they understood our drama. They used every kind of container they could find, dipped into the stagnant water, took the risk of running to the train, with this gift which was so precious to us. After some serious jostling, I succeeded in getting to one of the apertures myself and drank the water, poured into my mouth from the spout of a watering can pushed in between the barbed wire.

The joy, the well-being that flowed into me, was beyond all describing. The fire was extinguished, which had been burning in my throat for hours. I could have stayed there forever, drinking this miraculous water, but soon, far too soon, I was pushed to one side by others who needed to drink. Animal instinct dominated all of us.

Thank you, my brave, anonymous peasant friends, for this water you gave us, which made it possible for some of us to survive.

The water we had just had made us sweat profusely, and the intense heat transformed it to a suffocating vapor around every body.

Our skin turned scarlet and burned us. It took all the strength I had, but I succeeded in taking off the few garments I still wore. My trousers burned my legs. I saw a vision of hell before my eyes. We were all naked, swarming and steaming at the bottom of the devil's cauldron, and in spite of our nakedness, our bodies were devoured by fire.

Some of the men broke completely with thirst. They urinated into their mugs or in their hands and drank this liquid which quickly enflamed their throats and stomachs, and they cried like demented souls.

Another man cut his hand with his knife, and avidly drank his own blood.

Total madness came closer and closer.

When I breathed, my nostrils, throat and lungs were burned. My tongue was so swollen that I could only breathe through my nose. I felt that I was suffocating, and my feet burned in an acid sea of excrement and urine. My legs could scarcely support me. If nothing happened to relieve our plight soon, I felt that for myself and for many others, our voyage would soon be over.

11:30 a.m. to 2:00 p.m.—Saint-Brice.

Georgette Cher and Geneviève Barthélémy were paying formal calls—flowered dresses and patent leather shoes—on this Sunday, as on almost every Sunday. Georgette, nineteen years old, had been invited to lunch by Madame Antoine, her future mother-in-law. Three houses further on, Geneviève was visiting her best friend. Both of them, with water jugs in their hands, ran toward the cattle cars. Georgette was turned back by the sentinels, once, twice, three times. Geneviève climbed over the barriers and was able to reach two of the air shafts with her water pitchers.

"Where are we?

"Where are the Americans?"

Then Geneviève and her friend ran to the garden to pick carrots and tomatoes—the first tomatoes.

"How kind you are," said the deportee, who took the vegetables.

The Lutz Car.[1]

What time was it when suddenly one of the hundred in this car collapsed? I don't know.

I heard a crescendo of cries, and saw hands waving around. That happened at the other end of the car, in the corner opposite mine. An epileptic fit? I took a chance, and called out: "Don't hold him by the arms. He might break a bone. Let him thrash about, and give him space...."

I've taken care of an epileptic. I know about that, but not much else.

It was as if an electric current had passed through this mass of humans, and it stimulated a rumor.

"There's a doctor. Here's a doctor. Shut up, you! Let the doctor handle it."

I started to protest, but then I saw the positive role of this mistake. "If that could help to calm down the crowd...." and so I said, "Not a doctor, a medical student...."

That was all these poor guys needed!

They pushed back against each other as much as they could and left an opening for me to reach the convulsing form. They kept silent. I was able to lean over him, open his belt, and order a little stale water. It was handed to me without any objection, although a moment before, these men would have beaten each other up for a supplementary ration.

I almost panicked. What next?

The epileptic crisis came to its normal end. This was the moment when I had to do something, or the game was up.

I stood up and ordered, "Place this boy next to an opening. Make this one larger, this one here. It was located on the side of the car, and one board had already been pulled loose. I directed the action.

They obeyed. They listened to me.

Afterwards, in the calm, we agreed on survival arrangements, and accepted the necessary discipline. They would take turns, half of the occupants standing, half

1.   Unpublished manuscript of Jacques Lutz, January 1970.

sitting. Rotation on access to the openings. Silence. Distribution of water, etc.

And the most beautiful trickery of all—I had bits of sugar in my pocket that I had received in a package at Compiègne, and had guarded as a treasure. I crushed them together with an aspirine that a companion gave me, and I was able to dole out a pinch of this medicine, as needed.

No "medicine" was ever more miraculous than this.

* * *

André Page suddenly called for silence.

"There's a sentry in front of the airshaft. I'm going to try to talk to him. Help me up."

Lamirault and Lecène hoisted him.

"We have a sick man in here. His condition is very alarming."

The German replied by a question.

"How many dead?"

"How many dead? We don't have any dead...."

"Well then, shut up."

Pierre Pelet said, "If he's asking how many dead, it means that the situation is worse in the other cars than in here."

The three "Responsables" of the car: Lutz, Lamirault and Tesson, got together close to the door.

"André Tesson was a real force of nature.[1] He weighed about 260 pounds. Bald, he always used to wear a felt hat. I can see him now, with his almond eyes, high cheek bones and round nose. He forbade anyone to shit in the slop bucket. All the hats were requisitioned, and if anyone couldn't hold out any longer, he would call for a hat. Tesson offered his own, to the first emergency. Two bottles of Vichy water were reserved for urinating. I was one of the last to get into the car, and was therefore near the door. It was my job to empty the bottles through a crack. For three days, I emptied the bottles, seated at the level of the door, with my nose close to a bolt-hole which let in some air. André Tesson kept watch. He

1. Unpublished manuscript of Pierre Ropiquet, already cited.

maintained the calm. I remember, he spoke to them as if they were school children. He would say, 'If you behave well, I'll tell you the story of the little Chinese cook.' That would keep them quiet for a while. They waited for this famous story of the Chinese cook. But it was never told."

"Without warning,[1] a violent fight flared up. My friends from the Lamirault team were trying to make a hole in the car. There were vociferous objections. Those who didn't dare escape, or who couldn't escape were afraid of being shot. They remembered the warnings that had been issued at the departure. A man who had been a police commissioner was the most opposed to the project. He was cornered by some prisoners who recognized him. He was thought to have killed a Resistant during the course of an arrest. He defended himself and claimed that the man was a common thief; that he was in a state of legitimate defense, and beside, the man in question had not been a Resister."

"I remembered the voice[2] of a twenty-year-old kid begging to be released. He called for his mother, and he cried 'Let me go. I swear to you, I didn't do anything. I'm innocent....' A sort of madness started, not too acute at first, but growing in fury, took hold of a dozen other unfortunates. They shoved each other. They exchanged violent threats. One of the men near me, his eyes bulging, threw himself at me with a switchblade knife in his hand. I just had time to deflect the blow. I went crazy myself. I grabbed him by the throat, and I squeezed, and I squeezed.
"Once again, from his observation post, André Page called for silence, and got it.
" 'There are some peasants with water. This way, please, please. Help. Water!'
" 'Thanks. Thanks.'

1.   Unpublished manuscript of Gabriel Rykner, April 1970. He was a member of the Ajax-Micromégas network, arrested April 30, 1944, while he had, on him, the plans for the setting-up of the Gestapo in the southern zone.
2.   Statement of Gilbert Hamburger, L'Ordre, 1948.

"The peasant passed two bottles over to Lamirault.

" 'Where are we?'

" 'Where are the Americans.'

"In his corner, Pierre Pelet thought, 'I'm going to have to open my haversack. It's dripping. It's the melted butter running out with the granulated sugar.' He passed his hand through his hair. 'Yeah, that's what it is.' He remained seated. Drop after drop, the haversack dripped onto his head.

"The grandson of Millet, the painter, shook with hiccups, and kept repeating, every ten seconds, 'It's really super in here. Really super.'

"Pierre Lecène and Pierre Encrevé fainted."

11:30 a.m. to 2:00 p.m.—Saint-Brice.

"Who are those people?"

"Jews?"

"No, they're English prisoners."

Madame Morizet was waiting for the train to start so that she could pass over the tracks at the Saint-Charles grade crossing. She said:

"The simplest way to find out would be to ask them."

She pushed through the gate at the foot path.

"Are you prisoners?"

"I didn't do anything, but they took me. They've packed a hundred of us in here, but we'll pack in two hundred of them. There are hostages and Resistance Fighters. We're thirsty. Give us water...."

From the next air shaft came cries and pleas.

"One of my comades has just cut open his veins."

At that moment a guard hurled a stone at Madame Morizet, shouted and picked up a bottle... Madame Morizet ran toward the front of the train, and the German returned to his observation box.

"It seemed to me that he was drunk.[1] I found myself alongside other cars. The people of Saint-Brice gave water and bread to the prisoners. The guards tore open

1.   Unpublished manuscript of Madame Morizet, May 1970.

the bread to make sure that nothing was hidden inside
the loaves. A little further on, I heard cries toward the rear
of the train, and the stuttering of a submachine gun."

The Puyo Car.[1]

"The voyage will be what you want it to be." But we
hadn't wanted this, not us. We hadn't deserved this.
These are not human cries any more, they are the
howling of animals dying, but who do not want to leave
this cursed earth. "Help me." "Water." "Pigs." "I'll kill
you, yes you." "I'll poke your eyes out." "Why don't you
croak, you're too ugly to live?"

Yes, those pigs. They're on the platform, laughing at
us, our guards. They were all wearing Edelweiss in their
caps. Pigs. They shouldn't let us die like this. At each
stop they walk up and down the whole length of the
train. They heard us. "We already have ten dead—twenty
dead—thirty dead."

"Das macht nichts," was their only reply.

Although a few comrades died peacefully, most of
them had a hysterical and terrible passage. The dying
men were possessed of an unbelievable strength just a
few moments before the end. The disordered reflexes
were aggravated by our crowding. In the midst of our
physical and moral helplessness, even the strongest and
most lucid were overcome....All of these memories,
which I treasure jealously, like a personal and atrocious
possession, constitute my capacity to think of man, not
only with fear and with pity, but also with an enormous
love.

*   *   *

About one-third of the car had gone violently mad.[2]
The first victim was a very young man who had just
come out of a sanatorium. He was suffocating; he

1.   Unpublished manuscript of Colonel Puyo, already cited.
2.   Unpublished manuscript of Commander Henri Billot, May
1970.

wanted to get to the airshaft at any cost. He got there, after a struggle...and then he wanted to stay in that blessed spot, but it was impossible.

"Get him out of there," the men shouted. "He's blocking the air. We're all going to croak."

They forced him away from the window, and he went back to his place and began to whimper. Fifteen minutes later, he was dead. His brother, who was in the same car, went into a furious rage. He accused the others of being to blame for his brother's death. He howled. He cursed them.

"You've killed my brother!..."

A pitched battle followed, and there was a second death. The other brother.... Then there was an immense brute who got up, with a distorted grin on his face. He seized the man next to him by the neck and strangled him between his enormous hands. Terror immobilized us all. We feared for our lives. We had to defend ourselves. We all had to get together against this poor, demented giant.... The spectacle was terrifying in the semi-darkness. Bodies gripped each other, fell, rose up again. The men cried, "Separate them."

The fighting couldn't be stopped. Some of the fighters fell and died of exhaustion a few minutes later. My neighbor, Dr. Allard of Saint-Pal-en-Chalençon, got up, took a towel, and hour after hour, waved it to renew the air. Thanks to him, the dying stopped. The cries of rage from one corner of the car had turned into calls for help. The men felt that the end was near.

"Mother."

"Marie."

"Louise."

The men called the names of women and recalled their faces in their last hour...and they pleaded, "No, no, I don't want to die."

Those still half conscious were prostrated by the scenes around them: a Dante's inferno of the mad, the dead and the dying. Sanity could not survive here.

*   *   *

It was Georges Fauconnier who finally overwhelmed this pathetic brute with the enormous hands. The men tied him up, and he died a little later. Then Marcel Ballesdant, standing near Jacques Bronchard, burst out laughing, singing and dancing, and then collapsed. This broke Bronchard's will, and he crumpled. Our brave Dr. Allard held up his head, made him breathe, and forced him to live. Albert Pelot pulled two handkerchiefs from his pocket, fanned himself and fainted. François Wicher clung to one thought: "Keep standing." "Keep standing." Claude Laval made use of a hand towel to "ventilate" seven or eight comrades. Mazic and Migeat drank in the moving air. Martin, a heavy-load truck driver, repeated over and over:

"Come on guys. Don't lose your nerve. You mustn't lose your nerve. We're not babes. Don't fight. Don't lose your nerve. We'd better sing a song...."

Migeat, slightly jostled by a kid from Limoges, lost control and slapped him.

"I sensed Claude Laval's eyes on me.[1] We had promised each other, on our honor as scouts, that we'd hold ourselves in check, no matter what happened. Then I took this kid by the shoulders, and I really cried, and asked him to pardon me."

His name was Bruno Balp, and he was probably the youngest kid in the car, not yet eighteen. He had been arrested with his brother, Jean, and his father, Pierre. Pierre was sixty. His two sons stood by him for the whole trip, protected him from attack and blows, hoisted him up for air.

After Dachau, all three of them found their way back to France.

11:30 a.m. to 2:00 p.m.—Saint-Brice.

Madame Lapierre's uncle left the house, carrying the little kitchen blackboard in his hand.

"What are you doing with that?"

1. Jean Migeat, already cited.

"We aren't allowed to get near. We can't talk to them, but they're all asking where they are...."

So Uncle Lapierre took his chalk and wrote on the slate, "between Saint-Brice and Reims."

He held the blackboard high above his head, and walked along the tracks.

The Guérin-Canac Car.

Marcel Guérin still hadn't touched his canteen, filled with water at Compiègne. He decided to distribute a sip to the thirstiest.

"I started a chain of horrors. There was a rush to the water flask, and the first fights broke out."

The train had stopped at the grade-crossing of Saint-Charles.

"Ah! To be able to drink![1] To plunge into the water.... Just at this moment a brave gate keeper, with the help of her children, succeeded in passing us a few bottles of water. Other track workers joined them. Meanwhile some of us were hastily scribbling a few words on bits of paper, thrown out in the hope that they would reach our families.

"With the first bottles, fighting became general in the car. Whoever had the bottle in his hand wanted to drain it at one gulp, deaf to the pleas of his companions. It had to be taken from him by force. At times like this, nothing counts: not friendship, not solidarity. They're dry words in this crisis. For the few of us who could still see things clearly, the spectacle was infinitely sad.

"The first to go....Adjutant Didelot, my faithful colleague in the military school of Tulle, staggered toward me, his face livid, his eyes rolled back. He paid no attention to the men he bumped into or walked upon. With a desperate thrust, he made his way across all these fallen bodies from the opposite end of the car, and collapsed at my feet.

" 'He's going to die. He's suffocating,' I said to my comrades. We have to try to save him. But how?

1.   Albert Canac, already cited.

"We lifted him up toward the air. I was half unconscious myself, but I tried to practice traction of the tongue with my handerchief. It was no use. All we could do was to let him die, and wait for our turn.

"Cries, groans, chokings came out of the darkness all around. The full horror of tragedy. A tangle of arms, legs, prostrate bodies. Those on the floor, gasping where there was no air to breathe, were trampled under the furious feet of the men who were still standing. Bedlam! Sudden shocks of madness tore through the car, died down, resumed again and again.

"'Shoot us. For Christ's sake, shoot us.' The voices rose sometimes, even above the tumult. 'Finish us off.'

"Some men lowered their heads, bashed down anyone in the way, rammed against the walls and fell. They never rose again. Others rushed to the openings and pulled at the barbed wire with their bare hands, and howled....A burst of submachine gun fire from the observation box of our car....The men fought with everything they could lay their hands on, boots, bottles, punches, knives. They struck at the writhing mass. The men strangled each other, tore out eyes, broke skulls, and cried all the while for their mothers, fathers, women and children they loved.

"Those who were still sane flattened themselves against the walls, and tried to protect themselves when they had to. Sometimes they had to knock out a mindless aggressor. Death was the price paid for falling down.

"Cries from every side. 'I'm dying, Mamma.' 'I'm innocent.' 'Vive de Gaulle!' 'Long live France.' I was splattered with blood....Beaudiffier and André, two young teachers from the boarding school at Tulle, made their way over to me. 'I can't go on; no longer, no more,' Beaudiffier said. 'Stay calm. Don't move. Stay close to the aperture.' But they only lasted for a few minutes more, and then fell back into the heap of bodies at the center of the car. I still hear their dying gasps, these hiccups convulsively moving this welter of bodies. Poor kids, scarcely eighteen.

"Standing close to the wall, toward the middle of the car, I miraculously escaped the butchery. All of a sudden my ears rang, I heard bells, and I saw before my eyes, the hanged men of Tulle....I dropped. It was my great luck that my comrade, Boulant of Tulle, was close to me, he calmed and supported me. I know that I owe him my life. He wasn't as lucky as I was. He died of oedema at Dachau in February 1945. What happened next? How long was I unconscious?"

Albert Charpentier counted the dead.

"Sixteen already dead at Saint-Brice,[1] and this stop lasted three hours, under a molten sky, a few minutes from a shadowless clump of trees without a leaf that moved. I lived, half dead, unconscious, unaware."

"I fainted, I don't know when;[2] I recovered, I don't know how. I saw my comrades with their mouths foaming, eyes starkly vacant. I was afraid. I lurched clumsily toward the slop-can, walking on dead bodies. The can was full, overflowing on the floor. I couldn't stop. I vomited into it."

"Now it was each man for himself.[3] I had managed to hide a knife, and I used it to make a slit between two floor boards which let in a little fresh air. Then I must have passed out, because I don't remember anything more."

"Peasants were hoeing their beets[4] in a little field near the grade-crossing. They filled a few bottles with water from a stagnant pond. I was surprised that the guards allowed them to be handed in to us. I grabbed a bottle, but before I could get it to my mouth, it was snatched out of my hands. The impact shoved me to the left of the car were I found Pierre Germaine, Doctor Bouvier and Marcel Doré, who told me that he was going to try to get close to the window. But he fell before he could reach it.

1. Unpublished manuscript of Albert Charpentier, already cited.
2. Unpublished manuscript of Jean Barbazanges, March 1970. He had escaped from the hangings in Tulle.
3. Unpublished manuscript of Roger Grenier, May 1970. F.T.P. (Sharp-Shooters and Partisans) in the Ondaine valley of the Loire. He was arrested January 8, 1944, while transporting arms.
4. Unpublished manuscript of Maurice Baltet, already cited.

I took just the time needed for one deep breath, and then pushed everybody aside to try to reach my friend. His eyes were riveted to the left side. I called out for Doctor Bouvier who bent over him, just as I had done a few seconds before. He listened for the heart, looked up at me, and said, 'Marcel is dead.'

"We moved back. I made the sign of the cross. A young man began to cry, 'Let me out.' Dr. Bouvier warned him, 'It is my duty to order you to remain calm. This is the rule of the miners when they are buried alive....' A voice from the back of the car answered him: 'Close your trap.... They should've strung you up.'"

11:30 a.m. to 2:00 p.m.—Saint-Brice.

Ledru, the market farmer, attached his hose, opened the faucet and aimed a stream of water at the air-shaft.

Madame Pinel took advantage of the absence of the sentries to pick up a little pasteboard from the track. It was a union card from a factory in Tulle. About twenty names and addresses had been written on it. That evening the mayor of Saint-Brice, Monsieur Vaillant, sent twenty letters to Tulle.

There were still no guards. Madame Pinel filled cooking pots, buckets, watering cans. A shuttle system was set up by neighbors, friends, passers-by.... Pierre Manjeau, Jean Billaudell, Louis Heutard, Réjane Pasquier.

The Sirvent Car.

"Don't fight. Don't fight any more. The peasants are bringing us water."

The man next to Roger Bellot took off his boots and passed them to Albert Cognet. The boots were filled with water, but they half emptied themselves coming back through the barbed wire of the aperture.

"That's mine." A young man grabbed a boot and poured the water over his face.

"Son of a bitch."

Déclaration

Les soussignés Lorrains de la Résistance déclarent que monsieur MULHERR François, demeurant à Mannheim, Max-Jose Straße 2o, a rendu d'éminents services pendant l'occupati allemande alors qu'il était capitaine, officier de gare à Sarrebourg, notamment en juillet 1944 où il a obtenu aprè une vive altercation avec le chef-Gestapo d'un train de déportés politiques que les wagons scellés soient ouverts, que les 75% des survivants soient ravitaillés en eau et nourriture, que les morts soient mis dans un wagon spécia et que les compartiments soient nettoyés.

A la suite de cette intervention MULHERR fut traduit devant le tribunal militaire de Wiesbaden et ne doit sa v qu'à l'intervention heureuse d'un général du complot cont Hitler.

L'affaire ci-dessus a fait bruit à Sarrebourg et envi et la population française a su gré au capitaine MULHERR.

C'est pourquoi les soussignés demandent que la prése déclaration soit remise à l'intéressé pour lui servir de pièce justificative devant les autorités militaires alli occupantes.

Sarrebourg, le 8 juin 1946.

Dr. René Muller
Conseiller Général de la Moselle
Président du Comité de Libération

Jules Martin
[illisible]

Robert *[illisible]*

[illisible]

Konrad M.
[illisible]

[note manuscrite illisible]

pour légalisation des signatures
posées ci-dessus.
Sarrebourg, le 11 juin 194[6]
Le Maire:

Statement given by the Lorraine Resistants to Frantz Mulherr. "Commander Mulherr knowingly had the Death Convoy stopped for as long a time as possible, to allow as much help as circumstances would permit to be given to the unfortunate men piled into the cars of the convoy." Testimony of M. Loestler, the locomotive engineer who drove the train from Sarrebourg to Hagenau.
Author's Archives

Jean Mercier, Jean Lassus and Guy Forestier,[1] in the second half of the car, succeeded as best they could in keeping order. They were assisted by a group of officers of the Resistance Army organization.

* * *

There was never an answer to our calls for help.[2] We held a teacher from Alsace up to the aperture. He spoke to the sentry, who was obviously indifferent. The exchange was in German, and the teacher could understand every brutal word. First the guard answered that we were about to leave, then that we were all going to get out; then that he couldn't do anything for us; and finally, that we were all going to croak anyway, and it would be a good thing.

We were doomed to die, and doomed to die insane.

Was this all decided in advance? Or was this stop in the middle of the July furnace unplanned? But the sentry was sure of being unpunished, maybe he'd even be promoted, because he was simply following orders, or maybe because his chiefs would approve this extermination, or perhaps only to satisfy his own hatred. Whatever

---

1. Statement by Colonel Jean Mercier, July 1970: "In June 1943, I was the chief of the S.S.M.F.-T.F. network (of the army general staff). The history of this network was recounted by Colonel Brouillard in his book, *Mes Camarades sont morts* (My Comrades are Dead). I was arrested on March 29, 1944, at the Café Madrid (Boulevard Montmartre in Paris). I was going to a meeting with two of my post chiefs, Captain Denhaene of Lille and Captain Proton of Le Mans. After long interrogatories at Fresnes, I was transferred to Compiègne. I was somewhat comforted to find comrades from our organization who had been arrested earlier, and who got into my car at the departure: Ship's lieutenant Yves Le Henaff; infantry captain Joseph de Peich; artillery captain Paul Denhaene, as well as Pierre Dubuc, Henri Rousselin, Charles Bellet, Henri Lemasson (he must have been nearly seventy years old), and Alex Le Donguet, a young submarine radio officer."

Jean Lassius, professor of archeology at the university of Strasbourg, relocated for safety at Clermont-Ferrand.

Guy Forestier, director of the Clermont-Ferrand hospitals.

2. L.E. Sirvent, already cited.

the motives, circumstances had put him in an unhoped-for position to assassinate us.

The Alsatian teacher cried out for a moment, "*Schade, schade,* have pity, have pity. Water. Help." He turned from the transom, his face emptied of hope and of life. He coughed blood and fell, with the rattling in his throat.

Now we began to hear the anguished cries from the other cars. Our car was piled with corpses, and those who were going mad, who had been among the sane just a minute before, surged up, struck blindly and drew new recruits into the hell of death.

I thought of Géricault's painting of the Raft of the Medusa, of men trapped in submarines, of miners buried in the shafts. When did I think of them, before, after, during? When was it in my delirium? Half-unconscious, I only remember one thing: that Pascal gripped my wrists, lay on top of me, held me from leaping into the mass of the dead.

"Don't you see, they're going to shoot at us? You're out of your mind. They're going to kill you. Don't jump!"

I had a vision of my wife, my son, and everyone I love. This is impossible. I cannot die here. I cannot die like this. I struck out, defending my dream, and Pascal and I rolled down into the same pit.

Where did the strength come from, finally, that let me speak to him gently, to calm him, to get him to lie down on a sack, to hold his hand. I thought that he was going to sleep. A reddish froth foamed on his lips. From then on, I was alone in this madness.

Death was with us, in the screams, in the rattlings.

There was almost no one left standing at the air openings. The coffin was closing.

A Hercules, a miner whom I knew in Compiègne, father of three children, was still on his feet, stumbling around with a broken bottle in his hand. He missed me by inches. He rushed a young man, but he was already staggering. The man grabbed his bottle and killed him.

* * *

Raymond Decourcelle of Amiens,[1] implored his tormentors to give him a breath of air, in the name of his pregnant wife and his children.

At the start of this trip, our comrade, Léopold Rousselle, gave final proof of his great spirit of solidarity and devotion. He tried desperately to take care of and comfort those who were sicker than he. He was a man who spent himself without counting the cost, up to the limit of all human possibility. He gave all he had in the care for others and collapsed of exhaustion after only a few hours. He made his way back to our little group of Picards at the rear of the car. There was nothing we could do to keep him from doubling over, nothing we could do to save him. The loss of consciousness was fatal.

Abbé Leblanc, the curé of Framerville (Somme) saw the inexorable evolution and knew that it was almost impossible for us to come out of this inferno alive. He reacted like the priest he was. In a strong voice—very strong for a man so sick with a stomach ailment—he called upon us:

"Let us pray, my brothers, for we are going to die."

Sadly enough, this man of great good will provoked a terrible shock, the reverse of his intentions. The end of his life was comparable to the martyrdom of the early Christians. He had wanted to lead us to a dying worthy of our faith, and instead, before he died, he witnessed the utmost of demonic tragedy.

His call to prayer unleashed panic. Some men began to scream, to weep, to beseech. What madness was still latent flowed out in blood in an indescribable hecatomb.

Something had to be done to neutralize these dangerous madmen.

I was the impotent witness to an abominable spectacle.

I won't name those who acted out this tragedy, out of love for the memory of what they were. They were two good friends, like brothers, united in their political loyalties and by the Resistance.

1.   Unpublished manuscript of Pierre Dhenain, already cited.

The older suffocated and collapsed. A sudden murderous frenzy engulfed the other. He pressed his foot on the
throat of his fallen friend. He looked at this irrevocable
act with wild eyes, and kept repeating, "I'm killing!...I'm
killing!...I'm killing!"

Then it was his turn to be felled, by a boy of sixteen or
seventeen whose naked body still showed the wounds
inflicted by the "special attention" the militia of Darnand
had lavished upon him when he was arrested.

I saw Gaston Leroy die, alone in a group of the raving
insane. Hands gripped him, pulled him down, he shouted,
he fell.

Already many were dead, piled on the floor, and we
stepped on them whenever we moved.

Then I saw two comrades, at a distance, each armed
with a bottle. Before I could get to them, one of them
brandished his improvised weapon. "Don't be an asshole,"
I yelled at him. He lowered his arm and answered
something that I couldn't understand. Did I still look
somewhat human? Perhaps that was why he spared me.

It was hellish. I managed to slide over to the opening
and get a few breaths of air.

11:30 a.m. to 2:00 p.m.—Saint-Brice.[1]

I was a market farmer and for the last few years I had
been working with my widowed mother. My name is
Raymond Viret, and at that time I was twenty years old.
My mother, Marthe Viret, was fifty-three. My sister,
Denise Tisseur, twenty-six years old, and her husband,
Robert Tisseur, twenty-seven, were both there with me.

1.   Unpublished manuscript of Raymond Viret, July 1970, completed by the statements of Marthe Viret, Denise Tisseur and
Robert Tisseur: "We collected watering cans, buckets and bowls.
By climbing up on the buffers we were able to reach water up to
the deportees and speak to them. Men were lying all over the
floor, almost naked. There was a horrible odor. They asked us
questions, especially about the Allied advance. A German non-
com told us not to hang around there. We answered that the men
were dying. He said, 'Soon it will all be over.' A priest, physically
exhausted, gave us the address of his family in the Charentes...."

The heat was unbearable. The train had stopped just behind our house. From our garden, across the grilled fence, I could see the train standing still and hear the moans coming from it. The German sentries, guns in hand, walked alongside it. I came closer, fascinated, and through the openings in the cars, I caught sight of blanched, contorted faces. The men begged for water. We had a water pump close to the railway tracks.

I picked up a container and walked apprehensively toward the train. First the sentries stopped me, took the water, and drank it themselves. Then they told me I could give some to the men in the cars. My family helped me. My sister brought some more containers and she pumped steadily. My mother passed the water to us and we made our way, barefooted, toward the cars, keeping an anxious watch on the sentries. They were keeping a distrustful watch over us.

It was so hot that the rails burned our feet. As we approached the air openings, we saw frightened staring, hollow eyes, burning with fever. All these men were crowding against each other, trying to get a little water which they gulped down and poured over themselves.

Standing on the buffers of the train, we were able to see some of them lying in a corner, motionless, the dying and the dead. We worked as fast as we could, but we didn't have enough containers for the whole convoy. We didn't have time to talk much, but we learned that the train had left Compiègne and that the men didn't know where they were going. Some of them had letters and begged us to take them. My brother-in-law succeeded in hiding five of them, one being from the priest. Later, on, he sent them, but it was too dangerous to keep the addresses, or indicate his own.

For nearly two hours, we pumped and distributed water. We pumped so hard and so long that the water became cloudy and impurities were drawn from the well. Also, the water level had gone way down. The underground water level in the chalky soil was way down because of the drought. My brother-in-law, who had seen the dead inside the cars, told one of the Germans, who answered him in bad French, "Don't worry about that. We're going to take them out and put them in the last car." What an atrocity, and what a revelation, and we were so powerless! Little by little the villagers came and approached the convoy. They were carrying food, but they were frightened about giving it to the deportees. They were right to be afraid. Whenever one of them stepped forward, the sentry aimed his rifle at him and ordered him to stay where he was. Then they conferred briefly, and in less than five minutes, the train was moving. The men were still pleading for water. We could hear their voices and saw their arms and heads behind the barbed wire of the openings. The men's faces reflected their fate. They knew that there was no more hope for them.

We tried to encourage them, to give them a little hope, but they knew they were lost. We kept bringing them water and trying to encourage them, up to the last minute. The Germans ordered us to leave, and with our arms dangling at our sides, we saw the convoy part for an unknown destination. A few deportees shouted "thanks," but we could hardly hear their voices above the strident grinding of the wheels on the burning steel. The Germans hastily climbed onto the train, keeping their guns trained on us.

The Fonfrède Car.[1]

... I felt suddenly ill, with the anguished sensation of not being able to catch my breath. I had also begun to feel pricklings in my hands and feet, then the symptoms became generalized, and reached my stomach.

I got up as quickly as I could, explained that my case was urgent and that I had to be lifted up to the air vent. I tried to grip the bars, but my swollen hands refused to obey and remained rigid, as if dead. A sentry, running along the roadbed, signaled me to draw back and threatened me with his submachine gun. I was forced to obey. Then the comrades near the sliding door squeezed

---

1. Unpublished manuscript of Marcel Fonfrède, June 1970. Arrested for Resistance on February 3, 1944. Six months in a cell in Montluc, the military prison of Lyons.

over and made some space for me. There was some air,
and it revived me....

But as the day dragged on, it grew hotter and hotter. It
must have been about noon, but nobody wanted to eat.
Our concealed fears increased with the heat.

We started another distribution of water.

The train had been standing there, probably for hours,
and it seemed that it would never leave. The cars,
standing in the burning sun, had become furnaces. The
floorboards scorched us and nervous tension soon rose
to a peak.

There were further discussions about water. Some of
the men claimed that they hadn't had anything to drink.
The distribution began again, but the arguments became
bitter, more and more venomous. One of us, who spoke
German, was elected to maintain order and act as
interpreter, if necessary.

A semblance of calm was re-established, but already
nobody was in his normal condition, and the slightest
incident could upset the precarious balance.

And then, without warning, a big guy, bloody, his face
red and congested, fell unconscious. He must have been
arrested very recently, because he looked strong as an ox.

We opened the water barrel, again. Wet, tepid rags
passed from hand to hand. His neighbors slapped his
face with them and fanned him. The little barrel was
almost empty....We meted out the water, but as soon as
we had drunk, we were thirsty again....Most of us were
naked to the waist and sweat flowed along our chests.

We had to react...we had to do something...but there
was nothing we could do, we were powerless. Everyone
hoped that the movement of the train would bring in
some air, and the most despairing kept saying, "The
train's not going to leave!"

It was decided to take down all the clothing hanging
from the ceiling of the car, which could impede the
circulation of air. It was difficult to move at all. We were
crushed together. But we had to do it, just the same. We
took down the coats and jackets and made heaps on
which we all sat.

Order was achieved again, and then we wanted to
drink. Now there were only a few drops of water for

each. The evaporation was rapid and saturated the little air that remained with a noxious gaz.

A fetid stench rose from the slop pail. Almost all of us were fanning ourselves with our handkerchiefs. Our interpreter climbed up to one of the apertures to explain to the sentry that we needed air and asked for a door to be opened. The sentry just laughed. We couldn't hide from the truth. We were doomed to suffocate in here.

Just at this moment we learned of the death of one of our companions. He was a youngster from Clermont.[1] His brother was sitting near us. The news shattered the remnants of our courage. The brother went out of his

1. The following is the statement of Georges Bixel covering the same incidents (unpublished manuscript, June 1970).

"A young companion from Puy-de-Dôme showed disturbing signs of insanity, flailed about, cried and tried to strangle a comrade. At the cost of a tremendous effort, helpful friends succeeded in averting the worst. After a brief scramble, calm was restored. It was a momentary respite because the poor fellow who had been so full of frenzied energy, suddenly slumped and fell to the floor. Death came quickly. His stunned brother grasped the full horror of the drama and, in turn, became the prey of an overwhelming delirium, shouting incoherent words, imagining that we had killed his brother, and then he also fell down and quickly died, with a rapidity which amazed and frightened us. At the other end of the car, two other comrades were dying in silence, but with equal rapidity.

"It was not so much panic in the car, as profound dismay. We didn't know about the horrors in the other cars. Who were my comrades in misfortune? I only remember a few of the names. How could it be otherwise? We were hurriedly pushed on board, grouped into hundreds at random. However, I remember Bouzigues, a teacher from Clermont-l'Hérault; two pals, Bandel and Cheuneval; the prefect of Haute-Saône who was close to me and who never lost his self-control....I can still see all those anonymous faces in their suffering. The ceiling of the car was broiling, and covered with a gluey condensation.

"The sentries were stretching their legs. There was nothing to hope for from these taunting brutes. One of them spoke French well. He said, 'Now is the time for you to resist, you of the Resistance.' The track workers were not permitted to approach the convoy. Bandel, who spoke German fluently, was suddenly

mind. "Why did you kill him? You're killers. You're all assassins. Assassins!"

"Why are you talking like this to me?"

"Why do you want to kill me, too?"

"I'm suffocating....No! I don't want to die. I want to see my family again....Assassins! Assassins!"

"But what did I ever do to you?"

"Oh, my God, have pity on me...."

These words were repeated like the refrain of a song. He was mad!

Now others fainted all around us. From every side, there were calls for water to splash their faces. Wet rags were held to their lips, their faces were slapped. There was general panic....

The car was a menagerie. All we could hear was a cacophony of animal cries. The madman was still howling.

The anguish climaxed...he became violent. He managed to get up, swaying on his legs. There was no room for him to move around. He stepped on the others, and they pushed him back.

In the darkness, in front of me, a young comrade struggled and whimpered.

"He's smothering me. He's sitting on my chest. Get him off. I'm dying...for God's sake, get him off...." Then, gathering his strength, he began to cry, "Help, help."

This poor, insane creature was finally thrown over to the other side of the car, and there was an immediate concert of shouts. The battle started again. During the brief moments of respite, we could hear a voice calling out, "A comrade is dying here, in this corner. For Christ's sake, send us a drop of water...just one drop."

But there was no more water.

Two volunteers who had been standing up, waving towels to try to get the air to move, exhausted themselves and fell.

seized with anger, and called out to a sentry: 'Warum das? Wir sind keine Juden.' His words shocked me. Was he saying that it would be all right to treat Jews like this, or was he just trying to soften up the sentries? Fortunately for us, there were no reprisals for his ambiguous words...."

Near us, still another man died. We could no longer count the dead.... It was terrifying!....

Our interpreter again called out to the sentries. We tried to keep silent. The only reply they gave could be translated as: "Stop your yapping, or we'll shoot into the car."

The cries started up again, more fearful than before.

What an empty threat.... What difference could it make to men who were dying, if they were killed by a bullet.... It would be a liberation....

The madman was still raving. His monologue had changed into incoherent howls.... Little by little his violence increased and soon we were forced to defend ourselves without pity for him. He was trying to strangle us. He leaped on the men near him, his hands tense, he caught them by the neck and gripped their throats.

At one moment I even felt his hands reaching blindly for my neck. I had a chill of terror. Without thinking, I pushed brutally and punched him in the face. He fell back with an animal cry. Then I saw how little I had accomplished, for he immediately threw himself on another comrade and crushed two or three others under his feet....

Gradually, I crouched down in my corner, my belly contracted, my chest constricted, my legs twisted under the fallen mass of bodies. I disappeared into nothingness.... Then in a flash of half-consciousness, I heard screams alongside me... cries of sheer terror, the rattling gasps of the dying, the curses of those who still held to their sanity. Weaker and weaker, I fell into total unconsciousness....

With a spasm of last awareness, I kept repeating, "No, I mustn't.... I mustn't...."

2:00 p.m.

In eighteen cities of France the meteorological services of the German Army checked the outside temperature. These eighteen readings were then sent to Hamburg, the army meteorological center. When we examine this map of Sunday, July 2, 1944, and the graph established by the French meteorological commission for the department of the Marne,[1] we find that the two cities which, on that Sunday afternoon, recorded the highest temperatures, were Reims and Châlons-sur-Marne: 34°.[2]

1. *Meteorological Year 1944.* Imprimerie-Librairie de l'Union Républicaine, 27, rue d'Orfeuil, Châlons-sur-Marne.
2. At 2 p.m., Paris 24°; Dijon, 28°; Sarrebourg, 23° C (*Täglicher Wetterbericht des deutschen Reichswetterdienstes.* Published by Deutsche Seewarte, Hamburg).

The Furnace of Reims

2:15 p.m.—Reims Station.

T he station chief Jacquet dialed the telephone number of Mademoiselle Fernande Pierre, who directed the Red Cross reception center.

"A train of deportees will be coming into the station in a few minutes. There are a lot of dead....We don't know exactly what happened."

"I'm coming."

2:35 p.m.—Reims Station.

The 7909 bypassed the "blast-hole" at Saint-Brice and rattled into the tangle of station tracks between two ranks of soldiers, facing outward. The platforms were submerged in a tide of uniforms—all that Reims could boast of "official services" must have been present. The station resounded with instructions, orders, errands, running feet. This colorful bustle hardly slowed at all for the arrival of the train. The regular escort left the observation boxes and compartments with only a token force of the armed guards on duty.

"Where's the cantine?"

At switching cabin No. 2, Jean Rousset, postman *'Mixte'* [1] had replaced the saboteur, Roger Ollinger. Jean Rousset first put the 7909 on central track No. 9 and then left his box and walked toward the tail van, about twenty meters away. The wailings from the cars increased. Rousset, impelled by the tragic chorus, spoke sharply back to the sentry who blocked his approach:

"We'll see about this. I want to speak to an officer."

The soldier pointed to the front of the convoy. As he passed by each aperture, Rousset shouted: "We're going to take care of you. We're going to help you guys."

There was an officer there, right in the middle of a group watching him.

"What do you want?"

"I want to give water to these...."

"What's stopping you?"

Lucien Pelican and three track workers of the operating service were standing near the water pump for locomotives at the front of the train.

"Let's go?"

"We have to go."

"Open the spigot."

Three bottles. Two buckets. The first sentry smiled. Back and forth three times. Then a second sentry ran toward the pump, broke the bottles and kicked the buckets over.

The Guérin-Canac Car.

A young employee held up a bottle of water. It was "suctioned" into the airshaft. The deportee railway worker, Marcel Guérin, was perfectly acquainted with the services of the Reims station. He pulled himself up to the barbed wire:

---

1. *Facteur Mixte:* F.M.X. These replacement agents could both operate the telegraph of a station and direct maneuvers generally performed by station chiefs.

"Quick. Quick. Go get an inspector at the station. I'm a railway man, like you."

A few minutes later.

"Things are pretty bad in there for you guys."

"Pretty bad. You can save us by getting a pump-barrel."

The inspector raced off.

"He came back soon[1] with the apparatus used to fill the water tanks of the toilets on trains. It was composed of a reservoir, mounted on a frame, to be pulled on wheels by a shaft, with a funnel for filling, a Japy pump and a tube for conducting water into the toilets. In a very short time, our barrel was full of water again. This brave railway worker did the same for the car to our right.

"Doctor Bettinger took Marcel Guérin's place at the opening.

" 'I'm Doctor Bettinger of Reims.... Go get a nurse. Get Monsieur Berthet as well.'

"Another worker answered: 'Don't worry, Doc, I'm going. What do you need?'

" 'Ether, sugar, mint...anything she has.'

"By this time there were six railwaymen grouped under the aperture of the car. Two guards got nervous.

" 'Leave; no one stay.'

" 'These are men from Reims, our friends, my family doctor.'

" 'All right then. But no noise. Quiet now.'

"Accompanied by the S.D. officer in charge of the convoy, Mademoiselle Fernande Pierre came running.

" 'Doctor, Doctor. I wasn't far away. I have some ether, sugar, a flask of Hoffmann liqueur.... Take it.... This is frightful.'

"A railway man took off his cap politely:

" 'Monsieur the Officer, they have no air. We must open the doors.'

"The nurse added, 'He's right. They must have air. They're dying of asphyxiation.'

"The officer looked dead tired.

" 'Everybody go back,' he said to the nurse, 'except you, Mademoiselle.'

---

1.   Unpublished manuscript of Marcel Guérin, March 1970.

"He called a policeman. Immediately six armed men took up their stations facing the door. The officer unsealed the latch.

" 'Mademoiselle, if you wish, go forward.'

" 'Come to me, Mademoiselle.'

" 'To me.'

"But Mademoiselle Pierre had only what she could hold in her two hands.

"The officer ordered the door of the next car opened.

" 'Come this way."

"She ran. She was all alone. Another bit of sugar, a bit of mint, some Aspirine.

"A deportee with a long, white beard jumped out onto the platform.

"The officer commanded him to stop.

" 'Médecin, Arzt, doctor,' the man explained.

"And Doctor Bent climbed voluntarily back into the car, with another precious bottle of mint in his hands.

" 'Close the doors.' "

The Bent-Solladié Car.

Everybody cheered:

"Bravo, docteur! Bravo!"

"Sugar. Can I have some?"

"Silence. Move back from those who are stretched out. I'm going to begin with them."

The white beard and broad shoulders of the doctor imposed respect. Space was cleared around the sickest men.

"Unfortunately,[1] there weren't only Resistants in the car. I remember a big blond who showed off by putting on pajamas and lying down at full length. He kicked everybody out of the way to get enough space. To protest in this weltering enclosure would have started the free-for-all which had to be avoided at all costs.

"This part of the car also contained an item which we were determined to avoid using—the slop bucket. A comrade and I worked out a solution. By this time we

1. Unpublished manuscript of Louis Favro, May 1970.

realized that our personal possessions had no more
value, and my comrade willingly contributed his jacket.
He folded it up over the bucket and made a cover. We
used this as a seat. We swore to each other to remain
calm, and we worked out a system. While one of us sat on
the bucket, the other mounted on its edge, supported by
the body of the seated comrade between his legs, he
would have his head at the level of the aperture, and
would get a little air."

2:50 p.m.—Reims station.[1]

During the stopover, while my comrades were passing
in water, I attached a rubber hose to a water outlet on the
platform and slid the end of it through the barbed wire
tangled across the air vents of each car. A German officer
rushed at me and shook me very violently. He forced me
to stop the supplying system I had set up. It wasn't easy.
I hung onto the hose, and I managed to mess the
German up a bit. He grabbed the hose, there was quite a
bit of pressure in it, and turned it full force on me. That
wasn't enough for him. He whipped me on the back with
the hose, fifteen times, maybe more, and I had to take
sick-leave for two weeks.

3:00 p.m.—Reims Station.

"Have you got the travel order?"
"Here it is."
Claude Gérard, the new train guardian for the 7909,
forty-three years old, a bit grizzled, left the office of
Service Rotation. The trackman who opened the door for
him advised him to keep off the platform.
"They're very edgy up there. They're afraid the Resistance is going to attack. They've posted S.S. troops every
hundred meters over the next three kilometers. You'd be

1.   Deposition of Louis Albert Bernard, cleaner employed by the
French railway system (S.N.C.F.), before the Research Commission on War Crimes, June 17, 1948.

better off if you swung around by the outside. Your van should be by the main switching cabin on the Courcelle bridge."

The last check-point. The last verification.

"Not climb in there."

"But this is my van. This is my job...."

Long discussion, just about the same as that which took place before the same van in the Compiègne station when Cyriaque Frizon came on duty. But Claude Gérard had more luck than his predecessor. He wouldn't have to travel on the flat car between the machine guns, but in the last escort passenger car.

"Comfortable. Seat comfortable."

Laughs. Black imitation leather. Bottles of wine. Greasy papers, and weapons lying around.

"*Gut*. No moving. No getting out!"

In the adjacent compartment, Italian soldiers were singing.[1]

1. An appeal was broadcast over France-Inter ("Radioscopie," a program of Jacques Chancel) on April 20, 1970. At the O.R.T.F. (Office de Radiodiffusion et Télévision Françaises) the next day, I received an anonymous telephone call containing information worth special attention. My correspondent stated that he had been a member of the escort of the 'Death Train,' and after he answered three or four of my questions, I was sure that he was telling the truth (objective events—in particular those we shall be tracing later on in this text, concerning stops at Revigny and Novéant—organization of the convoy and time schedules). My informant would only speak for a short time, and was even more unwilling to agree to a rendez-vous. I am going to try to reconstruct our conversation as accurately as possible.
Question: Are you German?
Answer: No, Italian, or anyhow, I was Italian in 1944.
Q.: You have no accent.
A.: I have the accent of the Midi. I live in France.
Q.: Were there many Italians in the escort?
A.: Eight, I think.
Q.: What was your unit?
A.: I can't tell you. You understand, I must avoid all questions that are too precise or too personal.
Q.: Were you based in Paris?
A.: Yes.
Q.: Were you in the S.S.?
A.: No.

3:10 p.m.—Reims Station.

Théophile Mulette and Jean Hauller were at the controls of the relaying locomotive. They exchanged only a few, hurried words at the station with the crew they were replacing, Corville and Dorgny.[1]

"They're deportees. They're dying like flies."

"With this heat, no wonder."

"The sons of bitches."

Richter himself unhitched the convoy.

Q.: Was the convoy chief an S.S.?

A.: No.

Q.: Can you tell me his name, or describe him?

A.: He was thirty-five years old, at most. He was an Austrian, a lieutenant. He was driven almost mad by what he saw, by what was happening to him. He must have telephoned to Paris a dozen times to ask what he should do. He wanted to unload all the dead and bury them on the spot. The events had gone beyond his capacity to handle them. He said several times, when I was there, "This is no work for a soldier, we're undertakers." He was pale and I was told that he had vomited several times. I think we were all on the point of nervous exhaustion because of the heat, the smells, and particularly the stops and the long delays. By the time we got to the frontier, we were twenty-four hours behind schedule. The convoy chief had brawled with other chiefs in command of war trains on their way to Normandy, who claimed that military reinforcements had priority over the victims of the Gestapo.

Q.: Were there any brutalities? Any assassinations?

A.: Yes, but not on the part of the Italians. The others must have gone crazy, with all the deaths, and the maddening delays. I got drunk at Novéant, at the frontier. I guess all of us were drunk in the trucks that took us back to Paris. And the next day, we were even machine-gunned. Then there was a general stampede.

Q.: How old are you?

A.: Fifty-three years old.

Q.: Why are you telephoning me if you don't want to give me your name, or any details?

A.: Out of curiosity. I'll call you again when your book is published. I can swear to you that I killed no one. I'm a Catholic. It was war. At Reims, my best friend, an Italian, began to weep. I permitted the track workers to bring them water, and even helped.

1.   The crew Corville, Dorgny, Frizon and Reider returned to the Compiègne station, hitching a ride on a gas buggy.

Steam governor. A burst of steam. The locomotive dragged the convoy very slowly through the maze of fissures blasted open by the American bombs in June.

The rails, resting on ties balanced across a board scaffolding, bent and creaked.

"We're going to turn over!"

"No, no, stoke your furnace! I've done this twenty times."

"I'm telling you...."

After the switch point at Betheny, the tracks became solid again.

The station switches were three kilometers further on.

The "Feldpolizei" evacuated the platforms of the Reims station. A military train had been announced.

The Guérin-Canac Car.[1]

I could see enormous craters alongside the track, as well as long sections of rails that the explosion had propelled into the trees. Further on there was a shapeless mass of crushed cars, piled up on top of each other.

1. Albert Canac, already cited.

3:20 p.m.—Reims.
Switch post of the Betheny depot.

Jean Hauller slowed down even more. The convoy came into the switching yard. The engineer slightly increased the head of steam. The radial truck of the 230 D took the new section of the track to Châlons. In his cabin, the switchman violently pulled on the control lever. The transmission cables stretched and vibrated. The movable switch element pivoted slowly. The first driving wheel of the machine turned in space, but the flange touched down on the iron and grooved in. There was a slight rocking that neither Hauller nor Mulette noticed. The switchman had already returned the control lever to its position. The second pair of driving wheels also passed over, but the rocking motion increased. The last pair: sparks. The two wheels of one meter, seven hundred fifty millimeters rested on one millimeter of rail, slid, derailed, sagged. A crosstie splintered. The switches clacked and attached to the rail they had just left two seconds ago at the passage of the radial truck. The back wheels of the 230 D plowed through the track bed.

Hauller and Mulette, badly shaken, grabbed the footboard and the handrail. The tender and the cars, with a single jolt, crushed a second tie with their derailed wheels. The buffers absorbed the first vibrations, and then with reverse action, released all the energy compressed by the shock. The tender, off balance, and pulled in opposite directions by the locomotive and the convoy, fell off the rails. The bogie of the locomotive blocked against a tie. The half-buried wheels of the tender did not have enough drive to get over the tie. Hauller "dispatched" the brakes, and the casings swelled along the whole length of the train. The 7909 was stopped and no defect in the roadbed was apparent. The 230 D and its tender, pistons throbbing, were shrouded in steam. The slide of ten meters had lasted, perhaps, two seconds. The switchman ran up, waving his arms.

A muffled rumor, at first almost imperceptible, echoed and spread, like the whisper of steam.

Mulette and Hauller crawled under the locomotive. They looked out at a circle of military boots and service shoes.

Sabotage!

"Sabotage," in every inflection.

Faces, shaded by visored caps bent down to the level of the damage.

Hauller and Mulette stood up.

" 'Responsable'? Who is to blame?"

The face was all mouth.

Babble and splutter.

The helmet backed away behind the cap of the S.D. officer.

"It's sabotage."

The switchman spoke up.

"I'm the one who put it on the track. Take a look yourself. Everything's in place. But look over there, two meters along, and there, under the tender, there are depressions. The bombs did that. There are holes everywhere. They have done a little patchwork so that the trains could pass. And plenty of trains passed, and here's the result."

"We are going to investigate the switching."

"Investigate! Investigate! Besides, the station chief will

tell you, when he's seen it. It's plain. There's no cracking.
Lucky for me that the switch didn't slip when the train
jumped the track, otherwise I'd be in for trouble."

Hauller began to catch on. He thought, "I hope he
dries up. He's laying it on too thick. I'd better cut in."

"That's not all. I can tell you that I felt the locomotive
digging in. That means a weakening in the roadbed. It's
normal. The whole area has been bombed over. Now
we've got to get her back on the track."

The officer bent down again for another look.

"How long a time before you can get going?"

Mulette closed his eyes and thought a minute:

"It will take us at least two full hours."

"Two hours. Not possible. I shall telephone."

"You'll have to go to the depot. It's not very far."

"Let's go. You come with me."

"I can't. I'm working on the switching track. My
comrade will go with you."

The officer and the stoker walked off.

"You'll have to find another locomotive. Leave this one
here."

"It won't do any good. Even if you get another, you'd
have to wait for the tracks to be free. Since the bombardment, we have no other way out to Châlons."

"Can you go around it?"

"I wouldn't know about that. You'd have to see
Monsieur Richter."

3:20 p.m.—Reims Station.[1]

After the train left, I went to see the station chief,
Monsieur Jacquet, to ask him to notify the Châlons Red
Cross, and to tell them, on my behalf, about the condition
of most of the prisoners, and what medicaments would
be necessary.

1. Report of Mademoiselle Fernande Pierre, Director of the
Reception Center of the French Red Cross, to Captain Sigala,
transport officer of Reims, dated February 28, 1945.

Reims—Betheny Shunting Yard. (Fully-Thomas Car.)[1]

The tragedy continued. Men lost consciousness and dropped down on the bodies of their neighbors, who sometimes tried to hold them up, sometimes tried to push them away, but soon collapsed under their weight. As soon as an arm or leg was caught under a body, it became impossible to move it, and sooner or later, they were buried under other bodies. Many died, suffocated under the weight of bodies from which they could not free themselves. Others went insane; Barrois thought he was playing a game of chess with me. His delirium was short, and he died as if going to sleep. I was there, but then I could do nothing.

Some became violent. They began to strike about them with their fists, their shoes, their mugs...they leaped up and ran from one end of the car to the other, trampling on their comrades, who tried to defend themselves and exhausted their little remaining store of strength and breath, and also died.

One man brandished a pocket knife. Delirium marked his face, his eyes grotesquely enlarged, popping out of their sockets, inarticulate cries bubbled out of his mouth. I trembled with fear that he would attack me. I passed a towel through a ring on the wall and knotted it to my left arm so as not to fall and be crushed if I fainted. With my elbow held up like this, I held my jacket over my forearm, like a toreador. I held a shoe in my other hand, ready to defend myself.

Finally he threw himself on his nearest neighbor, slashed his face, dug out his eyes, with a maniac's frenzy. Then he cut his own throat. This scene terrified me and calmed me at the same time. I no longer had to be afraid that he would attack me.

I lived in a haze. My mind couldn't focus. At the other end of the car, Bulher was completely naked. He fell to his knees, got up again, gripped one of the wall rings and lifted himself to the air vent to be able to breathe. He remained there, a few seconds, at the opening. A madman caught sight of him and grabbed him around

1. Statement of Lt. Col. Jean Thomas, already cited.

the waist. They struggled a few minutes, fell, and neither could rise again.

Everything faded before me. An immense torpor sucked me down. My neighbor, a Communist with three years of arrest behind him, revived me. He had a little water left in his thermos, and a bit of sugar which he gave me. Just before I fainted I had seen him compelled to kill the last man to go mad, choking him and beating his skull with a mug. Now everything was calm.

Only two or three men had been able to stay sane. Those of us who were on top of the heap of bodies, like myself, revived little by little. Most of our comrades had stopped breathing, so the survivors had enough air. At first we didn't realize the extent of our losses; it was so inconceivable. It was only when we saw the bodies, sprawled, heaped together, motionless, that we finally understood that they were all dead.... Each of us called out the name of a comrade, father, brother. No answers came.

3:40 p.m.—Reims, Betheny Depot.

The S.D. officer, furious, slammed the door of the closet which served as an office for the man in charge of the depot.

"They're sending a car for me."

Richter had ordered Betheny to get the locomotive back on the track and to handle the pull-back of the 7909. A dozen track repair men climbed onto the tool car and the hoist. The transfer table rotated under the canopy.

3:40 p.m.—Reims Station.

Mademoiselle Pierre no longer had the strength to battle alone against the "gold braid" in charge, who were already coming back into the station, barking orders. She telephoned Dr. Bouvier, the mayor of Reims and president of the local Red Cross.

"Dr. Bouvier is probably on the way to the station. He has just left to mail some letters."

*The Death Train arrived at its destination. This photograph
"was taken on July 5, 1944, by a guard at Dachau, after
the 'column of the living' had been removed. The
deportees themselves discovered this document in his
briefcase when the camp was liberated."*
The original photograph was made available to the author
by Dr. Stéphane Fuchs

Mademoiselle Pierre assigned a nurse to keep watch by the letter box.... Then she telephoned Madame Chatelin of the Red Cross Committee and told her to come with her husband, Dr. Chatelin, and to be sure to bring lots of medicines.

3:40 p.m.—Betheny Shunting Yard.

Nicolas Marceau and a dozen other repair men who filled in the bomb holes in the shunting yard decided to approach the train from the wrong side of the tracks. Each one filled a bucket with water. When they were within ten meters of the central cars, they were forced back by the submachine guns of the three convoy escorts.

3:55 p.m.—Reims Station.

The cars of the 7909, pulled back by a shift tractor, stopped at platform No. 3. Dr. Joseph Bouvier, held at the passenger entry by a feldpolizei, argued his point.

"My name doesn't appear on the list of the Red Cross personnel, simply because I am the director. Everybody here knows me."

"All right. Go ahead."

Mademoiselle Pierre, Dr. Chatelin and Madame Chatelin gathered around him and described the actual conditions in the "transport."

"We have to find the responsible officer."

"He's there, in front of the passenger car."

"Follow me."

The S.D. officer, obviously nervous and bored, ordered the two doctors to present their professional credentials:

"I handed him my papers.[1] He didn't give me permission to stay, but on the other hand, he didn't indicate that I had to leave.... An interpreter who arrived at that point,

---

1. Deposition of Dr. Bouvier before a commission of "Recherche des Crimes de Guerre" (Research of War Crimes), Reims, June 17, 1948.

told me that there were men dead in the cars. I intervened again with the officer who, as I said before, appeared extremely annoyed, to get him to open the cars. After some hesitation, he cut the seals himself with pliers, and unconscious men fell out onto the tracks. The guards rushed up, thinking that they were trying to escape, but they quickly saw that these men were dying or virtually dead. However, we did succeed in pulling out two bodies and carried them to a little shed near the convoy.[1]"

3:55 p.m.—Reims Station.
(Habermacher-La Perraudière Car.)[2]

Comrades were lifting their heads to the openings and calling out, "Open up. Open for us. We're suffocating. Some of us in here are dead."

"Useless. Who's going to pay any attention to us?" Just the same. Astonishment. The door of the cattle car rolled slowly open! I was right next to it. A torrent of air poured in. I could breathe at last.

A voice with a German accent: "Pull out the cadavers."

Some comrades extracted a few bodies from the tangled heap and passed them over the heads of those who, like myself, were seated. A soldier put his head close to mine and ordered: "Pull this one out, too."

Could I be dying? They took me out, because I could no longer move myself, and stretched me out on the platform. I had no strength, but at least I could breath. I revived.

"It's not a Jew. He's a priest!"

I heard some comrades speak these words, but I didn't grasp the full meaning at that time. Later they explained to me that they had saved my life. It seems that the German soldier had just said, "This old Kike. Don't waste time over him."

1. A railroad worker, André Dubois and Dr. Chatelin carried the stretcher.
2. Unpublished manuscript of Father de La Perraudière, already cited.

And charitably, to speed my departure from this world, he drew his gun from his shoulder strap and was about to break my skull with the butt. He was very surprised at the rectification made by my comrades, and arrested his gesture in mid-air and replaced his weapon. I didn't see anything. I didn't understand anything. I was just enjoying the feel of breathing.

The door of the car rolled closed again. A wild hope. The train would go on without me and leave me at Reims, and they would put me in a hospital.... No, it didn't work out like that. A moment later, when I was completely conscious, they told me to get up. I stood up trembling, knees shaking. A soldier on one side and a French nurse on the other, propped me up and helped me walk, with great difficulty, toward the rear of the train. I wanted to speak to her[1]. The soldier wouldn't let me.

"No talking!"

She didn't answer. Where were they taking me?

The last car was partly empty.[2] They made me climb in. There were already six comrades, just about as sick as I was. They closed the car door. What a luxury. So much space for the seven of us, who had been crowded like sardines in a can.

---

1. The nurse was Mademoiselle Fernande Pierre, the director of the Red Cross reception center: "The guards demanded buns of bread from those occupying the cars of deportees being removed to a half-filled car. Then they 'tossed,' actually 'tossed' the pieces at these unfortunate men (as if they were throwing food to a dog). There was a priest among them. Madame Chatelin and I had supported him to take him to the car. He wanted to speak to us, but the guard who followed us threatened us with his submachine gun, and we were forced to remain silent." (Unpublished manuscript of Fernande Pierre, May 1970.)

2. At least seven cars had left Compiègne without "passengers." The convoy chiefs insisted on this reserve in case of bombardments or attempts at escape. In this way, damaged cars could be immediately replaced. (Author's note.)

3:55 p.m.—Reims Station. (The Rohmer Car.)[1]

We could hear cries for help coming from the near-by cars. They were taken up in chorus by all the cars, including our own. Everybody called out:

"Help. Hilfe. Open the doors. Men have died in here."

Finally, the door opened. An S.S. appeared. First silence, then he shouted: "Was ist los? Ruhe, Schweine-hund."

I went up to the door and explained to him, in German, that two of our comrades had died for lack of air. He didn't appear at all surprised, and simply gave the order to unload them. The two bodies were passed out from hand to hand. We tried to arrange to have Nikis put into another car because he seemed to be in a very serious condition, and I pointed out to the S.S. that our water barrel was empty. The S.S. closed the door on our appeals.

3:55 p.m.—Reims Station. (The Weil Car.)[2]

I glanced out of the air vent and saw that the Red Cross was removing some bodies on stretchers. I signaled to Fuchs that things looked very bad out there and we gave the order that nobody was to stand up. We were afraid that they would panic if they knew what was really going on.

The first prisoner suffocated. By some miracle we made space for him to lie flat on the floor and we set up a rule: all sick men would be treated:

first, by slaps;

second, by a drink of water.

The procession began. It was hallucinating, but there were no deaths because the men were held motionless and there was no anguish; perhaps, also because they knew that there were doctors taking care of them, even if they fainted.

I slapped Dartout several times. He was a little Maquis

1. Francis Rohmer, already cited.
2. Paul Weil, already cited.

fighter, twenty-one years old, and something of a hippy. Later on he indulged in the luxury of "doing" twelve concentration camps and work details. I have to confess now that he got two full glasses of water, because we had been protecting him ever since Eysses, where I had first seen the heroic character of this hip kid.

Kienzler, who had placed a fuse bomb in the German employment office at Montluçon, paid for his loyal activity. He was gasping for air wildly, he had gone pale and his eyes rolled back in his head. I must have lost my self-control. I implored him not to die. He had been my companion ever since Clermont-Ferrand, since Combat, in all the prisons, all the hopes and all the rotten luck. He pulled out of it, because he knew that I still needed him.

* * *

Paul Weil was a giant, one meter ninety-three (almost six foot five)....

We all owe our lives to him,[1] to the authority he commanded, to the obedience we were glad to give him.

At Compiègne we had seen Dr. Rohmer and Professor Vlès, the patron of my friend, Weil, and several other friends from the prison camp, get into the car next to ours. During a stop in the middle of the afternoon, I heard Dr. Rohmer call, in German, pathetically trying to attract the attention of the guards and explain to them that there were already a number of dead in the wagon, and that they would all die if they weren't gotten out of the car.

Little by little, we began to feel that we were there to stay. But by great good luck, all of those enclosed in our car remained sufficiently calm not to yield to panic and madness. Dr. Paul Weil had explained it all to us. Without discipline, it would be death for all of us. He said: "We must hold out until night. We'll get there, and things will work out." I don't want to talk about how we felt then, but we were certain that this time we were all going to die. All we could do was to remember, or dream about the happy days of the past: our families, friends,

1. Unpublished manuscript of Dr. Kienzler, already cited.

parents, the joy of life of those who can breathe freely, or simply drink all the water that they want.

When we joined the Resistance, we knew that perhaps we would have to die. But what was atrocious was to die asphyxiated, powerless before a faceless enemy con-demming us to slow death, a death which we would have faced more willingly, if it had been brutal, violent and heroic.

I remember, during a stop, that a fat German officer, flanked by soldiers who kept their guns trained on us, came to ask if there were any dead, and how many, in our car. Many of us were sick, some unconscious, but none were dead yet. But it made us understand that things weren't the same in the other cars.

* * *

Yes, I had a lot of luck to be with Weil.[1] I remember especially the stopover at Reims, and the terrible cries that came from the cars near us. A nice, simple guy next to me started to wander in his mind. First he prayed, and then he cursed. Then he prayed again and ended his litanies by cursing out God and all the saints in Paradise. After that, he was so worn out, he couldn't move. He leaned his head against the wall of the car and breathed in vain for the air that wouldn't come.

3:55 p.m.—Reims Station. (Fully-Thomas Car.)

"The brawling grew ferocious.[2] I couldn't see any end to it. We'd all have to go through it. I wanted to cry, but I couldn't. I thought of all the people I loved. I called them aloud by their names. They would never know how I died. They would never be comforted. These thoughts gnawed at me and drove me mad. I couldn't see anything. I couldn't understand anything. I waited calmly for the blow that would put an end to me."

1.   Unpublished manuscript of Roger Dartout, July 1970.
2.   Statement of Dr. Georges Fully, already cited.

"We were hammering on the walls,[1] calling for water and help. After about half an hour, they opened the door. The insweep of air revived us. The Germans told us to pass out the three or four sickest.... Everybody raised his hand. Everybody wanted to get out. The Germans closed the door again. They had only authorized three or four.... A young Dutchman I had known at Compiègne continued to batter on the walls with fists and shoes, calling for water. 'Bitte Posten—Wasser, Wasser, zu trinken.' His wailing kept up obsessively, ringing like a death knell, broken into, sometimes, by other voices in the car: 'Shut up!' 'Close your trap.' And the raucous order of an S.S. guard: 'Ruhe, Schweine, Maul.' But he continued to whimper in the delirium which had taken him over completely. A German had threatened to shoot into the car to silence him. At last he stopped, exhausted."

4:15 p.m.—Reims Station.

On platform No. 3, Drs. Bouvier and Chatelin practiced artificial respiration on about fifteen deportees. The brigadier, André Dubois, holding his stretcher, asked if there were other bodies to load:

"It's not worth the trouble," answered a captain of the garrison of Reims.

"But...."

"Useless!"

Dubois laid the stretcher to one side.

"At least I can distribute the bottles of beer."

"If you like...."

4:35 p.m.—Reims Station.

The German station chief and the captain of the garrison climbed onto the footboard of the shunting tractor which they directed onto a siding two hundred meters away from platform No. 3. The siding was sheltered.

---

1.   Statement of Lt. Col. Jean Thomas, already cited.

The S.D. officer in charge of the convoy slumped exhausted in front of the telephone switchboard, waiting for his phone connections to come through.

For the first time, the Red Cross was "neutralized" by a cordon of guards.

4:35 to 8:00 p.m.—Reims Siding.
(The Helluy-Aubert-Villiers Car.)[1]

This new, prolonged halt worsened the situation in all the cars of the convoy, especially our own, where the maintenance of order deteriorated rapidly because no one could hold out any longer. During all this time, Georges Villiers had been expending his own strength without stint in caring for the others. He was at the far end of the car where the number of sick was alarming; it had increased dangerously since the halt of the train. He called out to an officer, through an air vent, and asked, in German, for help and water for them.

This is approximately how the officer answered: "You're Resistants. You should know how to resist." Georges Villiers retorted with a violence that was rare for him, his voice charged with the contempt and hatred that welled up in him: "You Germans, you're rabid beasts, that's all."

Villiers translated this conversation for us, and those comrades who still had the strength, started to shout, in German, "Verrückte Tiere."

It was at Reims that we drained the last of our water reserve, caring for the poor comrades who were so feeble that their immediate survival was endangered.

We were cooked by the unrelenting heat and felt our strength evaporate with our sweat. And all the length of the convoy we could hear the screams, howls and blows struck against the walls of the train.

1.   Unpublished manuscript of J.-B. Perreolaz, already cited.

4:35 to 8:00 p.m.—Reims Siding. (Rohmer Car.)[1]

The tragedy persisted, mounting from minute to minute. Within two or three hours, seventy-four of our comrades died of heat, asphyxia and dehydration. We had less and less air. The symptoms of asphyxiation were clear. The air was fetid with sweat. Mad, delirious scenes erupted.

Some howled despairingly for help and beat on the sides of the car. Others panted and jerked more and more spasmodically. But our little group from Clermont remained calm. Peupion, leaning against the door, seemed to be lost in a dream. He was over sixty years old and he knew that if you want to hold out, you have to husband your forces. A scuffle jostled me over to his side. Rollot and Professor Vlès were close to us and we leaned against the door, getting a little air through the cracks. This was the best place, at least when the train was moving. Each of us kept on constant watch, fearing the worst.

One of the Riom convicts threw himself on Mirabelle in a mad fit, and struck him in the face, drawing blood. He fell over backwards and others threw themselves on him, bodies rolling and whimpering with pain. The contagion of madness spread to half the car. The men grappled, strangled each other, struck out with shoes and bottles. One after another they fell exhausted and died in a tangle of bodies from which they could no longer free themselves.

Close to me was a little hairdresser who had been literally martyrized at Clermont. In dreadful mockery the Gestapo had pulled out all his hair. They transformed his skull into a mass of wounds and swellings by hitting him with hammers, "click, click click," like English radio signals. He looked at me tragically, and suddenly jumped up and screamed:

"You want to kill me too. I don't want to die."

I tried to hold him back, but he hurtled to the other end of the car, walking over chests and heads, toppled, fell forward, and never rose again.

1. Francis Rohmer, already cited.

A tide of sleep swept over me. Professor Vlès woke me up.

"Something is wrong with me. My pulse accelerated, and now it is very slow. It is hard to breathe. What can be done?"

I applied a rag, moistened with some of our precious water, to his neck, and he began to recover. Soon afterwards, I began to show disturbing symptons. My fingers tingled, I had cramps and my hands tensed involuntarily first on one side and then on the other. I wanted to speak, but my throat was too constricted. My hands were tetanic and I knew that the only thing that could help me would be to change my breathing rhythm. I slowed my respiration. The cramp eased, little by little. I was fully conscious, and I was only afraid of one thing: that somebody who had gone mad would plunge at me, and that I wouldn't have the strength to react. There were now fewer crises of acute delirium, but more dead bodies. We couldn't know how much of this relative calm was due to their dying of asphyxia and excessive fever.

The young man facing me had told me his story when we first left. He was a member of the "Maquis" in the Haute-Savoie. Now he was staring at me fixedly. His breathing was very slow. I examined his pupils which were very small and contracted. I wondered why the right side was dilating in spite of the fact that we were not moving, and the light didn't change. Then the left pupil dilated. The pupils occupied almost the whole iris, and respiration stopped. He folded in, like a burst balloon. I shook him, but there was nothing more to do. He was dead. Still another....

The delirium swept over again. The whole car had turned into an unpadded cell, full of madmen, strangling themselves and each other, trying to hang themselves, hitting each other with bottles, opening their own veins, and then falling across the prostrate bodies which suffocated under their weight. Permeating the horror, were the screams of the men, silenced only when they died: "Help, I don't want to die...."

By this time, more than half of us were dead. Their cries resounded in my head. I don't know if I slept or fainted, my thoughts ran to those I love. Was it a few minutes, was it a few hours?

The sun came through the air shaft at an angle, lighting up the dreadful picture of the distorted dead and convulsing dying. The silence that flowed back was as fearful as the raging. There was only one man, just one who was delirious. He kept murmuring, in a low voice, "I don't want to die. Have pity, O God."

He spoke lower and lower, more and more slowly, and then stopped, like a run-down Victrola!

I looked around for Professor Vlès. He had been next to me before I passed out. Now an unknown voice spoke to me: He gave me his spot. First he was sitting near here, but in a scuffle he was pushed further away. He's sleeping now, over there.

I dragged myself over to him. He seemed to be sleeping, but his breathing was too irregular. He half-opened his eyes and looked at me with great sweetness.

"You have to take my place," I told him. I looked back, but somebody else had already slipped into it.

"My dear friend, I can't keep going."

There was a long silence, and then he started to speak again: "I have to tell you about my research. I haven't told anyone about it. Fifteen years of work."

I leaned over him, but his eyes were far away. I was only able to understand a few more words.

"Laboratory. My wife, Blanchette, assistants."

He lost consciousness. I gathered all my remaining strength, dragged him to the air shaft, lifted him as high as the barbed wire, my fingers gripping onto them, and our two heads almost at the height of the opening. How long did I hang on? The train shook and I fell, completely used up. I stretched him out near the aperture. It did seem to me that some air came in, but he breathed more and more shallowly, and then his features relaxed. He looked peaceful and happy. Professor Vlès, my dear friend....

But I couldn't give up the struggle. I had to continue. I pulled myself up to the opening, but no air came in, defeated by the heavy, putrid heat of the car. All of a sudden, I was grabbed around the throat. I hadn't sensed my attacker coming. His hands tightened and blood throbbed at my temples. I fell, trying to pull loose, and fortunately, in the fall, he was forced to loosen his grip. He rose and went to sit on the dead bodies, staring at me with vacant madness.

I also saw my "buddy" who suffered from a pneumo-thorax. I had tried to intervene on his behalf at Com-piègne, hoping that he would be permitted to stay behind, but I couldn't do anything. So far, he had held out, but now his face had become congested and he breathed with great difficulty. I called to a guard who was patrolling the convoy. In German, I begged him for some water. I told him that there was a boy of seventeen who was on the point of death. "Maybe you have a son of that age. Think of your own mother, your father, and take pity on him."

"Yes, I do have a son that age, but what the hell difference does that make? You're getting what you asked for, and all you have to do is shut up and die. And if you're not dead when we get there, we're going to kill you." And he punctuated his sentence by threatening me with his submachine gun.

So that was how it was going to end. If we weren't dead when we got there, they would kill us....

What use could there be now in struggling and suffering? I made my decision, and lay down beside Professor Vlès, my old teacher, and I waited for death. Memories floated through—my childhood, my friends, my parents. I confessed: "Our Father...."

How easy it is to die like this. My life seemed so unreal. "Rohmer!"

Who called me? I guess it was my great friend, Rollot. I felt better. I mustn't die. I had to fight to the end. If they wanted to slaughter us, we would try to make them pay dearly for our deaths. I got up and lurched over to my friends. My feet sank into the corpses, I stumbled on a head and fell with my nose near a slit in the floorboards. I lay across an unknown body. It was barely breathing. I fell into a coma.

*   *

Camille Rozan came to Rohmer's aid, shook him and slapped him.

"Hang on. Here'a bit of sugar."

Camille Rozan was still wearing his heavy sweater with a rolled collar. He had followed the advice of Professor Vlès:

"You must avoid evaporation at all costs. Above all, don't undress. If you can't stand wearing a sweater, at least keep your shirts on. In the Sahara, the Touaregs are always warmly dressed...."

Professor Vlès had died wearing his coat and scarf, with his funny little crumpled hat pulled down over his ears.

"I was only eighteen years old,[1] and maybe I owe my life to a large, ugly boil in my armpit. Every time I started to pass out, a sharp pain revived me. Without these stabs, I would have drifted off, like a lot of the others, and not awakened. I was in the right, rear corner, the least troubled. My companion, a Spaniard arrested at Montpellier, had succeeded in getting a little water at the previous stop and we were able to wet our lips from time to time."

Lucien Pascal and Daniel Gros fainted with the first exchange of blows. They fell with their faces against the base of the sliding door—if they had been a few centimeters further to the left, they never would have awakened. Above them, clinging to a tiny slit in the door, and paying no attention to what went on behind his back, stood Joseph Barlot.

4:35 to 8:00 p.m.—Reims Siding.
(The Metal Car of André Gonzalès.)

Not a sound. Not a cry.

1. Unpublished manuscript of Robert Cette, April 1970. He belonged to the N.A.P. Resistance network. He was arrested by the militia at Puy, May 1944. Passed through the prisons of Saint-Etienne, Vichy, Bellerive and Riom.

4:35 to 8:00 p.m.—Reims Siding.
(Garnal-Mamon Car.)

A young police officer of Montpellier, Pierre Mamon, and a doctor from Cahors, Jacques Garnal, had maintained order in the car during the whole first period of the voyage. The discipline they had imposed, reinforced by a sizeable collection of beer bottles at Saint-Brice and when they first arrived at Reims, suddenly broke down.

"A big,[1] powerful guy suddenly surged out of the back of the car with a heavy shoe in his hand and battered down his first victim. He lurched back into my corner and repeated his murderous gesture several times....I was against the right wall, with three scared youngsters. I had a big boot in my hand and was ready to meet any assault.

"Two of the kids, Georges Bernado and Didier Boueilh were shaken with nervous sobs. Henri Garcia fainted. Dr. Garnal and Mamon leaped onto the giant with the shoe to immobilize him. Garnal was knocked out. Someone shouted, 'He's a football player from Toulouse.... We can't take him on. I know him.'

"The giant took hold of the slop pail as if he were going to make a run with it, and then he grabbed the water barrel for a re-run. Garnal's head was bathed in blood and slop....

"Everyone started to fight, or almost everyone."

"I had been searched,[2] like the others, but had gotten away with a little penknife stuck under my left arm with adhesive tape. This knife saved my life. As soon as I determined the direction in which the train was traveling and reached a conclusion as to this heap of humanity; I took a position at the wall of the car and held stubbornly to it, as if glued.

"Altruism is a magnificent gesture, but life is something still more precious. A profound atavism, coupled with the awareness of the most primitive reactions and concerns

1.   Unpublished manuscript of Lt. Col. Gilbert Coulaudon, May 1970.
2.   Unpublished manuscript of Henri Fourcade, May 1970.

of mankind, led me to foresee the bloody tragedy that was fated to take place. What does food matter, and what importance does discomfort have, when you know that a little breath of air is enough to keep alive? While some around me were already in death agonies, and others were undressing, I made a little hole between two floor boards with my penknife, working patiently and silently. As soon as it was finished, I put my mouth to it. Until July 5, my horizon was bounded solely by this plank, and my greatest care was to hide it from the sight of others. Like a treasure out of One Thousand and One Nights, my hole was a diamond without equal. But the thieves in the car weren't like the ones in the story: they were madmen, grasping for life."

The giant was finally knocked out, and dragged to the sliding door.

"We had to tie him,[1] with our trouser belts, to the rings used for hitching cattle in the cars.

"Dozens of corpses were tangled on the floor. Garnal's leg was trapped under several bodies, and he called for help. Garcia fainted. The young Boueilh slapped him and fanned him with a handkerchief. Alain Marsille felt a sweet torpor invade him.

" 'Watch out!'

"Guitard, the giant, had broken his bonds. He screamed: 'We're going to die, we're all going to die. I don't want to die!' He was still attached by one arm."

"Jean Guitard, about thirty-eight years old,[2] had been arrested at Toulouse one night in May, 1944, while he was on his way home after having stood guard at the railroad tracks, legally authorized by the municipality of Toulouse. He was arrested by a service militiaman on a street in Toulouse and was imprisoned for 'verification of papers' and of a sum of money amounting to 32,000 francs, found on him at the time of his arrest.

1. Unpublished manuscript of Henri Garcia, May 1970.
2. Testimony of Pierre Mamon, February 1949, before the military tribunal of Metz, assigned to judge Friedrich Dietrich (see chapters on Novéant and Sarrebourg).

"He was locked in my cell of the Saint-Michel prison of Toulouse (No. 25, 2nd Quarter) where I had been since May 15, 1944. He was never questioned, in spite of the many demands he made to the prison guards.

"The final belt holding him to the ring, stretched and tore.

"He wanted to break out the plank nailed across one of the air vents. He managed to smash one of the boards with his bare fists. The convoy sentinels took this for an attempt to escape or as a clear act of rebellion. One of the guards circled around the outside of our car, tore the board off the opposite vent (located in the forward right side, while that destroyed by Guitard was at the rear left). Through the opening he had made, he fired his revolver at Guitard, who hadn't stopped trying to break through the opposite panel. He stood there, in spite of our warnings, and presented a perfect target for the guard shooting at him. The guard kept firing away, and the eighth bullet hit him in the right arm, and the ninth, in the head behind the right earlobe. The bullet came out through his left eye. Guitard fell like a log, and we thought he was dead."

"I was about two meters away from Guitard,[1] behind him. The first bullets buried themselves in the board near his head....He turned around and looked at us. The guard shot again. Our friend was hit in the right eye. He screamed and fell back. It appeared that calm had returned...but not for long.

"Another comrade from Toulouse, Gally, tried to tear off the barbed wire strung across the window where Guitard had stood. The guard's head reappeared at the opposite aperture. The second bullet shattered the frame of his glasses, but he wasn't wounded, and he hid among us, flat on his belly, to escape the shots.

"All of this contributed to increasing the tension in our car. Some of us were seized by despair, and the slugging began again. Then, I had to defend myself. In all this fury, I recognized my friend from Gers, Bernado. I pulled him

1.   Unpublished manuscript of Jean Deltrieu, May 1970.

On reaching Dachau, "the cars were opened, one after another, and we were the last. In this way we saw, as we passed in front of each of the others, an unspeakable pile of human waste. And we also saw human bodies. They had not all been collected into special cars. There were still more, and more. How many could there have been?" Statement of Father de la Perraudière. Original photograph sent to the author by Dr. Stéphane Fuchs

into my corner, where a little air came up between two planks. I made him breathe it. Things got better for both of us."

4:35 to 8:00 p.m.—Reims Siding.
(Guérin-Canac Car.)

"There was a guy crawling around on all fours,[1] trying to strangle everybody seated. He even tried to strangle the dead men. He couldn't tell the difference. We were in our corner, and completely spent. Steff's mind started to wander. I had to keep defending him against a fellow who accused him of having seduced his wife, and who wanted to strangle him. Another man stood up, pointed furiously with his index finger, and plunged it, with all his strength, into the socket of a comrade, tearing out the eye with a single motion."

"Black Sunday.[2] I never stopped thinking of my wife and my children, and that was where I found my strength to survive."

1. Unpublished manuscript, André Mas, June 1970.
2. Unpublished manuscript, written during the trip to Dachau, and in Dachau, by Pierre de Kegel. It was sent to me by Madeleine Ebène, the daughter of Pierre de Kegel (April 1970). These few slips of paper were saved by Marcel Guérin: "One of my comrades, Pierre de Kegel, before dying on December 8, 1944, entrusted to me a little notebook in which he had written, in pencil, the story of this convoy. I managed to save the notebook from searches by making it into a tiny roll (I must be excused for revealing how): I hid it by introducing it into the anal passage. Upon the liberation of Dachau, it was taken from me by the Americans, and I only got it back after great difficulties. Later on, I was sent to the Isle of Mainau and I didn't believe that I had long to live. The almoner asked me to trust him with this sacred souvenir and he promised to get it to the family, with all the consideration required. I had the good fortune to survive and found that he had been true to his word."

4:35 to 8:00 p.m.—Reims Siding.
(Liotier Car.)

"The panic reached its peak;[1] eyes wide with suffering: the struggle to survive. When my back touched the wall of the car, it made me cry out in pain. My nostrils pinched back and my tongue was so swollen that it took an immense effort to breathe the vitiated air. Despite the threats of the guards and the bursts of gun fire, the men never stopped howling for water, for help, for pity, for care. No one wanted to die in that hell. The convoy stood motionless. I had been defending myself for a long time, an army boot in each hand, to protect myself against the men who had gone mad and wanted to strangle me or kill me with their knives. With all my remaining strength, my back torn to shreds against the wall, blood all over, on the floor, on my body and hands, I fought on and on.

"A man with bloody gaping wounds and distorted face came at me, swinging a broken bottle in his hand. Automatically, my arms swung back. I foamed at the lips. I struck at him until I didn't have the strength to strike again. The shoe I held struck him in the belly and he fell backwards under the trampling feet around us. Then I saw nothing more. The scene melted into fog. My strength ebbed. My head turned. I was vaguely aware of the mad beating of my heart. I dropped the boots and slid down along the wall. This was the end."

"All the Spaniards got together[2] in the back part of the wagon. There were about thirty of us. Antoine Garcia and Felipe Espino; Spanish republican refugees, were arrested in the mountains of Montségur. They were attached to the third brigade of Spanish Guérilleros of Fraychinet. Their specialty was clandestine passage into Andorra and attacking German convoys on the tortuous mountain roads of the Ariège.

"Garcia and Espino decided to make every effort to cheat death once again. First of all they 'economized': no energetic or useless movements, deep breathing, total

---

1.   Unpublished manuscript of Henri Liotier, already cited.
2.   Taken from the statements of Garcia-Espino, May 1970.

silence. Slowly Garcia pulled over to him the body of a young Spanish barber who had just died. He was wearing a splendid pair of rugby boots, without cleats. Garcia couldn't resist the temptation. His toes had been seeing the light of day ever since he had been arrested. He took off his torn, rope shoes and slowly, wordlessly, took possession of the barber's.

"At the aperture, a gaunt man kept repeating: 'I'm an Alsatian: I've worked for Germany, for the Germans. I want to go on working....I'm an Alsatian...'

"Garcia handed a tube of tooth paste over to Espino. Espino squeezed out a centimeter onto his index finger, brushed his teeth and wiped his fingers under his nostrils. Then Garcia helped himself. They repeated the operation every ten minutes."

"Some of the comrades urinated[1] into any receptacle they could find, and drank it to appease their thirst. We didn't have any way of stopping this practice, which often resulted in death. The car became a charnel-house and any comrade who was weak enough to slump within thirty centimeters of the floor was doomed if he didn't have the reflexes and the strength to get up again. With my comrades, Tajean and Teisseyre, I saw a father and son praying in the midst of this carnage, where the bodies were livid as soon as they fell. They were so sure that the voyage could have only one end, that they seized each other by the throat to achieve a mutual release by strangulation. In spite of our feebleness, we were moved by this and we were able to stop them. But they tried again a little while later.

"Our comrades fell, minute by minute, as the time passed, and there was nothing we could do to help them. The bodies piled up and their stench sapped the little courage we had left.

"Tajean and I took young René Teisseyre under our protection. He wasn't more than seventeen or eighteen years old. We told him not to lie down. All three of us stood against the wall of the car. There was a little more air for us now, because dead men don't breathe. Still,

1. Unpublished manuscript of Paul Tastayre, April 1970.

standing against the wall, Tajean dozed off, and a little later, without being aware of it, I did too. When I awoke, I couldn't find our friend, Teisseyre. I awakened Tajean and we both looked around, but we couldn't see him."

"A big, burly fellow collapsed against me.[1] Just an hour ago he had defended me when the Spaniards had stolen my piece of bread. As soon as I discovered that it was gone I yelled, 'Shit, they've swiped my loaf....' And immediately my stalwart friend, whose boldness I admired, began a lecture, which went something like this: 'My comrades, perhaps now we are looking death in the face. This is not the time for us to take advantage of each other and steal....' Two of the Spaniards began to mumble in a nasty way. The big guy picked them up by the nape of the neck and banged their heads together so that they knocked each other out. And now my protector was dead.

"Two brothers were arguing about their arrest. They fought over every technicality. Finally one of them literally tore the tongue out of his brother's mouth and shouted, 'Now you've got nothing more to say....' Madness spared no corner. I guessed that there were about fifteen dead. I saw one man stuff his entire piece of bread in his mouth, pull his hat over his nose and suffocate himself. I wasn't much better off myself. A comrade who must have been studying medicine took my hand and said, 'You're not doing very well, but you have to hold on for a bit. It will be cooler in the night, and you'll feel better.'"

4:35 to 8:00 p.m.—Reims Siding.
(Habermacher Car.)

"I slid between two dead bodies[2] near the sliding door, and didn't move from there. With my nose held to a crack, I breathed. Then I remembered my friend, Claude

---

1. Unpublished manuscript of Gabriel Gasset, April 1970.
2. Unpublished manuscript of Maurice Habermacher, already cited.

Mathieu, and I caught sight of him among the the demented men who were walking all over him. He didn't move any more. I succeeded in pulling him over, close to the door and stretched him out near me, his nose near the crack, and then I dragged two corpses over us. The fresh air revived him, and he was soon conscious again. Meanwhile, the killing continued and the bodies rotted in the heat. The odor was sickening and irrespirable."

"Do you remember when you were a kid,[1] the boxes you used to fill with insects, squirming, tumbling, climbing on each other to get some air? Or have you ever seen shipwrecked people, pulling each other down, trying to stay on top and hang on to life? There was nothing rational about it. Each man for himself, trying to protect his own life in any way he could against a band of maniacs. They stormed about furiously crushing and trampling, striking with bottles, hands gripped around throats, and all about, screams and the last gasps of life.

"Dying men, in the final death throes, lay on top of those already dead. If you were unlucky enough to fall down you were lost forever. The drama reached the point of frenzy. The floor was covered with corpses. My comrade was seated beside me. We had been able to stay seated because we were at the extreme end of the car with our backs against the wall.

"He leaned toward me and murmured: 'Old friend, I feel that I've come to the end, and before I die, I want to tell you what my last thoughts are. Please tell my wife how much I love her, how I wished to make her happy and live my life with her, it was so beautiful when we were together with our four children. My wife can take care of them, but a man's hand is always needed. The oldest is fifteen, and he'll understand, I'm sure.... They're so beautiful, my children. How sad it is to die so far from them, and without having done anything. Tell them that my last thought was of them.'

"Then he stood up with his rosary in his hand. It had been given to him at Compiègne, by a bishop imprisoned with us. He called upon the others to pray with him for

1.   Unpublished manuscript of René Prungnaud, already cited.

the salvation of us all. His eyes glowed hotly, saliva
dripped from his lips, he was mad. He started to thrash
about and was drawn compulsively into the maelstrom. I
would have had to have a heart of stone to have
remained untouched by such a scene. Every word that he
said left a scar. I still wake up at night, haunted by this
scene."

"I remember that,[1] if we put our fingers in our mouths,
we tore off bits of rotted skin. The one way to survive
was to drink our own urine. This eased our thirst for a
moment, but then we were burning again....We lost
Louis Reverdy, the mayor of Sassenage, and then a
comrade killed himself. He came from Villard-de-Lans.
The Germans had burned everything there, and he had
no news of his family. He kept asking us if we knew
what the Germans had done with them."

4:35 to 8:00 p.m.—Reims Siding.
(Sirvent Car.)

"I saw a bridge,[2] and on the bridge there were Sunday
strollers. A man and a woman, leaning on the parapet,
looked at this strange train. Did they understand what
was taking place? Did they understand the reason for the
inhuman cries that reached their ears, or were they
indifferent? What were they thinking about? I was
jealous of them because they were free, and able to
breathe.
"The stench rose with the heat. The corpses putrified
rapidly and we had to climb on top of them not to have
our legs trapped. It was hard to keep our balance, but it
was death to lose it. Despite thirst and fever, and the
odor of this inert, soft mass on which I stood, I could still
stay upright, and I was conscious. Then I got the idea of
passing my belt through a roof rail and holding on to it
for support. I buckled it, leaving a loop, and crooked my

1.   Unpublished manuscript of Jean Augagneur, June 1970.
2.   Unpublished manuscript of Pierre Dhenain, already cited.

left arm through the loop. Now I had less fear of falling. My position was bearable, although not comfortable."

"I was with a pal from my village,[1] Eugène Martin. He was having a lot of trouble breathing, and I think that he had some ribs broken when we were being 'questioned' by the Gestapo at Laon. He complained of violent pains in the chest. I tried to get him close to an air vent. This precipitated the second murderous free-for-all, because one of the guys who had installed himself permanently in front of the opening went completely crazy and began to hit and kick out at everybody, and he slashed with a knife that he must have hidden during the search.

"Then almost everybody went crazy. They all started to hit and kick at each other.... I tried to stay very close to Eugène, who was getting weaker and weaker. I cradled his head on my knees and held his hands. I begged for water for my poor friend, but the water was finished a long time ago. He suffered greatly. Suddenly an ice cold sweat covered his face. That's when I knew he was going to die."

"I caught sight of a comrade.[2] His eyes were wild and he had a knife in his hand. He lunged toward me and wanted to drive the knife into my belly, shouting, 'I've got to cut someone up before I die.'[3] I was surrounded by dead bodies. I managed to free a leg and pushed away my companion who howled like a terrified beast, and died. I fell into a coma. For how long?...When I came to—what a stink! I was buried under cadavers, with only my head out. I had a great deal of trouble getting up. My nose and mouth were covered with suppurating blisters."

1. Unpublished manuscript of Florian Bondois, May 1970.
2. Unpublished manuscript of Joseph Bert, June 1970.
3. A deportee in this convoy, Louis Favre, was well-acquainted with this "traveler" before they boarded the train at Compiègne: "My bunk mate was a fellow named B.R.... He was about forty years old, and a bum, by profession. He said to me: 'I'll bet you that two hours after I leave here, I'll have money in my pocket.'

"I thought I was going to die,[1] smothered. A body fell over me. He had been a big-bodied man, and he crushed me. I gathered all my strength together and I pushed him off. Where? Doubtless onto somebody else, since there wasn't a bit of free space in the car."

"I didn't believe in God,[2] but I knew then that only God could save me.... Pressed against the wall, I fought off everybody who tried to grab me. I stayed lucid the whole time. In contrast, Ludo, who was beside me, got drawn into the melée by some incomprehensible compulsion. He jerked forward, struck a few blows, and then fell, like the others...."

"Standing in a corner,[3] on a mass of bodies I forced myself to keep calm, not to panic, and with my feet and my fists, I pushed off the poor demented devils who came near me. It was the only way to survive. Nearby, I

His system was simple. In the first city he reached, he'd go to the national aid office and raise a rumpus until they gave him a pair of pants, a coat and a pair of shoes, which he lost no time in selling, and then moved on to the next town, where he pulled the same trick. One day he came up to Bishop Théas on the center esplanade. He had heard the rumor that packages had arrived at Building 7 and that a number of important people were there, such as Albert Sarraut, Georges Villiers, and a number of church dignitaries. Monseigneur Théas made an appointment with him to give him some things from the packages. From then on, the only person who counted for him was Monseigneur.... 'Have you seen Monseigneur? Hasn't Monseigneur asked for me?' There was nothing blameworthy, up to this point. Where it began to go bad (and I didn't understand about this until later) was when, toward the end of our stay at Compiègne, he said to me, one day, 'I have to go and bump off a few people. Some of them make me shit.' I paid no attention to his jabbering at the time. I only learned, much later, in Dachau, that he had killed twenty-five comrades in his car, by himself, with a knife, before being killed himself by a courageous man, who put an end to the carnage. (Unpublished manuscript of Louis Favre, May 1970.)
1.   Testimony of Roger Farelle (Chief of the National Service of Counterfeit Papers of the National Liberation Movement).
2.   Unpublished manuscript of Jean Samuel (April 1970), a member of the Roger Farelle network.
3.   Unpublished manuscript of Pierre Henri Drelon, May 1970.

recognized my comrade, Marcel Garroux of Tulle, a youngster of twenty, lying prone on a pile of bodies. I thought about his parents. I was deeply moved because he was their only son. Another from Tulle, Jean Martel, also fell. I grabbed him under the arms and dragged him with all my strength toward the only opening where I held him up several times. He was revived by the fresh air and was saved."

"There are some actions[1] which do honor to the human race. Summoning up the little strength they had left, the survivors, stunned and terrified, still thought of saving the dying. They chose the ones with the best chance to live. It took three or four of them to drag a single sufferer to the opening, and get him to breathe the pure, fresh evening air. I heard them say incredible things to their comrades, to force them to live. There must have been some splendid French faces at those airshafts."

*   *   *

In the chain reaction of madness, a few areas escaped destruction, incomprehensible though that may appear. Eight cars survived the holocaust of Reims and arrived at Dachau, without a single life lost....And still....

4:35 to 8:00 p.m.—Reims Siding.
(The Bent-Solladié Car.)

"I was able to save another young man[2] whom I didn't even know (for a time). He was suffocating, skin livid, lips foaming, eyes rolled back. I grabbed him, as best I could and dragged him over the other prone bodies up to the edge of the sliding door, where there was some air. I held him up on his knees, wiped his face with a wet handkerchief and slapped him lightly. His color and his breathing returned to normal. He was saved. I seem to

1. Unpublished manuscript of Louis-Eugène Sirvent, already cited.
2. Unpublished manuscript of N.R. Bidault, already cited.

remember that he was called Copenhagen, and I learned later that he was a common law criminal. He and a friend of his called Petit, wearing German military jackets and kepis, had attacked and robbed a woman at Larçay (Indre-et-Loire). At the end of 1945, this Petit was sentenced for the crime, but his stooge was never found. He had surely died during deportation. The only thing I accomplished by saving him was to postpone his fate."

The normal temperature[1] of the human body stays at about 37° C. We have a natural heat regulating system, like a thermostat, which makes it possible for us to adapt to extreme cold and intense heat, without our own inner temperature rising or falling to an extent that would be dangerous for the good functioning of our organism. We protect ourselves against heat by the evaporation of sweat, and by the increase in the number and profundity of our respiratory reactions. We sweated copiously in the car, but because of the lack of ventilation and the progressive saturation of the atmosphere, our sweat could not evaporate. Our whole thermostatic system was deranged. Our body temperature mounted. We became poikilothermic, that is to say, our body temperature varied with the temperature outside our bodies. When we know that at 39° C some become delirious, the fever causes them to lose control of their acts, then we can understand what happened in the convoy of death. Furthermore, the water that we lost rapidly in sweat was not replaced in the organism. However, our cells need the water and sodium which we were losing in such great quantities in our sweat.

"Having lived in Africa as a doctor in the Camel Corps, I was acquainted with the symptoms of heat stroke, and I foresaw what could happen and what, unfortunately, did happen in nearly all the cars. I succeeded in getting the comrades in my car to understand that water was a precious treasure to be most carefully conserved. A

1.   Dr. Philippe Bent in *L'attente de la mort dans les camps du Neckar.* Imprimerie régionale de Toulouse (1958). Available from the author, Montclar-de-Quercy, Tarn-et-Garonne. See also *Doctors of Mercy* for further mention of Dr. Bent.

vigilant guard was set up around the tiny barrel. Small quantities of water were distributed at long intervals. In my car, there were no dead. There might be other explanations for the scenes of bloody collective madness. Under the influence of the heightened internal temperature, our brains reacted to the caloric excitation exactly like those of laboratory cats. According to which zone is stimulated, the cat would remain inert and flaccid, or become raging mad, biting, foaming, leaping about with extended claws.

"What would have been the appropriate thing to do? In the Sahara a sub-cutaneous injection of salt serum was enough to stop these crises. In the train, where injection would not have been practicable, it would have sufficed simply to distribute water and to have sodium salt (chloride or bicarbonate) taken by mouth."

4:35 to 8:00 p.m.—Reims Siding.
(The Bernard-Troncin Car.)[1]

Before we left Compiègne, the Germans, during their search, discovered a knife hidden in the straw and so they deprived us of water. I believe that this punishment, although it contributed to our suffering, was largely responsible for the fact that there were no deaths in our car. The air was less humid with the evaporation of sweat and urine. This wasn't the only favorable factor. I am deeply sorry that I do not remember the names of the comrades who maintained a reasonable discipline over these one hundred men, controlling their changes of shift from standing to sitting. We moved as little as possible. The men rotated the task of waving blankets to keep the air in circulation. As for our general situation, it was that of the whole train: only one small vent for a car that was otherwise virtually completely sealed. I estimated, on the basis of brief experimental stays in test ovens, that the temperature reached 70° C (158° F). The day was terrible, but the atrocities have been described by others whose situation was worse than ours because of their lack of

1.   Unpublished manuscript of Pierre Bernard, already cited.

discipline. I was close to fainting when a comrade no doubt saved my life my lifting me up to the level of the vent I have referred to. I only learned his name a long time afterwards. He was the accordeonist, André Verchuren, and I shall always be grateful to him.[1]

4:35 to 8:00 p.m.—Reims Siding.
(The Lambert Car.)[2]

My car was completely calm, and I shall tell you the reason why.

There were twenty or thirty of us from Poitevins, and we had known each other for a fairly long time. At about noon, when the heat became intolerable, there was a rush on the water barrel, and we realized that it was already more than half empty. Understanding the danger that we were facing, all the men from Poitevins called upon me to ensure discipline in the car, and to make an equitable distribution of the water. It was easy to enlist the co-operation of the men because they were aware of the disaster that threatened us if we lost control. We estimated that we had a water reserve of three quarters of a liter per man. We decided, then and there, that everybody could drink a quarter-liter right away, and that there would be no further distribution before seven o'clock in the evening. The remaining water would be reserved for the rest of the trip.

I had everybody sit down, the first row with its backs to the wall, legs spread, and each next row seated between the spread legs of the men behind. Arranged in this way, ninety to ninety-two men could be seated. The remaining men stood, two at each side of the air vents. These men had the most favored position, but to make up for it, they had the task, two by two, of

1. A second deportee in this car lost consciousness, the pharmacist, Guillaume Troncin. Annex V contains his "hypotheses" concerning the massive generalized intoxication occurring during the day of July 2 and the following night, 1944. Unpublished manuscript, April 1970.
2. H. Lambert, already cited.

constantly waving a big blanket which ventilated those who were seated and made breathing easier.

It would be brash to claim that our situation was heaven on earth compared to the other cars of the train, because we avoided the same catastrophe by a very narrow margin. Nevertheless, we did avoid it.

At about five in the evening, nobody could hold out any longer. The men began to insist on getting their water. I reminded them of the promise we had made each other—not before seven.

The older men resigned themselves more easily. The most difficult was a kid of eighteen or so who had been arrested in a youth camp. He begged me, with tears in his eyes, to give him something to drink. At first my refusals were pretty tough, but I felt myself softening in the face of his misery, and then he hooked me with his final argument:

"You're not a father, because otherwise you wouldn't let me suffer like this."

I saw all the pleading, the innocent pain, I saw him quivering with what was probably the first real suffering in his life, and how emotionally lost he was, so far away from his family, perhaps for the first time. I couldn't go against my heart, and I said:

"All right. We'll drink a bit."

This uncharacteristic tenderness on my part almost resulted in disaster.

Several comrades got together and placed the water barrel on the slop bucket with the bunghole on one side, and the distribution began. The intense thirst, the frenzied jostling to be next mesmerized me, their flushed faces running with sweat, mouths wide open, lower lips drooping, eyes bulging and unfocussed, like the dying, whose souls have already left their bodies.

Each one wanted to be first. Everybody in the car stood up. Those assigned to ventilate stopped working. This mass of sweaty flesh in movement was the source of additional heat, and exuded a nauseous stench which made it still more difficult to breathe. The distribution was about half finished when one comrade collapsed, and then a second. I had them dragged over to the aperture, where they were promptly fanned. They came to in a few minutes, but then a third and a fourth fell. We applied the same measures to them, and they also came around a bit later, and seemed normal.

By this time the distribution was almost finished. There were only five or six left to serve. I felt too weak to continue to the end and I assigned the nearest comrade to take over for me. I went over to put my nose to the air vent for a few moments. I got over it and went to sit down in my place. I had hardly gotten there when four more comrades fainted, but we succeeded in reviving them all.

By now, it really was seven o'clock and the air was a little cooler. Heavy clouds covered the sun and a storm rumbled in the distance. It was possible to believe that the danger point had been passed and that we would find peace in the cool of the night.

4:35 to 8:00 p.m.—Reims Siding.
(The Car of Eighty.)[1]

Weiss succeeded in getting the attention of a sentry who was walking alongside the car.

"Open the doors. We have dead and dying men in here."

"Make plum marmalade out of them."

This exchange took place in German. Although the train didn't leave the station, it was shunted back next to a freight-load of straw, piled very high. Our plight was intolerable. The immobility of the car and the presence of the loads of straw kept us from getting any air at all. A comrade I didn't know became violently agitated and shook convulsively. Those who knew him referred to malaria. We passed him from one to another until he reached the opening. I saw him bite down with his mouth on the barbed wire entanglement until the blood ran. I don't know what happened to him after that.

*   *   *

1.   Unpublished manuscript of Maurice Voutey, already cited.

In the three other cars "without dead" (Lamirault-Lutz, Helluy-Aubert-Villiers, and Weil), discipline was always accepted and maintained, sometimes by force. The locomotive finally got back on the tracks and was attached to the 7909. The engineer and the mechanic, Hauller and Mulette, were ordered not to waste any time.

8:00 p.m.—Reims Station.[1]

Just as the train was leaving the Chief officer of the convoy ordered us to remove the two dead and place them in an empty car.[2] He pointed it out to me, toward the front, and said: "There's someone with malaria in the convoy. We should telephone to Châlons for some quinine."[3]

And the train left.

1.   Statement of Dr. Bouvier, already cited.
2.   "It had been understood, at one point, that these two bodies would be handed over to the French police by the German police, but at the last moment the convoy chief claimed the corpses. He had to have the count complete, whether composed of dead or living. The train started up again at about 8 o'clock in the evening. I have brought aid to a number of trains of deportees, but I have never seen any that presented such a spectacle of horror and dread. The dead, the dying and the mad were all piled together." (Report of Mademoiselle Fernande Pierre, February 28, 1945.)
3.   "It is our duty to add that the officer in charge of the train and his aides did their best to help the Red Cross, but the orders of the Gestapo were imperative, and the S.S. were on the spot to supervise the departure, so the officer of the Wehrmacht had to comply." (Unpublished manuscript of the Red Cross Committee of Reims, May 14, 1970.)

8:35 p.m.—Saint-Hilaire-au-Temple.
(The Guérin-Canac Car.)

"The train stopped[1] at a little pine wood that I knew at the edge of the camp of Mourmelon. I said to a guard on the embankment, 'We have twenty-five dead in here,' and he answered, 'What the hell do I care.' Then a man with a military bearing spoke to the same guard, but in French: 'Shoot me. It's a matter of honor.' But the other didn't understand. We were utterly astonished at our compatriot's bravery. We found his body the next morning. He had died during the night. Another guard opened the door of our car. He struck at everyone who was still standing and stumbled over the dead. He finally left us, muttering, 'Schweinestall.'"

"I became very dizzy[2] right before we reached Châlons. I fainted as everything dissolved in a haze. When I came to, I had a piece of sugar soaked in ether between my

1. Unpublished manuscript of Maurice Baltet, already cited.
2. Unpublished manuscript of Albert Charpentier, already cited.

teeth. A stranger was holding me up toward the air opening, facing toward the sky that was beginning to fill with dark clouds. Two men had worked together to save me, and I didn't know who they were. I recovered slowly. The car seemed calmer."

9:20 p.m.—Châlons-sur-Marne.

In less than ten minutes the locomotive had been changed. The S.D. officer had recovered a bit of energy and would let no one approach the train except Sister Marie, the Mother Superior of the Daughters of Charity, and three of her nuns.

"They telephoned us for some quinine."

"Very good, thank you. I have a male nurse who will take care of the patient."

The nurse wore a Red Cross arm band. He was part of the health service of Royallieu, a Czech by origin.

"Here's the box."

The nurse walked toward the "invalid car"[1] and had the door opened. When he got out, three minutes later, the S.D. officer ordered the departure of the convoy.

9:50 p.m.—Compertrix. (The Guérin-Carnac Car.)[2]

I know Châlons well. I did my military service there. After passing the station, the train stops at the junction with the branch line to Troyes. We heard screams from the cars in front and those behind us. It was still not dark and I used the time to go over to Jean Hurtaud. He told me that he was exhausted and I urged him to go to the opening and take a breath of air, the only way of getting a bit of oxygen. I also saw Alico, Buc and Loiseau, the

1. As far as I know, there were no survivors in 1970 of this "invalid car" which must have contained 28 or 30 deportees. According to the testimony of Abbé Goutaudier (at his arrival at Dachau and upon his return from deportation), only one man died during the voyage.
2. Unpublished manuscript of Maurice Baltet, already cited.

secretary of police commissioner Parvenchère. As I was making my way toward them, two young men who probably had a certain amount of confidence in me, grabbed me by the arm and just about forced me to lie down beside them. Their names were Fortier and Bernanos. The living were sleeping on top of the dead. They had no choice. They were asleep in less than ten minutes.

I worked my way back to Dr. Bouvier and Pierre Germaine. We had decided to get close to the opening and hang on there as long as possible. It was hard to tell the living from the dead.

The Lambert Car.[1]

For more than one hour I had been watching a young comrade from Niort with considerable anxiety. He was seated on the edge of the ever-present slop bucket, and he looked absolutely blank. Night was coming and it was already difficult to see in the car. I asked him: "How are you getting on? Is the coolness helping a little?"

He answered, "Me? I don't mind the heat. I don't think it's hot. I wish I had a mess tin so I could do what I did in Syria crossing the sands. I'd piss in it and I'd drink."

When I heard his outlandish dream I realized immediately that my poor comrade had gone off his nut.

At this time a customer arrived for the slop bucket and politely asked him to step aside, but our poor friend didn't take kindly to the suggestion. I knew him as the sweetest, gentlest guy in the world, and I heard him answer back, "Get the hell out of here, or I'll bust you one.... What are you trying to do, shit in the middle of the field kitchen?"

The "customer" didn't understand the mental state he was dealing with right away. An argument built up and the decibels mounted minute by minute, pushing the poor fellow to exasperation. I wondered if the free-for-all that we had avoided until now wasn't going to become inevitable. I succeeded in getting the one who could, to

1.   Henri Lambert, already cited.

shut up and help calm his deluded adversary. This he did, but there remained a considerable problem.

Now our friend absolutely refused to leave the slop bucket. It had become his field kitchen, and his desire to have a mess tin to piss in and drink from took on the dimensions of an obsession.

I found myself half way down the car, my back to the wall. I had just realized that the train was moving quite fast and that a little current of air was coming through the crack of the door. Then I tried to convince our self-appointed "cook" to leave his place and take mine. He absolutely refused. After a considerable time, I coaxed him to the center of the car where he stood with an arm against the wall, his head less than twenty centimeters from the current of air, but he showed no interest in it. Then I got up, gently took his head between my hands and put his nose right up to the slit, and said to him: "Take a look outside. There's lightning flashing in the sky."

I held him, by force, for a few minutes, making him breathe the air. The effect was salutary. He stopped trying to pull his head back, and in about half an hour, he had come to his senses. Then I gave him my place, so that he could sit, and a few hours later, he was completely normal.

The Car of Eighty.[1]

For a very long moment, I had the strange impression that I was completely alone. Most of my comrades were lying, one on top of the other. I had decided to remain standing, no matter what happened, and in spite of the fatigue of the day, so as not to suffocate. I was able to lean against the wall of the car and I found that, despite the high temperature, the humidity that resulted from our sweating was sufficient to produce condensation on the heads of the bolts.

Through the aperture I saw a train stationed near us, loaded with tanks covered with a tarpaulin. I heard a

1. Unpublished manuscript of Maurice Voutey, already cited.

sentinel move, we were separated by only the thickness
of a plank (he was perched in the look-out box). I called
out to him and we spoke together for a few minutes in
German. I asked him why we were being treated in this
way. He talked to me about the crimes of the terrorists.
And he used words that we would often hear again:
"Bandit—Partisan." All of this so calmly in this strangely
peaceful, almost serene night. Our discussion stopped
here, and I got a somewhat childish pleasure out of the
hatred that we inspired. To a certain extent it was the
consecration of the action that we had been able to carry
on, the effectiveness of which we had never been able to
measure.

5

Night—The First Night

The New Car of Father de La Perraudière.[1]

We were getting ready to pass the night and tried to gather enough of the straw tossed on the car floor, to lie on. There was a young comrade close to me, lying inert, without a word. They told me he was a policeman.

This night would be frightful for so many among us. By morning hundreds will have died in nightmare scenes; while I, in contrast, would pass it in peace, even if not in comfort. I even managed to sleep from time to time. It was only in the morning that I discovered that the young policeman beside me was dead.... The train continued to crawl, stopping from time to time, without any apparent reason, in the open country. Some of us starting guessing: "Maybe there was an escape."

As a matter of fact, every time we stopped, soldiers got out on each side of the train and surveyed the cars. I caught sight of one, an older man who looked somewhat approachable, and spoke to him in my bad German:

1. Father de La Perraudière and six other deportees changed cars at Reims, therefore there were only seven in this car.

"How are things in the other cars?"

"Alles Schlimm! Very bad," he answered.

This is how I learned that things were bad all over, and not only in the car where I had been.[1]

Attempted Escape.
Helluy-Aubert-Villiers Car.

Statement of Doctor Joseph Helluy.

The very tense situation threatened to take a tragic turn. Supported by some of my friends, I assumed the leadership of the car, on the basis of the fact that I was a doctor and an officer. I arranged that the men would take turns, some seated in the center of the car and all the rest standing as closely together as possible. This eased the situation somewhat.

During the night I ordered the men to make an escape hole in the wall. This led to a contest of wills which almost became a contest of force: some of the Communists opposed it. The train stopped frequently, and so did the work, of course. Time passed. The light of early dawn. I gave the order to push the plank out, and at the same moment, I realized that the train was stopping.

Statement of Edouard Aubert.

I am sure that, like myself and the other survivors, Georges Villiers will never forget those nightmare hours that we lived through together. On his return from deportation, Villiers became President of the National Council of French Employers while I became Secretary General of the C.G.T.'s Federation of Textile Workers. I'm sure that he remembers the men, Communists and Gaullists together, toughened by the clandestine struggle, who found ways to organize and impose a discipline which finally saved all of our lives during this terrible voyage.

1. Unpublished manuscript of Father de La Perraudière, already cited.

By luck, the two little air slits in our car were open....
Like all of us, he took his turn at being lifted up to
one or another of these air vents to breathe for a few
moments before resuming his place seated on the floor,
in the pre-determined rotation that had been imposed
with considerable difficulty, in order to avoid conflicts
and useless movements. From the first night on we used
this system. One of us made everybody laugh by calling
it the "midnight maneuver." It's a fact that even in the
most tragic circumstances there will always be someone
who has the gift of finding the quirky word which
comforts, nourishes hope, and affirms life.

Like all of us, Villiers received his allotment of water,
distributed at regular intervals in an orderly fashion,
under the control of a team assigned to keep watch on
the barrel, directed by the Communist worker, André
Morcel, who never came back from Dachau. He was also
a C.G.T. militant of the union of textile workers of
Lyons...he was one of the victims of the employer's
reprisals following the general strike of November 1938.

Finally, as to our attempted escape, certain details
stand out in our memories.... They contain many lessons,
I believe. While we were still at the camp, preparing for
departure, the organized Resistance planned to get tools
to me that could be used in an attempted escape on the
way: wood and metal saws, pliers and nippers, screw
drivers, hammer, etc. The plan failed. However, another
Resistance group was able to get somewhat similar
equipment, and among them, Dr. Helluy who was with
us in the same car. I didn't know Dr. Helluy or the
comrades around him, but contact was immediately
established. We recognized each other right away as
fighters for the same cause, imbued with the same spirit.
Thus, from the very beginning we had helped set up
discipline and had worked together to maintain it, and a
little later on, we laid plans for an effort at escape.

We discussed every aspect of the plan at great length,
what tactics to be used, what precautions to take in
cutting an opening, and most difficult, once the opening
was cut, what should be the order in which we left. This
was a matter of primary importance. It was simply
impossible to imagine that we would all be able simply to

go out, one after the other to the last man. Our car was hitched directly behind the S.S. guard and at frequent intervals during the night they swept the convoy with their floodlights. We would not be able to drop down onto the tracks and roll along the embankment without attracting the attention of the enemy. Everybody agreed that, even under the best conditions possible, only the very first men to leave would stand a chance. But then, who should be selected as first, second, third and so on? Logically, it seemed that the first should be those who had the greatest responsibility in the Resistance.... But how could we judge who that was, and in addition, how could we get an agreement on it under these critical circumstances?

Dr. Helluy certainly remembers this tragic discussion as well as I.... But I wish to emphasize, I wish to underline the fact that never did the Gaullists and Communists waver from the spirit of unity in joint struggle, which was their essential strength.

First of all, it was necessary to straighten out a few unruly elements who had no relationship to the Resistance (men who had been rounded up, common-law criminals). And the worst was they did not know how to accept discipline, and then they claimed that they too could make a hole in the car with their own tools without paying any attention to us or taking the elementary precautions we had insisted on to avoid alerting the S.S.

Then there was the problem of carrying out the work to be done by the team responsible for making an opening.... It wasn't easy... particularly because it had to be done without making any suspicious noise, and at the same time it was necessary to maintain order, care for the sick, boost the moral, supervise the distribution of water, and make sure that the disposal of excrement kept pace with the production.... And we were already beginning to smell that pestilential odor, the origin of which we still did not know.

Statement of Georges Villiers.

It was not long before the heat became unbearable and the lack of air was cruelly evident. The comrades grouped

The corpses of the Death Train were unloaded into the courtyard of the crematory. "The 536 cadavers fueled the crematory of Dachau for four days." Clandestine Photo.
Author's Archives

around us helped us, so we were able to set up a continuous rotation up to a little opening we had pierced through a wall.

In this way, everyone could take his turn breathing. But there were a hundred of us and the turns came around too slowly. Quarrels broke out as the men fought for their rights. Surprisingly, knives appeared out of pockets, indicating that some were on the edge of madness. Some of them had to be calmed, and some knocked out cold to make sure that they were harmless.

Time passed slowly and this day of record heat finally burned to its end.

Tension eased with the coming of evening and we were able to apply ourselves to the question of escape.

About twenty comrades said they were willing to make a try. It seemed possible as we were still in France and the train was moving very slowly.

Protests burst out. We were accused of being crazy. Some of the men said that they didn't want to escape and that we were going to get them punished, when they didn't even know why they had been arrested and that they were sure that finally the Germans would acknowledge that they were innocent.

New fights broke out as we took turns in opening up the hole.

Doctor X was the first to get his head and shoulders through the hole. I was right behind him with a C.G.T. delegate from the region of Lyons.

Statement of Jean-Baptiste Perreolaz.

Our panel was almost completely cut through, held only by a few points we had left to keep it in place. Long confabulations were held. We had to make a distinction between those who wanted to go, and the larger number who wanted to stay.... Anyway, my group didn't get mixed up in these sterile discussions where the arguments advanced were often simply excuses for the lowest kind of egoism. We, the young ones, had decided to jump, and nothing was going to keep us from doing it. All the rest was just old men gabbling in the Café du Commerce!

But voices grew shriller and tempers grew hotter, especially at the other end of the car where a strong opposition built up against the attempt to be made in the coming hours. "Useless and very dangerous, both for those who go and those who stay. There is no use trying to avoid suffocating to death if we are all going to be killed to pay for a deliberate act of a few." This argument, which was at least reasoned, was advanced by the frightened minority, which had become considerably more vocal now that the air was cooler. They also added a precise threat, but none of us paid any attention to it at the time: "We are going to alert the S.S. car if you try to go through with your mad scheme."

We didn't believe that they could be that vicious. It was a gratuitous threat, at most. The decision was taken. Twenty men would jump, and then others, if it was possible.

The train came to a slight rise, and slowed. We decided to go into action at once. The carpenters were to be the first to go. They completed the operation of loosening the panel which was flush to the floor, half way between the door and the end of the car, to the right. The group prepared to go, shook hands for a last time with friends to be left behind, received the last farewells, the last words of advice, and all of a sudden, when it seemed as if everything was working smoothly, violence broke out between the opposition, which had now gotten the upper hand, and those assigned to keep them under control. A near panic gripped one corner of the car. The chorus of screams grew in volume. We couldn't silence them immediately, in view of the preparations that were going on. The opposition elements screamed louder and louder, beat against the walls of the car, making all the noise they could to attract the attention of the S.S. car, directly ahead, and howling the word, "escape, escape!"[1]

---

1.   Other statements:

Julien Villevieille: "The decision to make the hole was reached by the majority. We were aided by three of the common law prisoners."

André Petit: "The train slowed down. One guy shouted out some words in German. He gave the alarm."

FIRST NIGHT:
THE REST OF THE CONVOY

The Rohmer Car.[1]

I regained consciousness.... Professor Vlès was wearing a gold wristwatch which he had covered with a bit of cloth at Compiègne so as not to tempt the...envious. I slipped it off.[2] Peupion called the roll. There were only twenty-four to answer.

We could stretch out. I couldn't keep going any longer and I went to sleep at once. During the entire night Rollot saved me from slipping between the corpses and suffocating against them. The night was sweet and cool. We were sleeping on the still warm bodies....

In the middle of the night a few of the men tried to escape. They had cut through some of the barbed wires, but they couldn't pull themselves through. They were too weak to climb up to the opening.

Dawn.—Sleep had restored some of out strength. We decided to pile all the dead into one half of the car. The work was infernal. In falling, they had become entangled and when we pulled, strips of flesh fell loose. In spite of the fact that the bodies were still warm, they had already become stiff. The pile grew higher and reached almost to the roof. We had to stop several times, exhausted and discouraged. It was nauseating to handle these cadavers and the fatigue and pestilential stench made us vomit. Finally the job was done. We covered them with their own belongings and their blankets. The odor was sickening.

How much longer were we going to have to stay in this coffin on wheels? Meanwhile, we stretched out on the floor and looked for cracks against which we could hold our noses and breathe.

Armand Serre: "Somebody called out, afraid of what was going to happen, and he aroused the sentinels."

(Unpublished manuscripts, April-May 1970.)

1.   Francis Rohmer, already cited.
2.   The watch was listed at Dachau, and was returned to Professor Rohmer at the Liberation. He gave it to Madame Vlès as soon as he got back to France.

The Lambert Car.[1]

Some of our companions, with truly admirable courage, built up the morale of their comrades. They pointed out that the train was going very slowly because of the massive destruction of the tracks by the R.A.F. And others still found the courage to tell jokes.

I smiled when I heard one of the exchanges, although it wasn't a joke. One of the men was complaining to a friend from Niort: "Why did they arrest me? I never did anything against the Germans. I never got mixed up with the Resistance."

With an expression free of all guile, my friend answered that he would have been better off if he had engaged in some patriotic activity. At least then he would know why he was there. That was the logic of things. It was the consolation of those who, knowing the stakes and accepting the dangers, were not afraid to join in the common cause with all their hearts.

The Car of Eighty.

"There was a roly-poly guy in our corner,[2] and much to everybody's surprise he woke up suddenly, just at the end of a wet dream...."

"During that night[3] I held a wine merchant from Le Mans, Marc Soulier, up to the airshaft. He said to me, 'Kid, you're an apprentice barber in Tulle. Anyhow, you've saved my life and when we get back I'm going to buy you a magnificent salon and set you up in business.'"

Paulin Tessiot and Antoine Vésir were talking about Martinique. A policeman was praying on his knees. Still seated on his slop bucket, Chapalain drowsed off.

1.   Unpublished manuscript of Jean Depraetere, July 1970.
2.   Unpublished manuscript of André Salle, May 1970.
3.   Statement of Jean Viacroze, April 1970.

The Fully-Thomas Car.

"I began to breathe better[1] as the air freshened. I studied myself, I felt myself. I could hardly believe that I was still alive, that I had passed through that hell. I had a few scratches on my chest, my watch was broken, my trousers were in shreds...and that was all. But I was still alive. And yet, I wasn't dreaming....

"We started to count off. 'One, two, three....' we spoke up one after the other, 'eight, nine, ten....' How many of us were left? 'Fifteen, sixteen, seventeen.'

"That's all. Nobody else answered. A few had simply fainted and might come through with the cool of the night. The final count was twenty-four, plus one who was seriously wounded, 'Twenty-five, out of a hundred....' "

"We slept,[2] with corpses as our mattresses. The bodies were swollen out of shape, violet faces, blue lips, diabolically distorted, horrible to behold. We couldn't even recognize our friends anymore....On top of this charnel pile a few lost, mute, brutalized and haggard men still survived.

"After the airless heat, an insidious odor had spread through the car. We covered our mouths and noses with rags, towels, shirts. Sometimes, when we moved and stepped on a body, we heard a sinister sound of the body guggling as it emptied itself, like a boot being drawn out of the mud of a swamp.

"In order to avoid any contact with the dead, I sat on the barrel which I had turned over....A man lying near me sucked, from time to time, at the knee of a cadaver, with an infant's smile on his face. This wasn't the delirium of agony, but pure madness."

"The body of a young boy[3] from Lille was near me. He had a gold medal around his neck. When somebody snatched this medal off, Barcos said quietly, 'Aren't you

1. Georges Fully, already cited.
2. Jean Thomas, already cited.
3. Jacques Remaury, already cited.

ashamed? Put the medal back right away.' The other knotted the chain behind the dead neck, looked up and said, 'Excuse me,' and moved off to another corner."

The Fonfrède Car.[1]

I was alive, after having passed the night with my mouth held to the floor at the slit of the sliding door....I had to suck the air in with force, because it didn't want to come in by itself....Every intake was a true delight. I can compare it to the sensation of drinking pure, fresh fountain water after a long walk in the sun....Two comrades were spread out over my back, drinking in the air that passed over my head.

I tried to move, but it was impossible....My legs were trapped under the human mass and my feet were wedged under the icy head of a madman...who had finally succeeded in dying, in spite of himself. As a matter of fact, I didn't realize that he was dead until after I had accidentally touched his face, and then I threw myself back in terror.

The survivors counted the dead. They stretched them out and piled them in the middle of the car to make room....Many were already rigid, in contorted positions and their faces were blackening. We covered them with a little straw....The smell was very bad and we feared that their bodies, extended with gas, might burst at any moment....

One of the comrades stood up and called for a moment of silence, out of respect for the dead, and then, addressing the believers, he asked them to pray with him.

"Our Father who art in Heaven...."

"Deliver us from Evil...."

---

1.   Marcel Fonfrède, already cited.

The Lutz Car.

"During the night,[1] we decided to escape. Some of us had metal saw blades sewn into their trouser legs. Part of the car caught on to what we were going to do and opposed it for fear of reprisals. What kind of men were they? I asked myself that, and I still can't answer today. Here we are, the total victim, paralyzed by the vitiated air. René Millienne, the director of the *Petit Parisien*, said to us, 'Go, if you still can.' I felt my hopes founder. What a cruel disillusionment. I was counting so much on escaping. I was crushed. This was the worst. Farewell, escape. There was nothing left."

"Why didn't the escape[2] take place—I don't remember. The torpor of the night, the fatigue certainly counted for something. I was taking care of people, trying to encourage them. I remember a young boy who seemed very sick, and who revived because his illness was really his overwhelming sorrow. He was afraid that he would never see his loved ones again, and he was weighted down by his own anguish. This is a good memory. Our two anguishes merged into one; the anguish I got him to speak about, and the one that I kept to myself, and both brought us calm."

The Sirvent Car.

"It was night.[3] I heard a strange noise of scratching and whistling. A heavy weight paralyzed my legs. On each side of my body I felt something flabby and slimy. A voice penetrated the humming in my ears.

"Little by little I regained consciousness, and with it came the ghastly memories. Even in the dark, I knew that this weight, this 'thing' burying me belonged to the realm of death. I was the prisoner of the dead. The voice that I heard became clearer and clearer. Someone was speak-

1. Bernard Poclet, already cited.
2. Jacques Lutz, already cited.
3. Pierre Dhenain, already cited.

ing to me. It was Jean Mercier. He brought me back to reality and awareness. He told me I had fallen. I remembered my belt, my fragile support. It must have given way under the weight of my body, or perhaps I had let go. My mind had wandered through my past and I had recounted story after story about my family and my feelings. Mercier was teasing me, despite the tragic situation, about my romantic adventures which seemed very close to me in this dramatic moment. The air became better as the night advanced. Words were exchanged among the living which overlay the inarticulated voidings of the dying.

"I called out to Jean-Marc Laurent who was my cellmate in the Citadelle d'Amiens. I was happy to hear an answer. He said that he was all right and that Ballin, a policeman from Rosières (Somme) was with him. Gaillet from Amiens, and Desjardin from Poulainville also answered....What about the others? Many were dead, and for a long time the survivors questioned each other. One of us gave the order: 'Count off. Begin with "one." ' Everybody who could answered, and so we found that there were thirty-six of us alive. But after thirty-six, all we could hear were death rattles, weaker and weaker. We waited for day, and in its light we saw what the night had concealed.

"Tangled bodies were piled a meter high. I pulled myself loose from my grotesque position. I had been seated between the thighs of a dead man, leaning on his raised knees. I didn't have my pants on anymore, but I recuperated them, only to lose my shoes in the delicate operation. We decided to collect all the victims at one end of the car. A painful task. Most of the dead eyes were open wide and the bodies crushed and bruised by the trample of feet. They were frightening to see.

"We few remaining men of Picardy covered the bodies of our unfortunate comrades. We found some of them still in the seated position they had adopted from the start. We recognized a few of them: Maurice Thedié, René Bernard, Pierre Delplanque, Jean Caron, Marcel Vion, Marcel Richeter, Joseph Trodat. Poor Trodet, the father of eight! He had been assigned to the Royallieu camp as a gardener. Out of loyalty to his prison mates, he had asked to be deported so as not to be separated from them. He didn't know then....

"Sixty-four cadavers were piled on this enormous mass, this monstrous heap of putrefying flesh which shook with the rhythm of the train. We covered them with all the blankets we could spare."

* * *

"Sixty-four bodies[1] that we had piled together, so as not to step on them. It took all of our united strength to do this. I'll never forget that night—to hear a few men chanting the 'Magnificat' in the darkness—I can tell you, it was really doleful. (A personal note: I hope that no one will have to make such a voyage ever again. But if, by some cursed circumstances, this were to recur, everyone who goes mad should be killed at once....)"

The Guérin-Canac Car.[2]

Now we had to count our dead. They were scattered everywhere in the car, in every position, faces purpled, eyes rolled back, bellies bloated, covered with excrement, horribly deformed. We summoned up our courage, and the strongest amongst us carried the cadavers to a corner of the car and we piled them up like fire-wood. We were so exhausted that we could hardly lift them. "Hey, look...it's so-and-so....Here, here's X....Over there, that's Y...." Each of us gave vent to his pain and surprise when he discovered a friend or a relative among the dead. There were forty-six of them in the car, forty-six out of a hundred!

We sat down in the rest of the car and stretched out our aching limbs. By luck, and what a derisive word to use here, by luck, it was raining now. We were still tortured by thirst. The straw on the floor and our bread were half-rotted in the tainted air. And we ourselves were changed beyond recognition: eyes sunken by fever

1. Unpublished manuscript of Henri Desjardin.
2. Albert Canac, already cited.

and thirst, faces flatulent and covered with sores. Our urine was completely red. Now that we were fewer, it was easier to take turns at the air openings to breathe, and to extend our hands to collect a few drops of rainwater dripping from the roof. What sheer delight!

The train stopped with a jerk. The guards marched up and down the length of the convoy. I took the chance of calling out to one of them and asked if it would be possible to remove the dead. "We have forty-six in our car," I told him. A grating laugh came back: "Es sind 46 Schweine weniger!" (That makes forty-six pigs less.) That was the response.

The Habermacher Car.[1]

During the night, with Claude Mathieu and a few of the other comrades who could still function, we took advantage of the fact that the insane had all gone to sleep to pile the cadavers in a corner. We counted more than thirty of them.... It was frightful: we weren't able to hold on to them, the skin slipped between our hands, their bodies were decomposing. After that, until morning, we breathed at the air vents. I was so thirsty that I knew I couldn't hold out and I would have given anything in the world for a drink. My throat was dry and foam began to form on my lips. I tried to tear my eyes away from the corpses which fascinated me, and to forget their smell. I dozed and saw water, rivers of water, which flowed and flowed....

Claude woke me up. He said that I frightened him when I was asleep, and also that we couldn't let go now because we would soon arrive and then we could drink. I didn't contradict him; I allowed him his sweet optimism. I couldn't understand this miracle. How was it possible for him to be building up my morale? Last night he was dying, half strangled and stamped on by the madmen.

Then he calmly took his eyeglasses out of his pocket. Somehow he had been far-sighted enough to keep them in a safe place. They were dirty, full of blood and other

1.   Maurice Habermacher, already cited.

matter; he tried to spit on them to clean them, but no spit came, so he soaked his finger in urine.... Then he shoved aside a corpse that leaned against me. He tapped it on the cheeks and said: "You lucky bastard, you're not thirsty anymore."

We talked about our home towns, Nancy and Lorraine, where we had spent our childhood. Claude told me about his parents, who thought that he was in Africa with the Free French Forces. He hadn't been able to get any word to them. Then, with thirst giving rise to images, we saw ourselves on the terrace of the brasserie of the "Deux Hémisphères" in Nancy, enjoying excellent half-liters of cool beer, and drifting on to the famous "Cave aux frites" on the place du Marché....

The Puyo Car.

"The bodies of the dead[1] were already distended and gave off a putrid odor. The men who could still function, myself and Dr. Allard among them, decided to separate the dead from the dying, carrying them to opposite corners of the car.... The fit occupied the rest of the space. We counted seventeen dead."

"I thought I heard the porters[2] on the platform where the train had stopped, and that I was in a comfortable sleeping-car. I wanted to go and get a drink at the buffet, but I couldn't seem to move. How would I ever get down from my berth? Later on I learned that I had fainted. My comrade thought I was dead and had placed me on the pile of corpses, and I slept like that for most of the night. I was saved by the very fact of being on top and able to breathe."

"I called out for my brother,[3] whom I had lost during the uproar. I found him at just about the same place

1. Henri Billot, already cited.
2. Unpublished manuscript of Eugène Clunet-Coste, June 1970.
3. Unpublished manuscript of Henri Cluzel, already cited.

where we had been at the start. There was a dead man
lying along the wall and I had no room to sit. I passed the
night sitting on the corpse which made odd gurgling
noises with every shake of the train."

The Metal Car.—André Gonzalès.

His face was coated with dried blood. He had to rub
hard at his right eye to get the lids apart.... The three
survivors of the metal train were standing together near
the sliding door.... The last to revive was the one who
talked most:
"I'm telling you, this train is the train of death. None of
us will escape. Do you hear what I'm saying. This is the
'Death Train.'"[1]

The Garnal-Mamon Car.

They piled the dead up like bundles of fire wood...
their legs tied together by their belts. Seventy-five dead.
Sitting against the wall, dumb-struck and gaping, was
Jean Guitard.
"Guitard could still get up,[2] and even speak to me,
with his left eye hanging out of its socket. He was
horribly disfigured. He told me that he felt that he was
going to die and begged me to see his young wife if I got
back to France, to tell her that he was innocent, because
he had never done anything, either for or against the
Krauts. I kept my promise when I returned from Germany, and I made a written deposition concerning the
circumstances of his death so that she could get the
death certificate. Just the same, Guitard held out for
a number of hours of additional suffering. In the
opinion of Dr. Garnal, Guitard could have recovered
from his horrible wound if he had had immediate
and adequate care, a care which, unfortunately, we
couldn't give him under the circumstances. But Dr. Garnal

1.   See the first pages of this book.
2.   Pierre Mamon, already cited.

added that even with such care, he would have been blind."

"We washed his face for him...with urine."[1]

The Liotier Car.

"I was brought back to reality[2] by the sensation of a glacial cold against my face....It was the cheek of my comrade, Pierre Port, who had died during the night."

"I wanted to stand up,[3] but it was impossible. I was blocked by eight tangled bodies. I extricated my legs with difficulty, but my shoes remained behind."

"Death, blind as justice,[4] and without pity, entered our car and mowed down the men in our ranks at random, thirty-two of my brothers in misfortune.[5] They were there, mingled with the survivors, who were struggling with their last strength to get out of this charnel heap. It took me more than half an hour to help them get free of the pile of bodies. Everything I touched was slimy, the bodies of my neighbors, whether dead or alive, the scattered clothing, the walls and the floor, everything swam in sweat, blood and shit. My hands and my body were drained of color. The sight of the others frightened me. There was not one single human face left among us. All were marked by fear, by madness and by the sight of death. Galled, blotched by asphyxia, nostrils pinched, eyes bulging out of their sockets, lips burst and enormously swollen, mouth open, tongue tumescent and thick, that was the condition we were in when day dawned on July 3, 1944.

"Our phantom train continued pitilessly on its way, jerking and jostling us against each other. The hours

1. Pierre Bourg, already cited.
2. Joseph Renouard, already cited.
3. Gabriel Gasset, already cited.
4. Henri Liotier, already cited
5. According to all the other statements, there were 36.

passed. It took an almost superhuman effort on the part of each survivor to put a little distance between himself and the dead strewn about the floor, knotted in their final spasms.

"The morning wore on but, thank God, the sky was covered; however, this wasn't enough to keep an overwhelming heat from accumulating in this cursed car. Each of us was huddled into himself, propped up like an abandoned puppet. The wheels clanged on. The low clouds let fall a little light rain on the convoy, which cooled us somewhat, but not much. The situation in our rolling casket was neither better nor worse. When we finally succeeded in overcoming our lassitude, we were able to gather the dead at one end of the car. This punishing operation gave us a bit more space. There were eighty-eight of us alive; eighty-eight who were worth not much more than the dead accompanying them.[1]

"For a period of several hours, some of the comrades used a tin can to try to capture a little water dripping from the roof. From time to time the S.S. guard fired a volley of shots to make them pull their arms back inside the car. It was the torment of Tantalus. It took hours to half-fill a bottle, and then the contents had to be divided among fifteen men. The water we drank was black with coal dust. It was foul, and what was worse—the little mouthful to which each was entitled was not enough to quench the fire in our throats.

"The rain had stopped now and those who had held their mess tins outside for hours examined their arms, lacerated by the barbed wire. Our convoy crept forward at a snail's pace, stopping and starting erratically. The air had become so drained that we were forced to keep standing so as not to breathe the carbonic gas stagnating above the floor. The bodies piled at the end of the car gave off a sickening odor. Would this infernal voyage ever end?"

---

1.   This car contained 120 deportees.

THIRD PART

ALL HOPE ABANDON,
YE WHO
ENTER HERE

1

July 3
The Frontier at Novéant

It is raining.

5:00 a.m.—The Helluy-Aubert-Villiers Car.

The panel, cut during the night, had just been smashed through. Two or three voices cried, "Escape, escape!"

The convoy stopped. Submachine guns were pointed at the heart of Dr. Helluy, halfway through the hole.

The S.D. officer unsealed the door. Two guards counted and re-counted the deportees.

"Very good," said the officer. "Now we shall close the hole."

The soldiers were already at work nailing down the planks and attaching barbed wire.

"We'll take care of you a little later. You will all be shot if there is a man missing when it is lighter and we check again."

The train started again—stopped for a long time—started again.

"This new defeat[1] robbed us of the last of our courage: prostrated and despairing, we didn't even have the energy to take any action against the 'informers,' or to give them the beating they richly deserved.[2] It must be admitted that there was some justice in their argument—that after all, the effort to escape would have had to fail and that we would all have been rounded up again very quickly.

"However, the 'informers' weren't riding high either, because we promised them that they'd lose nothing by waiting....But all of us, even the most courageous, wished that they could turn back the hands of the clock...for if we were all going to be shot, what good would it do to play at executioner? We almost stopped talking. There were only a few whispers here and there. We appeared to be resigned....We had just lost all hope and we were weary. We were defeatists, in spite of the words of consolation offered by some comrades in an effort to convince themselves that it would be better tomorrow. Mechanically, we went on taking turns, but the heart had gone out of it. We were unmanned."

Same time. The Lambert Car.[3]

Driven by the wind, the rain slanted down along one side of the car and a few drops came in through the air vent. Hands reached out, and as soon as a thimbleful had been collected, the tongue lapped in all directions, eager for a drop of this precious liquid.

One of us had a book and got the idea of tearing out the pages and making little funnels which he then slipped into the openings of the barbed wire grill, point down. The idea was to collect the water drop by drop at

1.   J.-B. Perreolaz, already cited.
2.   "The comrades agreed not to kill the man who had given the alarm, with the reservation that they would take care of him when they arrived; but I don't think he was recognized after the cleaning-up we were given at Dachau." (Unpublished manuscript of André Petit.)
3.   Henri Lambert, already cited.

the base, but there weren't enough containers to catch the heavenly brew, and the paper quickly grew soggy and useless. And so the system had to be abandoned.

The third system, which proved to be the most effective, was to place handkerchiefs, towels, rags of all sorts, up to the window, and then suck them after they had absorbed some water.

The badly joined roof of the car allowed little trickles of water to pass through, and thirsty mouths groped for them as they fell. The tiniest drop, filtering through between the boards, was picked up with the tip of a finger and carried to a mouth.

The Car of Eighty.[1]

Gaiters! The postman wears gaiters....Suddenly an idea came to us. Folded up, they could be slipped between the planks and the barbed wire and then spread out into the form of funnels. They functioned as a sort of drain pipe, and we were able to fill a bottle.

The Puyo Car.[2]

Someone found the wire strip which had served to tie up our bales of straw. We folded it lengthwise, bent it at appropriate angles and slipped it through the vent, getting it to join the roof gutter. The water flowed....

* * *

It rained. Then the sun shone. The 7909 felt its way onto one track...backed up, stopped.

1. André Tixier, already cited.
2. Jean Migeat, already cited.

11:45 a.m.—Révigny. (The Guérin-Canac Car.)[1]

The Germans shook the door of our car and it banged
open. "Raus! Raus! Los! Los!"—"Get out. Make it
quick." Staggering, drunk with the fresh air, we jumped
to the ground. They lined us up along the track, in a
potato field. Behind us the soldiers with submachine
guns, aimed and ready to shoot. Flight was impossible.
For that matter, we didn't even have the strength to try.
We were in the open country, far from curious eyes. And
then, what did we see arriving behind the backs of our
convict guards, concentrating on keeping us in order, but
an honest local citizen, pedaling his bicycle down a path
through the fields. He came forward hesitatingly, not
knowing what to expect, a bit afraid. But the Germans
saw him and welcomed him with a string of incomprehensible insults punctuated with very precise threats.

"Go back, go back," they barked at him.

The old fellow was so shocked and shaken that he just
escaped a spectacular spill from the bike, turned around
and disappeared without asking for an explanation. The
scene would have been funny, if the circumstances had
been different.

It rained in torrents. Most of us were almost naked. The
rain whipped our bodies, clammy with sweat. It didn't
matter. We were so happy to drink handfuls of the
muddy water from the ditch. During this time, the
Germans selected a few of the surviving prisoners from
each car to carry out the corpses and pile them in cars
left empty for that purpose. Even the dead must reach
their destination.

We watched forty-six bodies being moved from our car
to the one ahead. Those from the neighboring cars were
also piled in it. The same process took place the whole
length of the convoy. The officers supervising the transfer felt that it wasn't going fast enough. They cursed at
our comrades who, out of exhaustion, sometimes uninten-
tionally let a body fall onto the track cinders. These
representatives of the "master race" made believe that
they were highly indignant at the lack of respect they

1. Albert Canac, already cited.

claimed we were showing to our dead, for whose fate they, and they alone, had been entirely responsible. Curses and maledictions beat down on us.

"Juden! Lumpenvolk! Dreckhunde!" "Jews, bunch of bums, filthy dogs."

They tired of that. Then something happened that enraged them totally. A few dying men, taken from the neighboring car, had been set down surreptitiously on the embankment, a little to one side. They began to move again, coming back to life. The Germans rushed up when they saw them. Howling, the officers drew their pistols and finished them off with a ball in the head.

* * *

The survivors[1] had already come out of the car ahead. They joined us, on an order from a guard, and we were all led down the slope. We thought that they were about to "liquidate" us. Monsieur Loiseau gave us a discreet glance that we took to mean bad news. Wherever we had been, he had told us:

"If we see preparations for an execution, we are going to sing *the Marseillaise*—we mustn't die like sheep."

In the end, nothing happened. The guard chose six slaves including me; two got into the car ahead and passed the corpses out to us to be carried to the car I had just left. There was one dying man among them. Only his arms moved. The guard beside us put a bullet through his head.... André Maire was selected to get water, with one of the "new comrades." This operation was carried out with the slop pail from the new car, because there hadn't been any in ours. This latter was first emptied out onto the roadbed before we went to the well of the gate keeper to draw up the precious liquid. The convoy guards weren't in any mood to hand out presents: they wouldn't allow our comrade to wash out the slop pail. Maire came back with a bucket of absolutely foul water. Then they had us climb into our new car with our new comrades. The survivors of the two cars together added up to only eighty-six men.

1.   Maurice Baltet, already cited.

11:45 a.m.—Révigny. (The Weil Car.)[1]

A German officer assigned me the task of getting a bucket of water from a house. He came with me and questioned me. I told him that I was the son of a doctor, and that I no longer understood anything about the human plight. He answered something like: "You're a Jew. Isn't that enough for you?"

I told him that I wasn't a Jew, and that I had been a Christian up until now, but that now I wasn't anything any more; that I couldn't believe either in God or in man. I recall that he made no reply, but that he let me drink as much water as I wanted, and that he showed no violence toward me. It wouldn't have taken much more to make me believe that I had detected something human in his attitude.

11:45 a.m.—Révigny. (The Lambert Car.)[2]

Two comrades and I rolled our cask toward the gate-keeper's well. An armed soldier escorted us. There was a certain amount of confusion there. I looked at the well: a stone lip, a chain on a wooden roller, a galvanized iron bucket. It was located very close to the track. I can still see the closed barrier and the road that could have been the road of liberty for me. It would have been easy for me to let myself down toward the bottom of the well, hanging on to the chain, and then cling to the rough stone walls. I was tempted to try it... But I had left my shoes in the car. It seemed to me that this detail would keep me from saving myself, and I followed my companions.

11:45 a.m.—Révigny. (The Garnal-Mamon Car.)[3]

"Get down!"
They were counting the dead.

1. Doctor Kienzler, already cited.
2. Francis Fagot, already cited.
3. Pierre Mamon, already cited.

This was when we called their attention to our comrade, Guitard who lay helpless, wounded. One of the S.S. non-coms turned back toward us and ordered "Zwei Männer!" Two of us who understood German stepped forward. They were told to get the wounded man and bring him to the door of the car. As soon as this was done, the S.S. non-com virtually screamed at the two men, "Raus," and at the same time, he drew his gun. In less than a second two shots were fired point blank into Guitard's head, while the twenty-four survivors of our car looked on.

Then we were commanded to climb back into the cars and Guitard's corps was carried off to join the seventy-five dead. The guards made jokes and puns in German, laughing at the deaths. A survivor who understood German, translated the witticism of one of the guards, standing in front of the pile of corpses from our own car: "It's a veritable Todt organization." This pun had a bitter twist. Todt refers to the para-military organization for the construction of highways and fortifications, but the humor lay in the fact that 'Tod' and 'Tot' mean death and dead.

11:45 a.m.—Révigny. (The Fully-Thomas Car.)[1]

The three Krauts who opened the door, stood frozen with horror at the sight of the floor covered with a tangle of corpses. But their faces showed more stupefaction than remorse. The bastards! They made us get down, they lined us up on the embankment, they counted us, questioned us. They wanted to know what had happened, what had caused the drama. A Kraut officer came up and talked things over with the others....We wondered if they were going to shoot us. They were quite capable of it. At last the interpreter spoke up: "The Kommandant is willing to believe you, for this time. He pardons you." *(sic.)*

The pouring rain came down like a blessing. We literally came alive again. They let us go and get water in

1. Georges Fully, already cited.

a nearby farm. I went with a comrade, as fast as we could. A Kraut kept us company. We brought back a wash bucket full. Everybody piled in and drank like dogs. It seemed that we could never get enough of it.

Finally they put us into a different car with thirty-five other survivors, so we were only sixty. That was much better....

11:45 a.m.—Révigny. (The Habermacher Car.)[1]

When we had finished unloading the cadavers, a German soldier, originally Czech, who was on the hospital staff of Compiègne, and who knew me well, refused to let me get back into my own car after the shifting of the dead. He made me get into a forward car which was empty. He told me to set up a first-aid car—a sort of infirmary—naturally without any means of treatment. My clothing had been left behind in my original car, and I was separated from my comrades. I was wearing nothing except my shorts and was, consequently, fairly conspicuous.

In my new car, I found myself with Father de La Perraudière, a Jesuit from Tours. I was shown a certain number of the dying. A few of them revived in the fresh air, others remained in a coma until they were taken out at Dachau. One died.

11:45 a.m.—Révigny.
(The La Perraudière-Segelle Car.)[2]

The car began to fill, but only moderately. There would be only forty of us on arrival. That is to say, we were in the most enviable position of all in that terrible convoy.

They even put a man who was in good shape, Dr. Segelle, with us, assertedly to take care of us.

"What do they expect me to do?" he asked me. "At least, you can carry on your ministry, but as for me,

1.   Unpublished report of Dr. Pierre Segelle, January 26, 1949.
2.   Père de La Perraudière, already cited.

A

B

C

Three of those who disappeared: A*) Paul Ensuque;* B*) Georges Rix;* C*) Jacques Jakubovicz. A number of those who died during the voyage were difficult to identify, because most of the deportees did not know who the other voyagers in the car were. These three pictures were sent to the author by the families of the prisoners.*
Author's Archives

without medicaments, I'm like a violinist without a violin."

11:45 a.m.—Révigny. (The Liotier Car.)[1]

I found my shoes again in the straw they had tossed on the platform. I washed them at the gatekeeper's water spout. They were still good for a few more days. The skin tore off and stuck to the hands of the volunteers assigned to transfer the dead bodies. Thirty-six dead in our car.

11:45 a.m.—Révigny.
(The Metal Car of André Gonzalès.)

The door rolled open.
"Everybody 'kaputt' in there!"
"No, three of us are alive."
"Everybody dead."
The door rolled closed.

11:45 a.m.—Révigny. (The Fonfrède Car.)

Bixel and two deportees were sent to the La Perraudière car, Fonfrède to the 'invalids' car.'
"A comrade stared intensely at another prisoner,[2] which made us uneasy because we were afraid of the repetition of the tragic scenes of the night before. We were rather soon reassured. The two men were old acquaintances. 'Weren't you my old captain in the Bat' d'Af' (Battalion of Africa)?' Each one identified himself. 'That's what it is.' 'Oh shit...to find each other here like this—That's what it is.' The sun of southern Tunisia burned in their memories like a cool oasis in the midst of the stinking furnace where we now were."

Louis Lefrançois refused to get out of the car:

1. Gabriel Gasset, already cited.
2. Georges Bixel, already cited.

"I'd rather stay in here and die[1]....I'm too far gone. Finally, on the insistence of Louis and Quémerais, I agreed. They lifted me down and laid me out on the embankment. I remained lying there, waiting for orders, or to be shot through the head....I watched them unload all the cadavers. The bodies tore apart when they were thrown to the ground. It was frightful. Finally a guard came over and helped me to an empty car...."

"The gate-keeper looked astonished[2] and even aghast at the spectacle. I was close to her, at the kitchen door. For a moment I had the idea that I could jump out of the window and make off across the fields. But the guards were too near. I returned to the train."

3:00 p.m.—Révigny.
(The Helluy-Aubert-Villiers Car.)

"And how about us?"
"They put us on the back of the stove to make us more tender."
"But the others got water. They were let out. Not us."
"We, we're the ones who are condemned to death because we didn't succeed in escaping, and got caught at it."
"What are they doing?"
"Everybody's back in. I can't see anybody outside."
"Hell. What about us?"

3:05 p.m.

The 7909 left Révigny, with its hearse wagons.

---

1. Unpublished manuscript of Louis Lefrançois, May 1970.
2. Unpublished manuscript of Henri Huyard, February 1970.

3:15 p.m.—Between Révigny and Bar-le-Duc.
(The Helluy-Aubert-Villiers Car.)

"This time we're really going to get it. Our car is surrounded. I think they're all out there."

Dr. Helluy called for silence. The door clanged open.

Statement of André Petit.

They forced us out, with shouts, gun butts and cudgels. They led us out into a gravel pit and one of the officers ordered the saboteurs to drop their tools, which they did, very regretfully. Looking at the handful of pitiable objects, he couldn't keep from saying:

"It is only the French who can do so much with so little."

Then something happened which was truly sublime. The man who had led the work for the escape was on the point of disclosing his role to spare the others, but there was a young teacher standing alongside him who wanted to assume the blame because he knew that the older man was married and father of a family, whereas he was single.

Statement of Joseph Helluy.

The Kommandant of the train asked who had made the hole. Otherwise...everyone in the car would be shot. I am a doctor from Lorraine, an officer in a D.J.N.A., and a former prisoner of war. I knew how to deal with the Germans with the least risk. So I spoke out. I said that I had not made the hole, but that I had given the order to have it made. That, as an officer, I was the only one responsible for what took place in the car. But the Chief of Convoy overrode me and repeated:

"I order the man who made the hole to step forward."

I insisted: "I am a French officer. I gave the order to make the hole. I also ordered those who made it not to admit the fact. All these men are French. They'll obey a French officer, and not a German officer."

"Who made the hole?"

All of this was repeated a certain number of times, with more and more insistence in the voice.

Unexpectedly, a man stepped forward: Jamarin, a metal worker from Lyons who had not taken part in opening the hole. A magnificent reply to those who preach class struggle. It is very sad, but Jamarin, this hero with a great heart, did not come back to France.

The incident was terminated by a decision of the Chief of Convoy:

"Don't shoot them. They aren't worth the bullets. Beside, they'll all die when we get there."

Statement of Edouard Aubert.

A machine gun was set in place.

"Who had the tools used for cutting the plank? Either he confesses, or else...."

No one spoke, but all the men were thinking intensely. Some wondered what should be done. Was this a matter of intimidation? Should we or shouldn't we answer? And what would be the result?

Suddenly Dr. Helluy took a step forward and proudly stood at attention. In a courageous and firm voice, he said: "It is me."

Assuming the role of the magnanimous officer, dilating on the honor of a soldier, the chief of the convoy declared himself satisfied.... The interpreter translated it.

"You are pardoned.... Pardoned...!"

A short time later we had to get back into a car, this time one with metal walls... and the convoy started off again... with its increasingly cloying odor of cadavers.

5:00 p.m.—Bar-le-Duc.
(The de La Perraudière-Segelle Car.)

"That evening[1] we stopped for a short time at the Bar-le-Duc station. We hadn't advanced very far along the

---

1. Père de La Perraudière, already cited.

road, and we had had nothing at all to eat or drink. We tried to insist on water. A railway worker passed us a very small quantity. I looked through the opening. A big devil was standing on the platform very close to me. If I had stretched out my hand I could have touched him. He held a rifle with a long, slender barrel, a precision arm, and quite casually, he aimed at the windows of the houses facing the station, and fired. He probably wanted to keep them from looking at us."

"A Schupo (Schutzpolizei)[1] fired on a young girl who was watching our convoy from a bridge. Two shots...the first one missed her...and the second one missed fire, it was a dud."

1. Dr. Pierre Segelle, already cited.

6:00 p.m.—Novéant Station.

The two men looked so much alike, they could have been twin brothers.

The station chief, Oscar Triepmacher, advanced to meet them, thumbing through a sheaf of papers, and calmly preparing to meet the new storm which was sure to break over his head; for perhaps the tenth time during the day.... He thought to himself, "the best defense is a good offense: I'd better attack first."

"It's absolutely unbelievable. I am sure that they haven't sent me the new change in schedule...it's inadmissible!"

Heine and Dietrich were stunned by this welcome. They looked at each other in mute astonishment. Triepmacher, convinced that he had scored a point, wanted to consolidate his advantage without delay.

"Your phantom train is beginning to get on everybody's nerves around here....I know that you're not responsible, but since this morning, when it should have been here, I have had to change all the arrivals in the station and all the departures. About twenty trains have been delayed, and I have to account for it. You're highly placed, you should do something, I don't know what,—write or telephone—so that such incidents don't happen again. And I might mention that that track was not to blame, because it hasn't been bombarded nor machine-gunned for several days."

"Take it easy, Monsieur Triepmacher, don't get nervous...."

It was Heine, Little Heine, Fat Heine—'Bouboule,' 'Drag Ass,' 'Pig,' 'the Killer'—this Heine with thirty-odd nicknames, Heine, the Chief of the Gestapo of Hagondange, who had just appeased the station chief. Triepmacher, relieved by these honeyed words, noted with great satisfaction that Heine had called him "Monsieur" Triepmacher, for the first time. Heine continued:

"It's not our fault. Besides, you said yourself that nobody ever tells us anything. Furthermore, yesterday was Sunday. The only thing that Metz told me was that there had been some incidents. All I can imagine is escapes, or sabotage. But to get back to your first question on the change of schedules, nobody told us...."

This conversation was obviously getting on Dietrich's nerves, and he asked coldly:

"So then, at what time will it be here?"

"After 9:30 tonight."

"Are you sure?"

"I am certain that it will not come into the station before 9:30.

Dietrich looked at the clock.

"We have time to eat in town. Are you coming?"

Before they left the station, the twins instructed the police stationed in the outbuildings to have the sentinel cordon in place by eight thirty.

Oscar Triepmacher whistled as he sat down at his desk. Germaine Ferry, his secretary, astonished by his unusual behavior, looked up and asked: "Is it the prospect of passing the night waiting for the 7909 that makes you so happy?"

"Not at all. And anyhow, I won't wait for it here, but in my room. All that happened is that, for the first time, I told the chief of the Gestapo what I thought, and he took

it very well. Now I'm going up to my apartment. Donate[1]
will come by as soon as he's finished eating. No
particular orders? None? Nothing? Very good....

* * *

Until 1940 Novéant played a secondary role in the
S.N.C.F. railway system. But after the Armistice agree-
ments and the territorial partitioning, this little provincial
station whose only activity used to consist in switching
trains toward Metz and Nancy, became a frontier station,
with twenty times the number of working staff it had
had: security police, gendarmes, customs officials, soldiers' center. All of these many elements had great
trouble fitting themselves into the curious structures
—a colonial flight of stairs, with columns, circular
windows, seated dogs, balconies and balustrades,
gutter overhangs and chimney cowls in relief—designed
by some architect either given to revery or slightly
deranged.

Wilhelm Hollinger, the "Reichsbahn-Oberinspektor" in
his old age, was quickly exceeded as he confronted the
problems presented by the installing of the new admin-
istrations. In 1941, he took charge of the customs
service, and left the rest to Oscar Triepmacher.

The station of Novéant, under the direction of the
Saarbrücken railways system, was too important both
strategically and politically to be entrusted to civilian
functionaries. The way it actually worked out was that
everybody was in charge at Novéant: the army, the
security police, the Gestapo, behind its various faces, the
gendarmerie, and the economic spy services of the
Reich. Poor Triepmacher, for all his diplomacy, was held
responsible for all the oppositions and anomalies.[2] The
"twins," Heine-Dietrich, representatives of the lowest
caste, managed to create a reputation of being "untouch-
ables."

1. Assistant station master.
2. He was fired after the war and ended his career as a
salesman of women's underwear.

"Heine, the chief of the Gestapo at Novéant,[1] gave the order for dispatching the convoys of deportees. He was wicked, and all the employees of the station were afraid of him. He was fifty and measured roughly five foot two or three. He was very fat and his face was puffy and rather round. His hair was grey, his eyes blue-grey, and his skin was pale. He was so tough that even the other agents of the Gestapo tried to stay out of his way.

"Friedrich Dietrich, the other half of the Dietrich-Heine combine, was captain of the gendarmerie, and was always tightly stuffed into his field grey uniform with brown collar and facings. He sometimes accompanied the convoys of deportees. He had already been selected for five of these extremely special missions by his superiors in the Préfecture of Police of Metz.[2] Dietrich couldn't understand why the S.D. or S.S. in charge of the trains from Compiègne to Novéant didn't stay with them until they arrived at the camp of destination. He put the question to Brigadeführer Mueller of Metz, and Mueller had answered:

"'If those young fellows saw what was taking place over there, they'd come back transformed into defeatists.'

"Dietrich had only been informed on July 1 about this convoy to Dachau. 'Delayed in transit, twenty-four hours. Escort sixty armed men.'"

"My name is Dietrich, Friedrich Karl,[3] born March 6, 1885, at Schwetzingen, of Dietrich, Franz Xavier and Schmidt, Dorothéa, now deceased. Profession, captain of the Schupo, married, domiciled at Mannheim-Sechenheim, German nationality, never condemned.

"I have been a member of the (Nazi) Party since May 1, 1937, without office. I did not belong to any other Nazi political organization. I have been with the police since 1910. Before 1940 I was Revierführer of the

1. Statement of Germaine Ferry.
2. Friedrich Dietrich, prior to the 7909, had accompanied three convoys to Dachau, one to Buchenwald, and one to Neuengamme.
3. Interrogatory of Friedrich Dietrich, March 15, 1948, by the investigators of the Research Service of War Crimes and Criminals.

police at Mannheim-Sechenheim. About June, 1940, I
was sent to Luxemburg-Esch as captain of the police. I
had, under my orders, ten German police and about thirty
from Luxemburg. On June 13, 1941, I was shifted to
Metz-Hagondange, again as District Leader. On my
arrival fifteen German police were assigned to me, one of
them from Lorraine.... My functions included everything
that ensured public security. The arrests, interrogatories
and searches that I had to make had no political
character: they were simply police matters—theft, assault
and battery, 'crimes passionels,' traffic accidents. My
service was subordinate to the Préfecture of Police of
Metz. I was aware of the deportations which were being
carried out by the Gestapo, but we took no part in them,
because the Gestapo always worked alone. In the month
of May 1944, I was assigned to accompany trains of
French deportees coming out of France...."

At that time, the month of July 1944, Dietrich looked
younger than his fifty-nine years. A permanent, slightly
sneering smile, on a face otherwise without expression,
he was more or less the typical caricature of the standard
Prussian. He shaved his head entirely, once a year. His
eyebrows were thick and in his heyday he must have
sported a monocle. Slightly bow-legged, large nose,
parched personality, respectful of the order and rank of
power.

His favorite expression was: "Yes, I am hard on others,
but particularly hard on myself."

8:30 p.m.—Sarrebourg.

The telephone operator at the Sarrebourg station rang
the Fisteur restaurant:

"The Sarrebourg office, calling Captain Franz Mulherr...."

Franz Mulherr, railway transport officer at Sarrebourg,
picked up the phone.

"Tomorrow morning, at eight thirty, you will make
arrangements for the arrival of the 7909. It is a train
of civilians. They will be fed at the military platform.
Kindly have two thousand rations prepared in advance.

This train certainly appears on your scheduling for July 4...."

9:00 p.m.—Novéant Station.

The "twins," Heine and Dietrich, sat at a table in the Center, which was open, by exception, this evening. A dozen drinking Schupos sat up straighter and lowered their voices. Beer and smoke.

9:50 p.m.—Novéant Station.

Auguste Zimmermann surveyed all the platforms from his glassed-in control post. Right below him, he had just caught sight of station master Triepmacher in deep discussion with two plump officers, when his attention was attracted to a halo of light at the entry of the main track.

"They're crazy to have lit up the searchlights. That must be the 7909. If any planes catch sight of that, they'll have a wonderful time. The black-out is for everybody, even the special transports."

A German employee opened the window.

Triepmacher is waving his hands wildly. He's going to give them a good bawling out.

Under the heading of "Arrivals," Zimmermann inscribed: "7909—21 hrs 53 min."

9:53 p.m.—Novéant Station. (The Fonfrède Car.)[1]

This arrival was an unbearable frustration for me....I was boxed in, opposite the house where I was born. I recognized all the paths, streets and roads, and there, on the platform, I saw fellows I had known who had changed their S.N.C.F. caps for those of the German railway lines. I think it was only then that I was certain that we were heading toward the German Reich. I vowed to myself that I'd come back alive.

1. Unpublished manuscript of André Klein, already cited.

9:55 p.m.—Novéant Station.

Standing at attention. Military salutes. Handshakes. Introductions. An order rang out:

"Turn off the searchlights."

The S.D. lieutenant and the "twins," followed at a little distance by Triepmacher, headed toward the offices of the station, where they made themselves comfortable.

Dietrich's sixty Schupos took over from the soldiers who had come from Compiègne, in the three passenger cars, the observation boxes and on the flatcar.

Triepmacher left the three officers where they were and dispatched the 7909 onto siding III of the switch system. The train stopped eight hundred meters from the station.

In this way, there were no witnesses to the handing-over of orders and the background information that was needed. Four years later, when Dietrich was arrested and questioned by the investigating commission on war crimes, he replied:

"When I found out that there were four hundred fifty dead, I felt queer about it. It was very unpleasant. You see, I wasn't indifferent to this large number of dead because I telephoned to Metz right away to inform them. They told me that my job was to convoy the living and the dead. You can't know what it would have been to disobey under Hitler and Himmler.... When I finished the count, I telephoned to my service in Metz to get them to send me a truckload of lime to throw over the bodies. As for the S.D. officer whose shift I took over in the Novéant station, I reported his name as soon as I arrived at Dachau, but since then I've forgotten...."

10:00 p.m.—Sarrebourg.

Before leaving his office, Captain Mulherr telephoned Jules Martin, in charge of the Red Cross, and told him to supply two thousand additional rations. On that July 4 about a dozen military convoys were expected to pass through Sarrebourg, and the military kitchen generally stopped serving at 9:00 p.m. Mulherr also asked if that wouldn't be too late for the canteen.

"No. I'll be there myself from tomorrow morning on."

11:50 p.m.—The Novéant Siding.

"The night was rather cool.[1] We put on our shirts and pants, which we had taken off the previous day. In spite of the burning thirst which tortured us, we tried to eat— something that none of us had thought about since our departure. Then we became aware that our sausages had rotted, and the best thing we could do was to throw them out of the window. The bread was dry, and worse, it smelled of cadavers, which made it very disgusting. Nevertheless, some of us took a mouthful, but ten minutes later they were forced to vomit it back up. Our bodies were so dehydrated that the salivary glands were completely dry and it was impossible to get the necessary moisture to masticate.

"Faced by this defeat, we decided to try to sleep. The night was cool, which helped, and we had undergone so much suffering, that most of us succeeded in drowsing. There was a clashing and banging in the middle of the night as the door opened and a German officer, booted and carrying a whip, burst into the car. He whipped all the occupants to one end of the car, and then drove us back to the other end, by twos and threes. We learned later that he was our escort to Dachau, and that he had just counted us."

"There were the same screams and shouts as always.[2] The door opened abruptly. An officer of the Schutzpolizei, the security police, carrying a flashlight and armed with a blackjack came into the car, escorted by some soldiers. He got a blast of the fetid air straight in the face and couldn't conceal a movement of recoil and disgust. Then he counted us by making us pass from one end of the car to the other. There were one hundred of

1. Henri Lambert, already cited.
2. A. Canac, already cited.

us. 'Obviously these men have a skill for handling crowds
(Massenbetrieb).' "

"We were passed in review[1] in our cars by hurried,
arrogant and brutal officers. One of them, more stupid
than the others, struck all the circumcized comrades with
his horse whip. This cocky imbecile probably didn't even
know that not all circumcisions were ritual, when he
called them dirty Jews."

1.   Pierre Lecène, already cited.

2

July 4
The Righteous Wrath
of Franz Mulherr

6:00 a.m.—Novéant Station.

Wilhelm Hollinger, the director of the customs service, poked his head through the raised grill of the night watchman's cabin.

"Good morning. How was the night? Not too bad?"

"Oh, but it was. Can't you smell anything? Wait a minute. I'm coming out."

Hollinger had already noticed, as he crossed the outside yard of the station, a stale and noxious odor, somewhat sweetish and heavy.

"It's an infection, or a rotting...."

The employee pointed to the switching post.

"It's back there, by the shunting yard. You know the train of deportees which should have come in yesterday morning? Well, that's the one. It's stuffed with corpses. I tried to get closer, but I couldn't, because of the smell.[1] In the process of decomposition the corpses were literally liquefying. The Schupos threw lime on the cadavers. There are several carloads of dead. They told me that

1. From the statement of Wilhelm Hollinger.

they were Communists and Gaullists who had massacred
each other."

"I'm going to take a look."

"There's something else that we have to deal with. You
remember about the tanks of wine due to be dispatched
this morning....Well, a bunghole was unsealed by the
escort of the deportees' train. Some of the men got
soused. They left the tap open half the night. There's a
big pool...."

"I'll see about it."

Hollinger, red in the face, went to the office of the
station master. Closed. An inspector pointed out the
7909, and added: "If you're looking for the officer, there
he is."

Hollinger identified himself, and said:

"Some men stole wine from the tanks during the
night."

"I know. I drank some too. We had to drink to try to
forget the smell of death. Drink. Drink a lot Monsieur.
And we took wine where there was some to take. I don't
think you can build up a drama over that incident."

"No, no, excuse me.[1] I'll work it out. May I ask you a
question?"

"Yes, certainly."

"I haven't checked, but one of my men told me that the
corpses were completely decomposed. Why not bury
them before leaving?"

"We don't want to give the French population an
excuse to revolt."

7:15 a.m.—Novéant Station.

The "twins" shook hands with each other. Station
chief Oscar Triepmacher, without much conviction,
wished Captain Dietrich "bon voyage," and gave the
locomotive the signal for departure.

1. Hollinger was well-acquainted with Heine and Dietrich. He
stated, in his testimony, that he didn't know the identity of this
"officer." It is probable that Dietrich left overnight supervision of
the train to the police of Metz.

7:15 a.m.—Sarrebourg Station.

Fifty Schupos from the Sarrebourg garrison marched onto the military platform of the station.

7:30 a.m.—Imling (a little village three kilometers from Sarrebourg).

The engineer, Jean Koestler, and his wife Alice were having breakfast in the kitchen of their tiny apartment. Coffee with milk, black bread and jam. Jean Koestler closed his heavy leather sack:

"What's in here for lunch?"

"There are noodles and two eggs in the mess tin."

"What! No meat! That makes at least six days...."

"I'll cut into the July ration tickets tomorrow. I've added a big piece of cheese and some apricots."

Jean Koestler gave Alice a parting hug.

"Now you're to go back to bed, even if you can't sleep, you should stay lying down.... It's the last month, you know."

"Come on. I'm not the first woman to be having a baby. I'll see. Go along now."

"Until tonight. I'm on the reserve list. It's tough. I may have to wait six or eight hours, and then leave for Hamburg or Nancy."

Jean Koestler put on his big beret and straddled his bicycle.

8:00 a.m.—Sarrebourg Depot.

The sleeping quarters were empty. Jean Koestler put on his working blues, closed his locker, and set out for the office of Georges Martz, records chief in charge of transport.

"'morning Koestler. I have a dispatch for you. You are to take the 7909 as far as Haguenau.... Departure, I think at about nine o'clock. No confirmation has come in yet."

Georges 'Martz handed the engineer the key to the locomotive and the transport bulletin on which all the incidents along the route are to be marked.

Coming out of the office, Koestler took a long look at the notices tacked to the walls of the corridor: "Nothing particular between Sarrebourg and Haguenau."

"Perfect, he thought. For once, I'll get home early."

Greasing, inspection, a bite to eat with the crew, wait for the signal from the Sarrebourg station regulars. The depot is a world to itself, far from the shunting, seven to eight hundred meters away, a clique of the train crews who pay no attention to, and often look down on, the poor sedentary pen pushers at the station.

10:15 a.m.—Frontigny.

August Lang, the tracks-and-buildings boss of the Peltre-Remilly sector, rejoined his crew in the Frontigny trench. Lang, sweaty and short of breath, spread his blue handkerchief over a rock:

"Stinking day!"

"Yeh, stinking day and stinking sun for working in this sink."

"It's an oven!"

With a final sharp blow, Edouard Boime tapped the last axle-box bearing with a resounding bang, followed by a tinkling of iron against the pebbles of the track bed. In this fault five hundred meters long, cut into ramps of eight meters, Boime and about ten others changed the crossties of Metz-Strasbourg track II. The slope was held by a cut-stone facing. Not a breath of air. The tracks were burning hot.

"I've never seen anything like this. You could cook an egg on it."

Lang folded up a piece of paper in his hand.

"An unscheduled train is going to pass through here at about ten forty-five. It's a queer train, a train of dead men." The men gathered around Auguste Lang.

"I heard about it from the marshalling yard at Metz. Over there, they refused to let the train through. They sent it around by the outside tracks. It smelled too bad.

They made it stop in the open country. It's guarded like a bank safe."

"A train of dead men?"

"Yes. The guy from Metz told me over the 'phone that they were bodies they were going to burn in Germany."

"The bastards!"

"Let's go. It isn't going to last much longer. Perhaps these are the last deaths."

"Let's hope."

Edouard Boime walked along with the crew chief for a few steps.

"I want to ask you for a favor. You're going to pass by the station at Courcelles. Please telephone my wife. Almost all the trains stop at the barrier signal, often for a long time. My little daughter is with my wife. She mustn't be allowed to see that."

Edouard and Eugénie Boime had acquired the cottage at grade crossing 123 in 1936. The silvered bell, the white and red warning signals of the barrier, the faded stucco, tiny garden, white lace curtains, enameled coffee pot, green with a long spout, green like the shutters.

"Hello!"

"Speaking from Courcelles. I'm telephoning because the train scheduled for ten thirty or so is loaded with corpses and it stinks of decay. It's impossible to bear it. Close up everything, doors and windows. Close everything. Block all the holes...."

Andrée Boime, nine years old with a shock of light blond hair and a smile, was playing on the steps of the cottage.

"Bring your dog in."

10:20 a.m.—Peltre.

The inspector, Joseph Vogein, the only Peltre station railway man authorized to go onto the military platform, eastern sidings, couldn't believe his eyes.

"Check the couplings! Check the couplings, and then we'll see. First we've got to get some water to these poor buggers. Half of them must be dead already. What a putrid smell. And the train's even dripping."

A voice:

"Water."

... and then dozens of others.

"Water."

"Where are we?"

Vogein pushed past the guard, rushed to the water hydrant and began to fill a bottle. The guardian interposed his bulk.

"It's verboten."

"Forbidden? I don't give a damn. This hydrant was put here so that we could water the animals.... We can damn well give it to the men."

Dozens of tins, mugs and bottles were being held up, being waved at the air openings.

The guard lowered his gun. Vogein ran toward the nearest car.

"Where are we going?" "What time is it?" "Where are we?" "Quick, bring us water."

He returned to the hydrant and lined up the containers. By this time, three soldiers had joined the guard. One of them kicked over the tin cans. "Verboten."

Then the big moustaches of Joseph Vogein began to bristle. He turned red, and then white. His hands shook. He puffed himself up, and said, in German:

"I'm sixty years old. I've been a railway man since 1907. I've never seen anything like this—such barbarian behavior...."

"Shut your trap."

"I'm going to talk. Barbarians.... You've lost the war. The war is ended. You're worse than gangsters. You bastards. You Krauts. You Schweinehunde."

Flying fists, kicks, gun butts. Vogein collapsed on the platform. A whistle.

"On board. Leave him there."

"We ought to put him in with the others. That's what he deserves."

10:35 a.m.—Frontigny.

On the work site of the Frontigny sector, the men gathered up their tools:

"Everybody on the embankment."

The train had been taking the Sablon-Courcelles slope for ten minutes. Klein, the engineer, shouted to the stoker:

"Load her up. We're not going fast enough. We have to give them some air...."

The stoker piled on the coal.

"We've got to go fast enough to stay ahead of the smell."

Twenty kilometers per hour, perhaps twenty-five.

"The work crew climbed onto the retaining wall.[1] From the height of the wall we were able to look down into the cattle cars through the air openings. There were at least forty cars. It was horrible. The first three or four cars were full of dead bodies, piled up to the roof. Blood and water leaked out. Unbearable sight. Unbearable stench, I swear. Next came the cars full of living men, clutching the barbed wire, silent, white as paper. They were like living dead, zombies. Those poor guys. It was at least 50° C in the cars, I'm sure. There were armed soldiers between the cars. They, too, were nasty to see. After the train passed, the smell was so strong that we couldn't start to work again. We had to climb further up the embankment to be able to breathe."

* * *

Whistle. "Signal?" .... "All's well."

For the past three months, all the day trains had stopped at Madame Boime's grade crossing 103.

"That one didn't stop.[2] The barriers had been closed for ten minutes. We had to stay inside with my daughter, Andrée, and then curiousity got the better of me. The smell! What a smell! Unbearable. Andrée made a face. It seems as if I can still smell it. Two hours after the train had passed, the air was still foul. We thought there were only corpses in the train. We were amazed to see men hanging onto the barbed wire of the openings. They

1.   Unpublished manuscript of Edouard Boime, February 1970.
2.   Unpublished manuscript of Eugénie Boime, March 1970.

didn't say anything. They didn't shout out. Probably they were just trying to get a bit of fresh air."

11:56 a.m.—Sarrebourg Station.

Jules Martin, chief cook for the Red Cross aid, came out of the canteen and noted that it was still hotter outside than next to the stoves, which had been loaded with eight hundred liters of pea soup since seven in the morning.[1]

At the central switching post, Eugène Dreidemy, chief of the routing service, switched the 7909 onto track XV, reserved for supplying military convoys.

The engineer, Joseph Klein, took charge of the convoy at Blainville. He passed over the shunting of track XIII and closed down the head of steam.

Bernard Kitta, security chief, couldn't tear his eyes away from the opening through which he could see enormous, swollen masses....

"God in Heaven!...They're all dead bodies in there."

The 7909 stopped between a coal train and the barracks of the military platform. Dietrich's police leaped out onto the flagstones of the quai and rushed to the toilets.

Auguste Oliger, chief of the work crew checking the coal train for hot-boxes, heard a military policeman from Sarrebourg ask his counterpart from Novéant:

"Who are those guys shut up inside there?"

"They're all Communists and terrorists...."

A powerful voice, from inside the car, shouted in German:

"That's not true. We're not Communists and we're not terrorists. We're honest Frenchmen and honest people... we're people just like you."

The M.P. from Novéant barked: "Shut up, bastard."

---

1. According to Jules Martin, more than 30° C. The readings of the meteorological services of the German Navy give, for Sarrebourg, 25° at 2:00 p.m.

11:56 a.m.—Sarrebourg Station. (The Lutz Car.)[1]

Was it the end of the morning, or the beginning of the afternoon when we reached Sarrebourg...on my birthday, the fourth of July.[2] I was twenty-five years old. I had already lived through turbulent times. When I was fourteen, both my father and mother had died. I left high school at eighteen to enlist. I was a prisoner of war and escaped from Germany in 1942. This is the second time that I was going back there, but just the same, the first time wasn't so tough. I'm not myself any more, nobody knows where I've gone. True enough, aside from my brothers, who was there to miss me? And now, Germany....I thought I knew what it was. I was alive. I had saved my skin.

11:58 a.m.—Sarrebourg Station.

"Is that the 7909?"
"Yeah, that's it."
Jules Martin had just spoken to a non-com. He went on:
"I have to feed these men."
The German burst out laughing.
"Well, you're the lucky one. There are five hundred dead. Five hundred dead means five hundred less rations to distribute...so you've got less work. Do you know where the toilets are? I have to go and throw up...."
Jules Martin walked toward the passenger car. The Schupos of Sarrebourg, without haste, stationed themselves along the train. A voice shouted:
"No one is permitted to approach."
Jules Martin stopped in front of a group.
The last guards were leaving the passenger car.

1.   Unpublished manuscript of Gabriel Rykner, already cited.
2.   Eleven "travelers" celebrated their birthdays in this train between Compiègne and Dachau. The youngest, Noël Schmerer, seventeen on July 2, 1944, was so profoundly marked by this experience that for the rest of his life he put off to July 2 all the major decisions of the year: buying a car, renting an apartment, etc.

"Hey, you, who let you through?"

"The Red Cross has prepared...."

"What Red Cross? What's this about the Red Cross. Listen to that.... The Red Cross."

"We've prepared two thousand rations on the order of the Sarrebourg center...."

"And we can tell you to shove them up your ass."

"But the soup...and the water...."

"Up your ass. With or without water, they're all going to be dead. Get the hell out!"

Noon—Sarrebourg Station.

Franz Mulherr, delayed in his office by the making-up of a train of the German armed forces, received two telephone calls, one from Jules Martin and the other from a mess corporal.

"Come right away. It's imperative. We can't get permission to take food to the train.... There are at least five hundred dead. They want to start up again as soon as the locomotive is changed.

Mulherr rang the depot.

"Monsieur Martz? Very well. Has the 7909 engine gone out?"

"Just this minute."

"Contact the engineer at once. Let him couple up, but he must not leave until I give the order. Do you understand? Only when I give the order. You tell him that."

Noon—Sarrebourg Depot.

Locomotive 040 D. G8 (AL) of Jean Koestler slid under the shed of the depot, letting out a whirlwind of steam.

Creeping forward slowly. Halfway along Koestler crossed Joseph Klein's locomotive which was backing up.

Klein signaled with his left hand, pointing back. Koestler understood. "Down there, at the heading-up...."

Klein waved his right hand at the level of his lips, twisted in a grimace. Koestler translated: "Back there, at the heading-up...something's screwy."

Steam closed. Steam builds up. Whistle. A gentle touch on the buffers. Koestler is startled, and whispers to the stoker:

"Be careful how you hitch up. I've just caught sight of Mulherr arriving, in person. That's not normal. So I think I'll get down with you, and we'll do the hitching together."

12:04 p.m.—Sarrebourg Station.

A railway worker who didn't know Koestler climbed up on the locomotive.

"I have a message from Monsieur Martz at the depot. You can start up when Captain Mulherr gives you the order...and only him.

Mulherr came over: "Hey you, up there."

The engineer leaned out toward Captain Mulherr.

"No use coupling up right now. I'll let you know in a little while."

Captain Friedrich Dietrich loomed up behind Mulherr's back.

"What's going on here. We're late. We're leaving right away."

A dozen Schupos surrounded the two captains. Each identified himself. Cold, formal presentations. Mulherr took Dietrich by the arm. "Let's step over there for a minute." They moved about five meters down the line.[1]

"We are not going to argue in public. We would simply

1. Several witnesses, among them Koestler, Martin, and a dozen first aid workers and railway workers I was able to contact, heard the exchanges in the discussion between the two. Franz Mulherr drew up two reports on the events in Sarrebourg. The first was addressed to the German officers of the prisoners of war camp at La Begude on April 16, 1945; the second on April 4, 1946, presented to the investigators of the Service of Research on War Crimes at Neustadt. Finally, on June 9, 1970, Roderich Mulherr handed me "a true and exact statement of the facts" unpublished and drawn up by his father shortly before the latter's death.

attract an audience of rubber-necks, and pretty soon the whole town would be talking."

"Well now, see here. You're not going to continue with all these dead."

Dietrich felt himself in a weak position. He kept wiping off his forehead with the back of his sleeve. Mulherr continued:

"What I saw as I walked along the train filled me with horror. All these dead...and the living! There's nothing human left about the living. You can't go on any further with these dead. They poison the air around them. There's a risk of epidemic."

"I must accompany to Dachau both the dead and the living. That's an order, an order from Himmler, 'dead or alive.' I took over this train at Novéant: the escort skipped out without giving me any explanation. And they left me with four hundred fifty cadavers on my hands."

"But we must avoid other deaths."

"The faster we leave, the quicker we'll get there, and the fewer deaths there'll be."

"I have had two thousand rations of soup prepared. They're hungry and thirsty. We're going to give them some water...."

Dietrich burst out:

"And I say you're not. No. No. We're going to start up right away."

Windmilling arms and cap. Mulherr backs away, and shouts, in turn:

"I'm the one who gives the orders here. The train will be fed, the dead buried, the cars cleaned."

"And I give you the order to leave me alone. This train is placed under my responsibility."

"Considering what I've seen, and listening to you, I'm ashamed to be a German. As for me, it isn't Himmler who gives me orders."

"Shut up!"

"No, it's not your Himmler. I get my orders from the transport authorities. And today, maybe you don't know what's happening in Normandy—military transports have priority. Even Himmler would understand."

"You're going to hear from me again. I swear to that. Shut up."

"I don't give a damn. I'm going to say one thing more: soon there are going to be more streets called Rue de la Paix or Rue du Pardon in Germany than streets called Adolph Hitler or Heinrich Himmler."

"Lousy bastard!"

Mulherr turned on his heels and walked in front of the locomotive: "You can couple up when we have finished supplying the train."

12:04 p.m.—Sarrebourg Station.
(The Guérin-Canac Car.)[1]

Howls and shouts. What could be happening? For this time the howls came from the platform. I saw two German officers bawling each other out. One of them lifted his arms to the sky as if seized by a violent rage. He shouted: "Poor Germany! You have gone completely crazy. (Armes Deutschland! Sie Sind ganz verrückt...!) Dragging around loads of dead bodies like this...." The other, mad with rage, answered with threats. He told him that we were all dirty Jews, terrorists, Communists and that we were getting just what we deserved. Then the first answered that he was in charge here, and that as long as the train stayed in the station, he was in command.

12:15 p.m.—Sarrebourg Station.

Dietrich placed two phone calls to Berlin.

From a nearby office Mulherr called the chief surgeon of the hospital of Sarrebourg.

"Dr. V... Can you come immediately to the station? I need your help. A decision of a medical nature must be taken. It is serious. Very serious."

"I'm coming at once."

1. Albert Canac, already cited.

12:25 p.m.—Sarrebourg Station.

"What's happening?"

"The escorts are refusing to let us start the distribution."

Robert Mangin relieved Jules Martin, the Red Cross delegate, and advised Martin to leave the station.

"You are responsible for the service during the entire night, so take a rest. You'll need it. How many dead?"

"No one knows exactly."

"I'll go and see."

Robert Mangin, his hands in his pockets, walked right through the cordon of guards. When he got near the tail wagon, he recognized a Schupo from Sarrebourg:

"Do you know the number of dead? I need to know, because of the rations."

"No, but that's easy. The cars containing them are marked in chalk with a white cross, and alongside the cross you have the number of cadavers. Come!"

Robert Mangin and the Schupo walked alongside the train.

First stop.

"It's marked one hundred twenty-one. Does that mean one hundred twenty-one dead?"

"Yes. You can check."

Robert Mangin climbed up on a buffer and looked in through the opening.

"This is terrible. How could such a thing be possible?"

The Schupo didn't answer.

By the time he reached the locomotive, Robert Mangin had noted down seven figures. He added them up:

"Four hundred eighty-one. 481. Dead."[1]

---

1. In his unpublished manuscript, Captain Mulherr confirmed this figure. However, two more dead should be added. They were discovered during the food distribution. Hence, at the Sarrebourg stop, there were four hundred eighty-three dead.

12:35 p.m.—Sarrebourg Station.

Doctor V..., chief surgeon of the Sarrebourg hospital, followed Captain Mulherr onto the military platform.

"They have just told me that there are four hundred eighty-one dead on this train."

"So what. I'm interested in the living, not the dead."

"But look, doctor, the living are all mixed up with the dead. We must bury...."

"I am not an agent for a funeral parlor."

"I don't think this is a moment to joke."

The chief surgeon put his cap back on:

"My dear friend. I know the kind of a person you are: honest, deeply human, and even a little defeatist, I think. I have a great deal of admiration for your high sense of...."

"Please, doctor. We must save these men. You can. All you have to do is find the officer in charge of the convoy and tell him that, considering the risk of epidemic, you have decided to bury, as quickly as possible...."

"...as quickly as possible, all these dead. Is that it? How you carry on! I have already told you that only the living are of interest to me. Furthermore, I might add, I have never had the least idea of transgressing an order, and least of all, an order from Himmler. You told me yourself that the leader of the convoy was hiding behind Himmler's phrase, 'dead or alive.' He is correct. I regret to tell you. I really must be going."

Mulherr closed his eyes wearily. The passenger car, which Friedrich Dietrich had just entered, was less than thirty meters away. In a few seconds Mulherr made up his mind.

"I must do it. It's my duty."

The mess corporal was standing in front of the canteen door. Without stopping, Mulherr ordered:

"Bring out the camp kettles. We are going to start the distribution."

Mulherr opened the door of Dietrich's compartment and asked:

"Have you gotten a reply from Berlin?"

"That's my business."

"Very well. I have decided to make a distribution of the soup intended for this convoy according to the orders I received from my superiors."

"You're stubborn. All right. One of my men will unseal the cars. But I warn you, you are responsible, and you alone, for any escape attempt. When can the train leave?"

"The tracks won't be free before three o'clock."

"We'll meet again."

12:40 p.m.—Sarrebourg Station.
(The Guérin-Canac Car.)[1]

The doors slid open, but in place of the usual guards, mean and threatening, we saw nurses of the German Red Cross before us. On the faces of these women, I thought for one moment that I could detect an expression of great sadness, a flash that revealed their disgust, their shame at the sight of such inhumanity, such cruelty, useless and stupid bestiality. They distributed soup and brought us buckets of water. This was our sole nourishment during the four days of this hallucinatory and tragic "anti-odyssey."

12:40 p.m.—Sarrebourg Station. (The Rohmer Car.)[2]

The Red Cross nurses distributed a half liter of soup to us in paper cups, absolutely delicious....When I heard a

1. Albert Canac, already cited.
2. Francis Rohmer, already cited.

nurse say to her neighbor, in Alsatian, "It's a shame to treat people in this way," I seized the opportunity to give her the address of my family and I asked her to reassure them that I was still alive. I found out later that she had transmitted my message.[1]

12:40 p.m.—Sarrebourg Station.
(The Garnal-Mamon Car.)[2]

During the soup distribution by the Red Cross, a suddenly prurient guard struck me and one of my companions with the utmost savagery, although he had ordered us to get down and help the nurses carry the soup kettle. This was because we were naked to the waist. He spoke fluent French, and even used Parisian slang to jeer at us for our undress: "You want to strut around stripped in front of the broads; I'll ram it in you, you bunch of bastards." (Ah! vous voulez vous balader à poil devant les gonzesses; je vais vous en foutre, bande de salauds.)

12:40 p.m.—Sarrebourg Station.[3]

The train stood under the beating sun. At one moment I noticed that several deportees had gotten out of the train, doubtless they had been ordered to do so. They carried one of their companions and laid him on the grass close to the kitchen. I took him some water, but I wasn't permitted to speak to the deportees who were standing

1.   This refers to Madame S. Konanz: "We were working under the orders of a German captain who told us that the dead should be buried immediately.... One of the Gestapo told him to close his mouth, or he would be stood up against the wall. However, we were authorized to distribute the soup. While we were doing this, several prisoners furtively slipped us letters, which we sent later. Among them was the son of a pharmacist from Colmar (Francis Rohmer).... I'll never forget that train...." (Unpublished manuscript, March 1970.)
2.   Pierre Mamon, already cited
3.   Jules Martin, already cited.

A

B

CONVOI DE LA MORT DU 2-5 JUILLET 1944

COMPIÈGNE

DACHAU

F

77 608

C

D

In the center: badge belonging to Monsieur Panchetti. These were distributed, after the war, by the F.N.D.I.R.P. to all the survivors of the Death Train. Their registration number at Dachau is written on it.

These are four of the survivors.

A) Gabriel Rykner, member of the Ajax-Micromégas network arrested while he was carrying the plans for the establishment of the Gestapo in the southern zone.

B) Jean Migeat, "Peace on Earth to Men of Good Will." He saw this inscription at one of the windows of a citizen of Compiègne on his way to the station. It was a life-giving comfort, and he regained confidence. In his car there were seventeen dead.

C) André Gonzalès. Ninety-nine dead in his car. He was the only survivor.

D) Albert Charpentier. At the station of Jonchèry-sur-Vesle, he succeeded in tossing onto the platform a piece of paper addressed to his family. A station agent saw it, and picked it up.

Author's Archives

around him. The only clothing that they wore was their pants. A deportee with a cross around his neck came and prayed. The man on the grass died almost immediately after that.

12:40 p.m.—Sarrebourg Station.
(The Perraudière-Segelle Car.)[1]

A paper cup, not even a fourth of a liter per man. The soup was fairly thick, but highly seasoned, which increased our thirst. And there was no water....

Among the forty sickest men I saw arrive at Révigny, I recognized my watch-maker from Paris. He still hadn't taken off any of his clothing. He was suffering from pneumonia and was on the verge of dying, "decently" dressed, as he had said at the beginning. I leaned over him, but he didn't appear to hear me. When he had breathed his last, I asked the Catholic comrades to join me in reciting "Our Father."

The soldiers guarding the train were notified of the death. We had to carry his body to another car, as we had done with the gendarme-deportee. We carried him, holding on to four corners of a blanket. Horror! The car was stacked a meter-and-a-half high with bodies. All they had done was spread a little quicklime over them, which gave the mass a grey, muddy appearance. The arms and legs, stiffened in contorted postures, bore witness to the frightful sufferings in which they died.

I wanted to save the blanket, after having laid the body of the poor watch-maker on the pile. A German wouldn't allow it, and forced me to throw the blanket in with the cadaver.

2:30 p.m.—Sarrebourg Station.

About twenty Serbian prisoners, guarded by six police, walked along the length of the train and threw fistfuls of lime on the puddles which had formed under the cars.

1. Père de La Perraudière, already cited.

Madame Rohfritsch, as was her daily habit, tucked her little daughter, Simone, into her baby carriage and began her afternoon walk down Winkelhof Street:

"This is the neighborhood near the railway.[1] Simone was two and a half. There was a group gathered at the little chapel overlooking the rails. I came up and I caught sight of the train. Three prisoners who tried to drink from a water hose were pushed back to their car. Then the German soldiers came up to us and told us to get moving."[2]

3:10 p.m.—Sarrebourg Station.

Captain Franz Mulherr left the military platform on the run. He stopped once to vomit behind switch cabin No. 2. Then, twenty meters further on....
"This way, Herr Mulherr, come this way...." He looked up and saw the smiling faces of two of his neighbors from the Rue Jeanne-d'Arc, and fainted. While one of the two men supported him, the other went to look for a pot of coffee.
"That's better, I think. Drink some more."
"Thank you, my good friends."

3:12 p.m.—Sarrebourg Station.

The postmen, Paul Krumenaker and Joseph Dillen-schneider, finished loading the Strasbourg-Paris van on track II. The military quay was just three hundred meters away.
"It smells funny...like cadavers."
"You must have a cold. Two sacks more."
Dillenschneider straightened up:
"It's true. You're right. I've just smelled it. I think I'm going to vomit. What a stench!"
The postmen stopped a railway worker.

1.   Unpublished manuscript of G. Rohfritsch, March 4, 1970.
2.   Charles Hiebel saw this same scene from the window of his apartment on the rue de l'Entente (the street ran four and a half meters above the military platform). (Statement, March 8, 1970.)

"What is it that stinks like that?"

"There's a train of prisoners at the military platform, and a lot of them are dead."

Dillenschneider held out the last sack of mail to Krumenaker:

"I'm going to take a look. Do you want to come?"

"No. I'm going back."

Dillenschneider walked onto the Hoff bridge which spanned the tracks and joined a group of women. The oldest of them told him the story:

"The men in there are in a wretched state. A little while ago, I saw one of them try to separate the planks across the air opening with an iron bar...the car was full of dead and living, both. Somebody went to bring them buckets of water, and two women came who had fastened sponges to the ends of sticks. Five minutes later the police chased everybody away, with the butts of their guns. I heard someone shout out, 'Anyway, they got some water.' My God, how can things like this happen in the world?"[1]

3:14 p.m.—Sarrebourg Station.

Friedrich Dietrich clacked the door of his train compartment closed. The escort police climbed into the observation boxes and balanced themselves on the footboards. A nurse called out:

"Wait, wait, we haven't finished yet."

Dietrich snapped at a non-com from the Sarrebourg garrison: "We're leaving. Get up to the locomotive."

3:18 p.m.—Sarrebourg Station.[2]

Captain Mulherr stepped out onto the military quay as the 7909 started up. He was still pale, collar unbuttoned

---

1. Unpublished manuscript of Joseph Dillenschneider, March 11, 1970.
2. Hour of departure of the 7909, recorded in the Sarrebourg station registry by Captain Mulherr.

and cap in hand. Jean Hebeisen, a Sarrebourg contractor, who directed the repair work on the platform, heard him say: "When you see things like that, it makes you ashamed of being German."

A nurse came up to him: "How can we still look each other in the eyes, after this?"[1]

3:20 p.m.—Sarrebourg Station.

The task force of Serbian prisoners began to spread three hundred kilos of chloride of lime over the tracks.

Robert Mangin shook Captain Mulherr by the hand.

"I don't think that any other station commissioner would have had your courage...."

"For the first time, today, I looked into hell. I won't ever forget it. Now, I'll have to wait for the last judgment."[2]

1.   Inquiry of R. Schoeser. Sarrebourg agency of the *Républicain Lorrain*, March 4, 1970.

2.   It is certain that the telephone calls of Dietrich, the reports of the Sarrebourg S.D., and the calls for an investigation by the Kommandant of Dachau (as we shall see later) were responsible for the opening of a file on this case. Here is the statement of Franz Mulherr:

"The terrible news spread quickly through Alsace and Lorraine. The Gestapo started an inquiry in the subdivision, which referred it to General Hogl of the Wehrmachtskommandantur and he, in turn, designated me as being the only one capable of providing it with certain and authentic explanations. I replied to these gentlemen that, unfortunately, this was not a matter of false rumors but of sad reality. The chief of the S.D. and the chief of the Kreisleitung censured me violently for my attitude and told me that they would denounce me, not only to Gauleiter Bürckel, but to Himmler himself.

"The Gauleiter Bürckel came to Sarrebourg himself on July 20, and certainly did everything necessary to see that the government was informed. He condemned the incident in the following words: 'I do not believe that there is a single sane German who could approve of such things.' July 26 must have been my lucky day, because Himmler came to Sarrebourg, and I was to have been questioned at the Château of Kolsing. But the general commanding the 12th A.K. at Wiesbaden, had me convoked with all urgency as soon as he learned of Himmler's impending visit. General Gerlach spoke to me, and said: 'I called you to me

3:25 p.m.—Locomotive.

The engineer, Jean Koestler, took a last look at the travel warrant: required average, forty kilometers per hour. He turned toward his stoker:

"We're coming to the three-kilometer tunnel. I'm going to push her as fast as she'll go. In that way they'll get a little fresh air in the cars. There are five tunnels between here and Saverne. That will set them up a bit."

3:25 p.m.—The Lambert Car.[1]

It was a little cooler in the tunnels...but we could still smell the cadavers....I was very young. I was afraid to die, and I started to pray.

because I wanted to make your acquaintance. I want to tell you of my satisfaction with your vigorous action on July 4. Because of you, this monstrous affair will not stain the reputation of the Wehrmacht. I consider it my duty to provide you with all the protection possible against any new attack.'

"However, an investigation had been started. I realized that I was the object of secret surveillance when I became aware that my mail was being intercepted. I had to acknowledge to myself that shortly after the assassination attempt against Hitler, a pattern of legal procedure was developing in which I might have paid a high price for my attitude. Like every member of the Army of the Interior, of which Himmler had taken command, I had to certify in writing that I had knowledge of the orders stating that whoever rendered any service to the enemy, was liable to be condemned to death, along with the members of his family. Actually, there was a German war council which condemned me to death in absentia, after I had been arrested."

On April 26, 1970, I received a letter from Roderich Mulherr, the son of Captain Mulherr:

"My father would have been eighty-one today. By an irony of fate, he fell seriously sick when he was a prisoner in the camps of Dijon and Vaucouleurs. He never fully recovered. He died fifteen years ago as the result of his treatment in prison."

1. Unpublished manuscript of Michel Léotard, May 1970.

5:15 p.m.—Haguenau Station.

Friedrich Dietrich was the first to jump down on the platform of track VIII. The lieutenant who commanded the Schupos of the Haguenau garrison held a police dog on a leash. Dietrich's orders could be summed up in a single sentence:

"Nobody is to get closer than twenty meters from the train."

He saluted and went back into his compartment.

Charles Krieger, the station inspector, and Ernest Reichmann, the service chief, supervised the inspection of the cars and change of locomotive in fifteen minutes. When Ernest Reichmann went by Dietrich's passenger car for the last time, he saw several of the guards drinking champagne.

The 7909 left Haguenau at 17:33.

3

July 5
The Final Run

I think I cried[1] when we crossed the Rhine: some say at the Kehl bridge, others say at Karlsruhe—what difference does it make? In almost all the cars, they sang *la Marseillaise*. I knew now that this was all over and that something else awaited us, perhaps equally horrible. Although I had no more tears, I know that I was crying. I cried all along the last stage. I know that I wasn't the only one.

*   *   *

During the night,[2] a storm broke out. A torrential rain poured down and cooled the car. We held our hands outside the openings, filled them with water and drank all we wanted. Then we gave some to the sick. We were happy. One of us chanted a canticle to the Virgin, and the others took it up in chorus, thanking heaven for this blessing. Everybody went to sleep, including the sick, comforted by the drink. That night nobody died.

1. André Page, already cited.
2. Maurice Habermacher, already cited.

* * *

I am one of the few prisoners[1] who didn't get sick during the trip, but my ankles and calves were the same size, and I couldn't hold out any longer.

It was my turn to lie down and Clauzade gave me his place. I dozed off for a few moments. I saw my wife, my little Madeleine, and held my little son in my arms. Suddenly, I awoke and sat up.

"What's the matter with you?" Clauzade asked. "At least you can stay seated and rest a bit."

Then I burst into tears and sobbed.

I had always forced myself not to think about my little family, and all it took was that damn dream to demoralize me. I shouldn't have gone to sleep.

"Come on guy, don't lose your nerve. Thinking about your family is exactly what should give you courage."

That maddening depression lasted for a few minutes, but I finally reasoned my way out of it and dominated my feelings.

Karlsruhe.

What struck me the most[2] were the station buildings, completely bombed out.

Pforzheim.

I knew Pforzheim[3] because I had been there in 1936. The women, at their windows, waved cheerily at the soldiers in the observation boxes, but they quickly saw that this wasn't a military convoy. It was a band of enemies of the Third Reich, terrorists and Jews....The hands fluttered down and the smiles faded and froze in scorn.

---

1. Robert Masset, already cited.
2. Albert Canac, already cited.
3. Georges Bixel, already cited.

Stuttgart.

Now the train was rolling[1] through a green countryside covered with beautiful pine forests, a landscape which couldn't have failed to charm us, if only things had been different. I saw a khaki uniform in a field, but washed out and dirty. A French soldier, no doubt a prisoner of war. I couldn't help envying him. I would have liked so much to be in his place!

Ulm.

Depression. We were in Germany. The houses were different, they were completely painted in neutral colors and merged into the fields. Without being able to foresee the horrible fate in store for us, we felt ourselves, this time, bereft of our country.

Daylight again. The sky was grey. We were gnawed by hunger and parched by thirst. We saw the fields and villages slowly file past, and the stations with names that meant nothing to us. How long could we keep on rolling like this? It didn't matter any more where we were going—but I just wanted to get there.

Then, a bigger station, copiously bombarded. This time the name was very familiar to French ears, Ulm. And just think, one of my great-grandfathers, a general of Napoleon's Empire, distinguished himself there in 1805. If only he could see his descendant at this moment....

* * *

A long halt.[2] The lights in the waiting room were camouflaged, and people passed before us on the platform. They were curious about the unbearable odor coming from our train. They looked furtively in our direction, held their noses, and moved away without saying a word, with a bleak and resigned air. Were they ashamed? In any event, there was no enthusiasm on their faces.

1. Père de La Perraudière, already cited.
2. Albert Canac, already cited.

Burgau.

It was raining.[1] We could breathe. We drank a little, I guess a spoonful. The train "Nach Ulm" (for Ulm) was waiting in this little station. A young girl stared at our phantom train. She seemed to be the only one, in the midst of the indifferent crowd, to take an interest in us. She kept on looking, backed up against the wall of the station, wiped away a tear and made a little sign of greeting with her hand. That was twenty-six years ago, and nevertheless, I still remember how extraordinary this gesture seemed. Maybe it was unique.

Augsburg.

The German reactions[2] to the sight of our convoy were very diverse. Some of them, particularly the young, pointed at us and jeered: "Juden! Alles ins Krematorium!" This was the case, for example, when we stopped at the station in Augsburg on the morning of July 5. Our train stopped near a convoy of youngsters, wearing the armband of the Hitler youth. They were enormously amused at the sight of us and threw stones through the air openings. These boyish faces revealed total hate. Others, particularly the older ones, glanced at us rapidly and then hurried away, their faces scowling and worried.

* * *

In spite of the fact[3] that this was a very important industrial city for the German war effort, we saw no signs of destruction there....
Where had the allied bombs landed?
A ruined city would have been the greatest consolation for us, but there was nothing like that here, nothing at all to mend our shattered hopes. Guesses ran riot in an effort to explain one thing or another. Our brave little Lajoix,

1. Roger Dartout, already cited.
2. Albert Canac, already cited.
3. J.-B. Perreolaz, already cited.

pulled himself up as best he could, till his shortsighted eyes were level with the opening. He searched from side to side, but not a single ruin. We're probably not in the right place, or perhaps everything has been cleaned up. The factories are certainly underground by now, or else the Allied aviators are bad shots.

All of this verbal play allowed us to forget our present situation and our lamentable physical state for a few hours. When our minds were busy, we were able to forget reality somewhat, to divert our thoughts from our manifold sufferings and our thirst, but the terrible smell which had served us as atmosphere for the past forty-eight hours was all-pervasive.

This spirit of vengeance and hate which we felt for everything German was to remain with us during the whole period of our deportation. It boomeranged back as glacial indifference to the terrible trials that these people would later undergo.

The moral contorsion and humiliating brutality shown by the S.S. toward human beings influenced us for a long time and made even the most sensitive among us harden and recoil.

Munich.

About eleven o'clock in the morning[1] we reached Munich.... München! Some of the men told us that this must mean that we were going to Dachau. Most of us knew the name, knew it almost too well. It was probably the oldest concentration camp in Germany. It should be well organized and equipped!... Dubious consolation.

It was almost noon. Maybe we'd get something to eat. But we stayed for over an hour, forgotten at the platform. We were worried, even anguished because we realized that we were getting close to the end of our voyage.... Our Raft of the Medusa was going to reach a shore, but what shore?

* * *

1.   J.-B. Perreolaz, already cited.

Final surprise.[1] I heard French being spoken on the platform. The men outside were prisoners of war. One of them approached and I gave him a brief account of what had happened and where we came from. I also told him that there were some dead in the car, and that we had lost forty-nine others en route. I asked him to notify my family. He seemed astonished. He said that the Germans had announced the arrival of a train of "French terrorists," bound for a camp called Dachau. Other comrades asked him to take their names and addresses in France, and notify their families. There wasn't time enough, because the Germans forced him away.

*   *   *

Munich.[2] It was raining. I noticed a soldier watching our car. He wore the "Luftwaffe" (air army) uniform. The German immediately told me that we were going to the concentration camp of Dachau, about twenty kilometers west of Munich. The word had a sinister significance for me. About 1935 my German professor had read us a book entitled "The Camp in the Swamps." It described the martyrdom of the unfortunate prisoners—Jews, Communists, Socialists, or German Christians, hostile to Nazism—who were building the first Nazi horror camp in the swamps of Dachau, working under terrible conditions. During all that time, the good folk of Europe were sleeping with a tranquil conscience and a soul at peace!

"Alles Schlimm!" the sentry said to me. "Yes, everything is very bad!"

*   *   *

In a locomotive on the track nearest to us[3] we saw a French prisoner of war.

"Hey, Frenchy, do you know where we're going?"

"Perhaps to Dachau. It's a camp about twenty kilometers from here."

1.   M. Habermacher, already cited.
2.   Albert Canac, already cited.
3.   Robert Masset, already cited.

We didn't want to talk too much with this compatriot because we noticed that he didn't seem too eager to answer. He was probably afraid of being called to order by the "Fritzes" who were standing nearby.

Dachau Station.

We started again,[1] going backward this time, and the train stopped an hour later. The doors opened. An S.S. officer, holding a handkerchief over his mouth and nose, ordered us out. The door was on the wrong side of the train and we had to jump. I jumped, but my legs refused to support me. I sprawled on the trackbed. A blow with a gun butt brought me to my knees. A dog bit my leg. I crawled on all fours, like an animal, to rejoin the flock that was shaping up along the track. It was three, by the station clock, when we arrived at Dachau.

* * *

Dachau.[2] It didn't seem that anyone reacted, but a shiver ran through me. It is true that before the war very few Frenchmen knew that name, which has since become infamous. Because of the relationship between the French and the German young Catholic movements, I was better informed than most about the Hitlerian system in the concentration camps. It was at Dachau that Probst, the leader of the German young Catholics, had been imprisoned and shot down. Naturally "in an attempt to escape," according to the consecrated formula. And so it was in this odious slaughterhouse that the survivors of our unfortunate convoy were going to be dumped....

The doors slid on their rollers.

"Raus! Schnell! Everybody out."

My God.... The cars were opened, one after the other, and we were the last. In this way we had to pass in front of all the others and we saw the grouped wreckage of the living men, and also we saw the dead. All of them

1. Henri Liotier, already cited.
2. Père de La Perraudière, already cited.

had not been piled into separate cars, there were more,
and still more. How many could there be?

* * *

Dachau.[1] I almost burst out laughing, and still I didn't
want to laugh.

When I was a prisoner of war, the civilian Germans
with whom we worked spoke in hushed voices of a
terrible place where the State sent its enemies. Schneider,
a chauffeur for the Vogelsang Firm and a member of the
Nazi Party, when he caught me trying to sabotage the
morale of the workers, would always say, "You're going
to end up in Dachau."

Well and good. Here we are in Dachau.

* * *

I had read an article[2] about the camp before the war,
so when I saw the name of the station, I turned toward
Kienzler and asked him if he caught the significance....

As we got off the train we both fell right into the arms
of Professor Lassus from Strasbourg, where he had
begun his outstanding series of professorships. First
there, then in Saigon and Algeria, and finally in the
Sorbonne. I don't know how he conveyed such a sense
of human warmth at that moment. Perhaps it was the air
of Bavaria, perhaps it was talking together about his
young children whom I had treated for a while before my
arrest.

* * *

The three survivors of the metal car rolled on the
roadbed.

"Stand up."

André Gonzalès didn't have the strength. His head
swam. All he could see were tiny lights dancing before
his eyes, under his swollen lids.

1. Gabriel Rykner, already cited.
2. Doctor Paul Weil, already cited.

He heard someone say, he didn't know whether it was in French or German:

"All three are dead."

A hand on his shoulder. A gentle voice.

"Come on, kid. One more little effort. Get up. I'm going to help you. I'm Abbé Goutaudier...we talked together at Compiègne.

"Monsieur l'Abbé...."

"Just one more effort!"

André Gonzalès staggered, and leaned on the shoulder of the lame old priest.

"Monsieur l'Abbé.... What about the two others? There were three of us alive in the car."

"I have looked at the two others. They are dead."

"But they were alive when the doors were opened."

"They're dead. Let's go on now."

Dachau

$\mathcal{S}$lowly,[1] those who had not been released from all this useless cruelty, and who were not "dead today, and forever dead," marched in file, with dragging steps, toward a crushing future, without hope.

These men who marched through the village of Dachau, under the hostile stares of the inhabitants, were completely different from those who had gotten into the train three days before.

They knew now that they had been caught up in the gears of a pitiless machine which would lead them through humiliations and degradations, and reduce them to their most basic animal instincts.

A few understood, as they trudged down the road to Dachau, that all that was left of them to show that they were still men was that which went beyond man—the soul.

* * *

True enough,[2] we looked like hallucinations of horror,

1. Jacques Lutz, already cited.
2. J.-B. Perreolaz, already cited.

more like professional beggars from the Court of the Miracles than like human beings. We formed a column of destitutes, just released from an asylum for scarecrows, with Easter-egg heads, and hairy, filthy repulsive faces, red, empty eyes, and our jerking, stumbling walk, like badly regulated, automatic toys.

The men and women along the boulevard that led to the "world apart" of the concentration camp really had a circus at which to laugh and jeer when they saw, passing by, these tumblers and mountebanks of death....

Children threw stones at us and shouted dirty words. I was at the edge of the column, and I saw a little boy, six years, maybe eight, all blond and rosy, who aimed at us with his tiny slingshot. His military cap of the Hitler Youth rested proudly on his head.

There were a lot of S.S. guards, and they were all laughing, too, with loud appreciation of the comments of the civilians, and I can say truly that I was unable to see the least trace of compassion in all that mass of Germans, who looked us over at their leisure.

* * *

Up front,[1] everything was regular: at the rear, a very old priest was being bitten by the dogs. I put an end to the show by having him take my place in the line...and I inherited the canine treatment. I started to walk faster. The kids threw stones at us, and one treated me to a magnificent gob of spit right in the face. Thank you. We weren't walking anymore, we were running....The first to slow down would get it....There was a butcher shop to my right. A woman, dressed in black, stood there alone, in her hand a bouquet of flowers the colors of the flag of France. I couldn't believe it. Two other comrades behind me also saw her. They said to me: "That woman... it's not possible."

* * *

1. Unpublished manuscript of Elzéar Gérard, August 1970.

Our faces were swollen,[1] so misshapen that we could not recognize each other. We saw, in the glances of some civilians that they weren't very proud, and a few of them turned away. Between the station and the camp two children, about ten and twelve, came up to me and said, in German: "Be brave, Mein Herr, the war is soon finished." You can't imagine how much good that did me.

*   *
*

At a crossroad,[2] a terrible poster held my attention, in spite of everything. A strange sort of bas-relief was mounted on a column about two meters high. It depicted a scene in which S.S. soldiers, looking warlike and resolute, dragged, toward the nearby concentration camp, a rapacious Jew, a chubby priest, and a fat and funny business man. In the background a crowd of splendid Aryans applauded.

*   *
*

A sharp order rang out: "Achtung! Mützen ab!"[3]
This is translated as, "Attention. Hats off." Almost everybody understood, and removed their headgear before arriving in front of the S.S. officer, but a few of them were lost in their own thoughts and walked on, with their heads covered.
Two S.S. on each side of the column were assigned the mission of snatching off the headgear of those who had forgotten to doff it, and to stamp it underfoot. Then they slapped the delinquent and kicked him brutally in the ass.

*   *
*

We passed in front of a number of civilians.[4] I noticed an old lady who looked at us with compassion. However,

1.   Unpublished manuscript of Albert Peolot, June 1970.
2.   A. Canac, already cited.
3.   H. Lambert, already cited.
4.   Père de La Perraudière, already cited.

some of my comrades told me that they had seen children shake their fists at us and curse us.

I was walking next to a French commissioner of police whose legs were almost paralyzed and could hardly support his weight, let alone move ahead. A young fellow from Sarthe was with me. I can still see him, with the seat of his pants in shreds. He told me that they were torn like that from being horsewhipped so much. We held the commissioner up under his arms and dragged him along with us. But we couldn't move very quickly. No matter how slowly the rest of the line hobbled along, they all passed us, one after the other. Next we were in the very last row, and then trailing. Now there was nothing behind us except the S.S. and...their dogs.

"The Devil take it."

From time to time, they shouted at us to keep us moving: "Schnell! Laufen! Quick. Run."

But how could we run with our cripple? And if we started, we'd have to keep it up. I made a sign to the boy from Sarthe that we should try to look as if we were willing, and walk a bit faster, but not run.

I tried to indicate to the S.S. that running was impossible.

The dogs barked ferociously, and nearer and nearer to us. In another minute we would be bitten.... It couldn't be helped. Running would be worse than anything else. We'd wait....The barks were so close that they were right at our heels. Without a doubt, the S.S. held their beasts back on the leash, because we weren't bitten. Then, before us, was the camp itself, with an inscription in colored tile on the roof, "Arbeit macht frei."

"Work is freedom—what a pious fraud!"

We enter the door. To the right of the column stood a haggard, headshaven wretch dressed in striped prison issue. He had escaped and been re-arrested, for he wore, around his neck a placart with a heavily ironic message, "Ich bin wieder da" (Here I am, back again). He had been placed there for our benefit, and would probably soon be hung. This ploy was to discourage any hope of flight. Yes, yes. "All hope abandon, ye who enter here."

5:00 p.m.—Dachau Concentration Camp.

Edmond Michelet, the clandestine leader of the French deportees, as he returned to the dispensary, saw Abbé Jost crossing the deserted Freiheitsstrasse. How had he dared to leave his office in the Political Department at this time of day? Something important must have happened to prompt such a displacement.

"What's happening?"

"Frightful. Hundreds of dead. A trainload of dead!"

And Jost disappeared.

The oldtimers among the prisoners,[1] like him, were always afraid when they had to walk around in the camp during work hours. They felt that they were personally targeted by the S.S. sentry in his watchtower, surveying all comings and goings. Obviously, every conversation was suspect. So I kept moving as fast as I could, curious and vaguely uneasy.

The Records Office in the infirmary was one of the most picturesque corners of the establishment, nestled between the morgue and the dental office, reserved for big shots and Kapos, who were received in a bright, clean room with a scrubbed floor. The *Zugänge* (new arrivals) passed through here to be inscribed in the Register. Dressed in medical board issue, they were measured, weighed and auscalted. Two secretaries, in prison stripes, slowly inscribed all the details on an index card which had previously been filled in by the *Pfleger* (administration officer). The inventory of gold teeth was maintained with particular care.

Ever since the inauguration of the camp, precise "medical" files had been established for each *Häftling* (prisoner). That made a big file record. Carefully labelled and arranged on the shelves, they filled all the walls of the room. During the days just before the final collapse, when the S.S. Chief Surgeon was terrified and ordered the destruction of these archives, we could get some idea of the tonnage by the length of time it took to burn

1.   Edmond Michelet, *Rue de la Liberté*, Editions du Seuil, Paris 1955.

them—and we could very well guess that they were full of interesting material by the alacrity with which they were made to disappear.

Joseph Jost and another Häftling handled the secretarial work of this surprising institution, which was a model of what can be done in the way of window-dressing. The comrade of Jost was an old German Communist, with a square head, like Marshal Hindenburg's. He had been arrested ten years before at Lübeck, and like Willy, had gone through unspeakable torture. Jost interpreted one day, when he gave me a ferociously mocking account of an "institutional specialty" that he had been one of the few to survive, as he told me. He described having been enclosed in a sort of strange closet or cupboard where they tried to asphyxiate him scientifically to extract confessions. The good Jost described him as a wild old boar with a tough hide. These two stalwart old men in the Registry Office superbly symbolized the famous alliance of the Cross with the hammer and sickle.

On this fifth of July, 1944, I found them in the middle of their dossiers, as they had been on the previous days, when I helped them to card-index the anatomy of the French from the convoy of Compiègne. Swida was there. He was one of the regulars in the Registry Office. He was gatling on, as usual, with a piercing and precipitous outflow, but we could see that there was something extraordinary about his emotion from his excessive gestures and the angry beating of his fist on the table. He was kind enough not to leave me in suspense for long, but immediately started to translate the end of his diatribe: the *Lagerobersturmführer* (chief camp director) himself was indignant at what had just happened, he told me.

"... I shall inform Berlin about this," he stated publicly upon the arrival of the train. "Those responsible shall be punished."

I linked these words with the enigmatic information provided by Abbé Jost. The truth only came through in scraps of knowledge in this strange world where nobody knew anything about anything and where the reconstitution of the slightest fact was obtained by making a sort of patchwork of the bits and pieces.

As Swida finished his speech, we looked out of the window onto the Appellplatz and saw a column of new arrivals coming into the camp. This convoy didn't look like the others. These Zugänge were abnormally loaded with baggage and what was even more astonishing to us was that, despite the black-jacks and the yapping S.S., they straggled in the most incredible disorder toward the showers instead of marching, as usual, in well-disciplined ranks. But what connection could there be between such strange disorder and the mysterious culpability that Swida had alluded to? I only learned later on: we were looking at the survivors of the Death Train.

* * *

Gigantic; Abbé Fabing was truly gigantic.[1] Square-faced, high, rosy cheeks, shoulders of a wrestler, heavy-boned and muscled, and always wearing an astonishing officer's cap which he had had made secretly with "Feldgrau" cloth, which he had picked up in the Jewish "surplus" stores—the tailor asked to be paid in three rations of margarine and two slices of bread. His suit was cut in "central European" style, and a cross of Saint Andrew was sewn between the shoulder blades. Abbé Fabing was the voice, the enormous voice of Dachau, on that July 5th. He was going to bellow out the roll call.

It was Schelling,[2] an Austrian priest, in charge of the chapel and dean of the churchmen, who informed me that I had been assigned to call the roll. He told me that I would have to act as an interpreter under oath and that I would have to be very careful because I would be under observation through field glasses to make sure that no objects of value or family souvenirs were handed to me....I had been very successful at getting away with it during the roll call of the previous convoy, with the complicity of Dr. Roche, who walked about among the new arrivals. I was the only one assigned to the roll call,

1. See the *Witches of the Sky.*
2. Unpublished manuscript of Abbé Fabing, February 1970.

and I had a number of secretary-interpreters responsible for getting individual data.

In the central assembly yard,[1] tables had been set up, and behind them were stationed German and Polish secretaries, deportees like ourselves. I had been selected for this task because I was the only one in my block of forty men who spoke German. I had to put the standard questions to the new arrivals. Family name? First name? Date and place of birth? Married or single? Profession? Person to notify in case of accident? *(sic)* Religion? Private address?...And the essential question: Number of gold teeth?

The survivors gathered in the assembly yard,[2] on the planting and infirmary barrack side. All the men in this convoy were almost totally catatonic and couldn't even have communicated to each other the hells they had been through in their individual cars. I had been through the terrible initiation of torture myself and so I could feel the terror that gripped them, the drama they must have lived through on the way here. The S.S. kept walking back and forth and told me to be extremely careful of my list of names because there were no other copies. I had to check off the names of the dead, or as they delicately put it: "Those failing to respond to the roll call."

*   *   *

A few drops of rain.
The survivors of the Death Train, left to themselves in this assembly yard, clustered in groups and tried to find their friends.

Young Jacques,[3] about nineteen years old, taken as a hostage at Tulle, had been my student in the grammar school of the Epinal troops. He was terrified and avoided looking at me. I said: "Look me in the eyes. What's

1.   Unpublished manuscript of Jean Berthelemy, March 1970.
2.   Abbé Fabing, already cited.
3.   Unpublished manuscript of Henri Huyard, already cited.

wrong with you?" He answered: "I killed a man, a
madman who rushed me....I cracked his skull with a
bottle."

Abbé Fabing stood up on a barrel and an S.S. non-
com stood beside him and sheltered him under a huge,
black umbrella. This would have been, doubtless, unique
in the history of any concentration camp, except for the
fact that he was simply trying to protect that precious
list....A hundred meters away from the gathering, the
S.S. general staff of the camp was plunged in deep
discussion. Sturmbannführer Weiter, usually so calm,
appeared furious.

The non-com with the umbrella told Abbé Fabing to
translate his orders:

"Line up in columns of five."

"Keep silent."

"Begin the roll call."

Abbé Fabing shouted out the names:

"Abadie, Maurice?"

Silence.

"Abadie, Maurice?"

A murmur.

"Louder."

"He's dead."

"Abadie, René?"

"Present."

"Albagnac, Gilbert?"

"Present."

"Allacouf, Maurice?"

"Present."

"Allègre, Pierre?"

"Died for France."

"Alliot, Marcel?"

"Died for France."

"Amery, Maurice?"

"Died for France."

In the distance, Sturmbannführer Weiter took leave of
his officers and walked toward his headquarters. An S.S.
came into the assembly yard of the deportees and called
out:

"There was a car in which everybody died except one
man. Where is he?"

The third deportee he questioned pointed out André
Gonzalès.

"Kindly follow me."

* * *

At his table Jean Berthelemy was questioning one of
the first men to be called.

When I asked him his religion,[1] he answered, "I am
Israelite." I was very embarrassed particularly because an
S.S. non-com was a few steps away. I suggested that it
would be more convenient to chose being either Catholic
or Protestant. But he had made up his mind and said that
he didn't want to go back on his word. At that point the
S.S. came over to tell me not to talk so much with the
comrades, and started hitting us. I tried to justify myself
by telling the S.S. that he was a friend. After this lively
little interlude, I told our comrade that this was just a
glimpse of what our prison life was like. I asked him if he
still wanted to stick with his decision. He replied, "Write
down anything you like." So then I said, "From now on
you're a Protestant."

* * *

André Gonzalès, in rags, covered with pus, blood and
shit, sat in the big leather armchair. On the other side of
the desk was the Kommandant of Dachau. The interpreter
remained standing.

I hadn't yet understood[2] what a concentration camp
was. Nobody had told me to sit down, but since there
was an armchair and I was tired....
He made me explain and tell him all the details about
the trip. I told him what had taken place in my car and
what must have taken place in the others. He was
surprised, actually astonished. He told me that the
convoy guards had explained to the S.S. of Dachau that

1. Jean Berthelemy, already cited.
2. Statement of André Gonzalès, May 1970.

there had been a settling of accounts between the
Gaullists and the Communists, F.T.P. and the F.F.I.
(Francs-tireurs et partisans and the Forces Françaises de
l'intérieur) .... I continued telling about the heat, the lack of
water, the suffocation, and the general madness. He
looked deeply affected, and he went on to say: "I'm
asking you to tell your comrades that the chief of the
convoy will be shot."[1]

André Gonzalès was taken to the showers, and then
directly to the infirmary.

In the assembly yard, Abbé Fabing was ordered to
return the precious list to a non-commissioned officer:

"You will continue the roll call tomorrow."

As Albert Canac left the central yard, going down
"Freiheitstrasse" (Freedom Street), he saw an enormous
tile inscription standing out on one of the roofs:

"Es gibt nur einen Weg zur Freiheit. Seine Meilen
heissen: Gehorsam, Nüchternheit, Sauberkeit und Fleiss!"
(There is only one road to freedom. Its milestones
are named: obedience, sobriety, cleanliness and hard
work.)

* * *

1. It is certain, see the chapter "The Righteous Wrath of Franz
Mulherr" that an investigation was opened, at the demand of the
top echelon (Himmler). The German records have disappeared,
so we will never know what conclusions were reached.

The first officer in charge of convoy of the 7909, that young
S.D. officer, it seems, was never sought by the various French
and Allied services assigned to pick up war criminals. As for the
second convoy officer, Friedrich Dietrich, he was called up
before the a French Military Tribunal in February 1950, because
Franz Mulherr, the Sarrebourg station commissioner had sent in
a report on the "Sarrebourg Incident" to the commander of his
camp of war prisoners, and this had been forwarded. Friedrich
Dietrich was condemned to death by the jury of Metz in the
course of a trial which, it must be acknowledged, fell far short in
its preparation and legal detachment. Three years later, Dietrich
died of pneumonia in his tiny apartment in Mannheim. In spite of
extensive search, I was never able to find any of his children
who, they told me, "changed their name and left the Federal
Republic."

We were led to blocks 21 and 23[1] and an exceptionally delicious soup of pearl barley was distributed to us. And as a final solicitude, we had the right to a "meat sack" wrapped in clean oiled paper. And the next day, reveille was sounded for us at six o'clock, instead of at four.

It took four days[2] for the Dachau Krematorium to devour the 536 cadavers carried to it by the Death Train.

For the 1,630 survivors, another life, another death had begun.

THE END

1. Albert Canac, already cited.
2. See Annex IV.

ANNEXES

Annex I

LIST OF ARRIVALS
AT THE CAMP OF COMPIÈGNE
(MAY AND JUNE 1944)[1]

Date of Arrival	Number arriving	Coming from
May 2	45	Lyons
May 3	1	Beauvais
May 3	27	Fresnes
May 3	58	Chambéry
May 3	39	Moulins
May 3	5	Amiens
May 3	10	Annemasse
May 4	61	Perpignan
May 4	18	Dijon
May 4	20	Caen
May 4	26	Saint-Brieuc
May 4	42	Périgueux
May 5	58	Saint-Etienne
May 5	27	Lons-le-Saunier

1. 98% of the deportees of the "Death Train" were interned at Compiègne during May and June 1944.

Date of Arrival	Number arriving	Coming from
May 5	25	Amiens et Saint-Quentin
May 6	19	Toulouse
May 7	24	Chambéry
May 8	37	Reims-Châlons
May 8	31	Fresnes
May 8	99	Blois
May 9	17	Montpellier
May 10	28	Fresnes
May 10	19	Dijon
May 11	9	Grenoble
May 11	57	Chalon-sur-Saône
May 11	407	Chartres
May 11	25	Saint-Quentin
May 12	493	Bordeaux
May 12	20	Fontainebleau
May 12	4	Brest
May 13	63	Rennes
May 13	67	Lyons
May 13	12	Compiègne
May 13	2	Vannes
May 14	146	Limoges
May 14	41	Nantes
May 14	96	Marseilles
May 14	16	Chambéry
May 14	171	Toulouse
May 16	21	Orléans
May 17	36	Amiens
May 17	27	Toulouse-Montpellier
May 18	159	La Rochelle-Tours-Poitiers
May 18	6	Paris
May 18	64	Fresnes
May 18	59	Dijon
May 18	56	Clermont-Ferrand
May 18	22	Rouen
May 18	9	Quimper
May 20	23	Grenoble
May 20	9	Charleville

Date of Arrival	Number arriving	Coming from
May 20	25	Saint-Quentin
May 20	28	Caen
May 21	59	Lyons
May 21	20	Nancy
May 22	16	Châlons-sur-Marne
May 22	27	Troyes
May 23	29	Angoulême
May 23	306	Montauban
May 23	66	Marseilles
May 23	6	Brest
May 23	35	Fresnes
May 23	2	Saint-Denis
May 24	60	Dijon
May 24	31	Fresnes
May 25	38	Alençon
May 25	63	Rennes
May 27	18	Saint-Quentin
May 27	15	Rouen
May 28	48	Limoges
May 28	89	Bordeaux
May 28	38	Montpellier
May 29	39	Saint-Etienne
May 29	57	Angers
May 30	66	Marseilles
May 30	37	Fresnes-Orléans
May 31	5	Caen
May 31	66	Le Mans
June 1	2	Vannes
June 1	63	Dijon-Châlon
June 2	29	Fontainebleau
June 2	33	Orléans
June 3	6	Brest
June 3	55	Moulins
June 3	106	unknown origin
June 3	62	Annecy

June 4   Departure of 2,058 prisoners for Neuengamme

Date of Arrival	Number arriving	Coming from
June 5	28	Fresnes
June 6	6	Chambéry
June 7	25	Béziers
June. 7	66	Châlons-sur-Marne
June 8	22	Evreux
June 8	122	Dijon-Besançon
June 8	56	Amiens
June 9	31	Nantes
June 9	30	Rouen
June 9	53	Fresnes
June 10	71	Clermont-Ferrand
June 10	60	Angers
June 10	21	Paris
June 12	14	Fresnes
June 12	8	Grenoble
June 12	16	Paris
June 13	34	Paris
June 13	26	Saint-Quentin
June 13	27	Fresnes
June 13	23	Saint-Quentin
June 15	283	Limoges
June 15	67	Montpellier-Narbonne-Béziers
June 15	27	Fresnes
June 16	30	Châlons-sur-Marne
June 16	1	Beauvais
June 17	65	Clermont-Ferrand
June 17	64	Fresnes
June 17	60	Angers
June 17	146	Blois

| June 18 | Departure of 2,145 prisoners for Dachau | |

June 19	293	Toulouse
June 19	53	Toulouse-Sanaut
June 20	29	Châlons-sur-Marne
June 22	154	Lyons
June 22	23	Laon

April 29, 1945: thousands of prisoners liberated from the Dachau camp by the Americans. Recoiling before the Allied advance, the S.S. troops had sent a large number of transports to Germany, under the orders of Himmler, who didn't want to leave a single man alive in the hands of the Allies. These orders could only be partially carried out.
Keystone

Date of Arrival	Number arriving	Coming from
June 22	25	Romainville
June 23	22	Perpignan
June 23	194	Poitiers
June 23	2	Compiègne
June 23	30	Châlons-sur-Marne
June 23	30	Fresnes
June 24	55	Rouen
June 24	118	Clermont-Ferrand-Dijon-Besançon-Chalon-Moulins
June 24	17	Rennes
June 24	6	Compiègne-Senlis
June 24	15	Rennes
June 24	98	Saint-Etienne
June 25	51	Toulouse
June 26	29	Fresnes
June 26	9	Beauvais
June 26	46	Le Mans
June 27	20	Charleville
June 28	39	Grenoble
June 29	1	Compiègne
June 29	157	Riom
June 29	33	Orléans
June 29	40	Fresnes
June 29	8	Rouen
July 2	55	Châlons-sur-Marne-Alençon

July 2	Departure of 2,166 prisoners for Dachau, "Death Train," see Annex IV

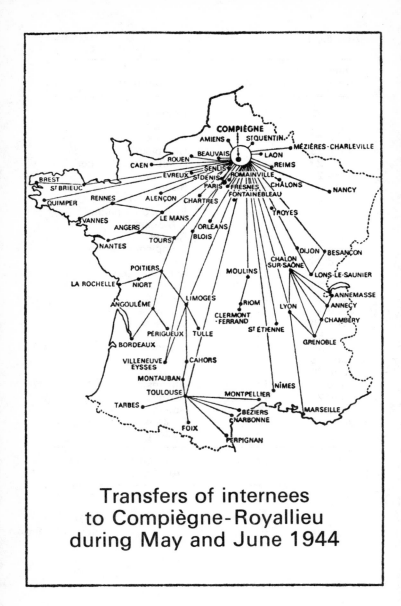

Transfers of internees
to Compiègne-Royallieu
during May and June 1944

CONVOYS LEAVING COMPIÈGNE

Date of departure	Number leaving	Destination
March 20, '42	178	Drancy
March 27, '42	1,112	Auschwitz
June 5, '42	1,007	Auschwitz
June 6, '42	1,034	Auschwitz
Sept. 23, '42	unknown	Brunswick
Jan. 13, '43	unknown	Buchenwald
Jan. 23, '43	1,604	Sachsenhausen
Feb. '43	700	Buchenwald
March '43	250	Buchenwald
March '43	222	Mauthausen
April '43	100	Buchenwald
April 16, '43	991	Mauthausen
April 21, '43	987	Mauthausen
April 28, '43	962	Sachsenhausen
April 28, '43	214	Ravensbrück
May 8, '43	1,003	Sachsenhausen
June 26, '43	962	Buchenwald

Date of departure	Number leaving	Destination
Aug. 7, '43	unknown	Buchenwald
Aug. 12, '43	unknown	Buchenwald
Sept. 3, '43	unknown	Neue-Bremm
Sept. 17, '43	1,004	Buchenwald
Sept. 23, '43	unknown	Neue-Bremm
Oct. 20, '43	unknown	Neue-Bremm
Oct. 29, '43	1,003	Buchenwald
Nov. 21, '43	unknown	unknown
Dec. 9, '43	unknown	Neue-Bremm
Dec. 14, '43	921	Buchenwald
Jan. 17, '44	1,940	Buchenwald
Jan. 22, '44	1,990	Buchenwald
Jan. 24, '44	121	Ravensbrück
Jan. 27, '44	1,581	Buchenwald
Jan. 31, '44	958	Ravensbrück
Feb. '44	650	Neue-Bremm
Feb. '44	160	Neuengamme
March 22, '44	1,219	Mauthausen
March 26, '44	50	Mauthausen
April 5, '44	unknown	Mauthausen
April 17, '44	unknown	Mauthausen
April 27, '44	1,654	Auschwitz
May 12, '44	2,052	Buchenwald
May 21, '44	1,986	Neuengamme
May 27, '44	unknown	Mauthausen
June 4, '44	2,058	Neuengamme
June 18, '44	2,145	Dachau
July 2, '44	Departure of 2,166 prisoners by the "Death Train"	
July 8, '44	unknown	Ravensbrück
July 15, '44	1,509	Neuengamme
July 18, '44	unknown	Ravensbrück
July 28, '44	1,651	Neuengamme
Aug. 11, '44	1,650	Buchenwald
Aug. 16, '44	1,251	Buchenwald
	(Last deportation train)	

Date of departure	Number leaving	Destination
Aug. 17, '44	100 women leave by bus for Ravensbrück	
Aug. 26, '44	300 deportees are liberated at Péronne. The engineer had directed his train behind the Allied lines.	

CONVOYS LEAVING FRANCE

There is no general study of convoys of deportees sent to Germany. The report of the French government (Document F 274, page 124 of Tome 37 of the Military Tribunal of Nuremberg) does not furnish "a complete accounting of the convoys, but provides a sufficient number to indicate the gradation of the process, not including the convoys leaving directly from Alsace and Lorraine."

1940:   3 convoys
1941:   19 convoys
1942: 104 convoys
1943: 275 convoys
1944: 326 convoys (from January 1, 1944 to August 25, i.e. an average of 10 convoys per week).

CONVOY OF JULY 2, 1944
"THE DEATH TRAIN"

Leaving Compiègne:	2,166
Dead en route:	536
Registered on arrival:	1,630

On the evening of July 5, 1944, the survivors of the Death Train compared their estimates of the losses they had sustained in travel....This was by no means easy because most of the deportees did not know the identity of the other "voyagers" in their cars. The word went from mouth to mouth, sustained by rumors, passed on by block leaders and camp personalities, that there were "more than a thousand dead."

By the next day the number had fallen to 870 (we were 2,500 at departure, 1,630 were alive at roll call, hence 870 died in transit). But nobody had actually held the departure list in his hand, except Abbé Fabing, and he confirmed the fact to me that he had not had time to count the names. The Kommandant of Dachau was in a great hurry to get the list back (the unique, one-and-only copy. Remember the umbrella held over the head of Abbé Fabing by an S.S. guard during part of the roll call.)

During the following days, the guess rose again to 984, without our knowing on what logic or what bases the deportees relied to arrive at this figure. And then Eugen Pfeiffer, who took part in unloading the cadavers (but didn't count them) confirmed the figure of 984. In addition, August Thillot, a deportee, said: "I was the first to the left of the column as we came through the gate of the camp. I speak German and I heard the chief of our convoy say, 'I'm bringing you 1,630 pigs from France who stink like the plague. Luckily, 984 of them died during the trip.'" This statement was accepted as true. Furthermore, he repeated this phrase during the trial at Metz and nobody (not even Dietrich's defense) contradicted him...which actually would have been quite easy to do: Dietrich had stayed on the railway platform at Dachau and the S.S. took over the "delivery" of the arrivals. The roll call was to determine the number present, and not the number absent. It had started on the 5th, but was interrupted and only completed on the 6th. However, Thillot's statement was believed at Metz as it had been at Dachau.

At Dachau we were content to accept the truth of the figure 984 (in spite of the fact that some deportees like Michelet, Roche and Lassus found this total too high).

At the Nuremberg trials the French Ministry of Deportees and Prisoners, in its document 274, confined itself to "more than 600 deaths" (Tome XXXVII of the International Military Tribunal, pages 126 and 127). The Tribunal arrived at this figure by comparing a first compilation of the Archives of the Camp of Compiègne with the Register of Enrollment of Dachau, which they had just discovered. (The 1,630 deportees registered on July 6, 1944, were given numbers from 76,418 to 78,047.) Those assigned to the task of preparing the French documents of accusation, had actually been informed, by the lists from Compiègne, that "under no circumstances could the train of July 2 have carried more than 2,200 deportees." To arrive at this figure it was only necessary to subtract the roll call of July 3 (the day following the departure) from the roll call of the last two days of June. Thus, 2,200 less 1,630 equals 570. This total was approximative and obviously logical, and not far from the truth. The figure of "more than 600 deaths" in the official bill of indictment was only a slight exaggeration to cover the margin of error always present in this type of problem.

The trial at Metz, in 1950, did not know about these first researches, which had, nevertheless, been printed in the Official Acts, and they accepted the "truth" of 984 dead. However, during the course of the proceedings, two body counts had been presented: 450 dead at Novéant, when Dietrich took command of the train; and 483 dead on arrival at Sarrebourg. These figures were confirmed by a number of witnesses and were further confirmed in the reports of the inquiry carried out by inspectors responsible for questioning the station railway workers. In spite of the fact that it was Dietrich who gave this "total," it appears credible. What appears considerably less believeable is Dietrich's contention that for the rest of the journey, there was only one additional death. In the chapter devoted to the events at the Sarrebourg station, we saw that Commissioner Mulherr was categoric: 481 dead (plus two deaths in the "infirmary car," La Perraudière-Segelle), which is 483 deaths. This figure was repeated by Robert Mangin when he totalled the numbers chalked on the doors of the cars, and it is also supported by the "jokes" of the convoy escort when on at least three separate occasions, they laughingly informed the Red Cross leaders: "You're going to have five hundred rations too many." And, actually, after the train departed there were about five hundred rations remaining (Metz Trial). Thus, the statement of 483 dead at Sarrebourg appears "acceptable." But since it is claimed that there were not many more deaths after Sarrebourg, the total at arrival must have been 483, minimum.

Obviously, the ideal would have been to have found the original list of departure from Compiègne. There was only a single copy of this document, some of the pages were typed, some handwritten, with many interlinear corrections. It was only in the possession of the Political Section of the Administration of Dachau for a few days, after which it was sent to the Sicherheitspolizei (Security Police S.I.P.O.) of Paris, drawn back to Württemberg. This document had been dispatched on October 9, 1944, (which seems to prove that an investigation had commenced). At the end of the war the archives were burned and the list disappeared forever.

Under these conditions, how would it be possible to make up a list of the dead, for the train of July 2...? Perhaps simply by consulting the death records of Dachau. I examined the original registry. There is only one name inscribed for the day of July 5: Franz Ryz (who had been in the camp for more than a year). It is clear that the bodies taken from the Death Train passed directly to the Crematorium, without being listed.

Since 1945, at the French veterans' administration, Pierre Garban and a group of investigators have been trying to reconstruct the archives of the concentration camps, and particularly the lists of names. They should be able to be successful in about 99% of this "impossible" research. The Death Train poses a number of problems and is the subject of a special study—incomplete, but interesting.

Beginning with the registry book of new arrivals at Compiègne and completing that information with other documents of the camp (roll call lists, barber's records, infirmary, work groups, transfers, partial departures, etc.) the investigators have been able to discover almost all the names of the prisoners of Royallieu. The register was maintained by prisoner-secretaries, more or less accurately, depending on the period, and generally contained the following information: name of prisoner, first name, assigned block, followed by the initial of camp A, B or C, date of birth, and date of convoy departure. This information was not complete in the case of hundreds of prisoners, but some of the data turned up on other lists maintained by the camp, particularly roll calls. After many months of systematic compilation and cross-checking, often with a magnifying glass, Monsieur Garban was able to draw up an alphabetical list of 464 dead, which has never been published.

In 1969 Monsieur Garban recommended that I take over his work which was "surely incomplete, but not too far from having reached the truth." When I accepted to try to reconstruct these records, I had no idea that it would require a year of work and the mobilization of a team of four.

However, even before I became involved in this effort, I had an "accounting" in my possession which seems to me to be as close as possible to the actual facts. An investigation had been opened for the purpose of finding witnesses and getting first-hand accounts, and finally I had a collection of one hundred sixty-one unpublished manuscripts drafted by the "travelers" on the Death Train. This was an invaluable source of information for me, and one which had never been available to any prior investigator. I had been given at least a thousand names of those who were alive on arrival and those who had died on the way. These one hundred sixty-one survivors had been located in different parts of the convoy and I thus had an adequate "sampling" from the whole train. They were able to tell me the exact number of dead in each car, since the dead had been counted several times en route. All that had to be done was to add up their figures:

(1) The metal car of André Gonzalès: one survivor on arrival, 99 dead.
(2) The Rohmer Car (according to seven statements): 76 dead.
(3) The Fully-Thomas Car (four statements): 75 dead.
(4) The Mamon-Garnal Car (nine statements): 75 dead.
(5) The Sirvent-Dhenain Car (eleven statements): 64 dead.
(6) The Canac Car (nine statements): 46 dead.
(7) The Habermacher Car (eleven statements): 44 dead.
(8) The Liotier Car (eight statements): At departure, there were 120 deportees in this car: 36 dead.
(9) The Puyo Car (twelve statements): 17 dead.
(10) and (11) It has been impossible for me to tell exactly how the seventeen survivors I contacted were distributed in each car and to reconstitute a list of occupants. However, it is certain that

the two cars counted (10): 8 dead; and (11): 3 dead.

(12) The "Infirmary Car," La Perraudière-Segelle: 2 dead.

(13) The "Invalids' Car" (according to Abbé Goutaudier): 1 dead.

(14) The Helluy-Aubert-Villiers Car (nine statements: no deaths.

(15) The Lambert Car (ten statements): no deaths.

(16) The Car of Eighty (Chapalain and fifteen statements): no deaths.

(17) The Bernard-Verchuren Car (nine statements): no deaths.

(18) The Lutz-Hamburger Car (ten statements): no deaths.

(19) The Weil-Fuchs-Kienzler Car (seven statements): no deaths.

(20) The Bent-Solladié Car (twelve statements): no deaths.

(21) and (22) Data on these cars is uncertain. I have located about twenty "travelers" whom I haven't been able to place in the other cars. Generally speaking, I have not used their statements in this book. Neither of the cars alter the "accounting," since there were no deaths in them. (21): no deaths; (22) no deaths.

It is obvious that many of the deportees were not in the places attributed to them in the train...however, the listing for the thirteen cars in which there were deaths is accurate.

Two qualifying statements should be made before adding up these figures:

(1) The survivors, after leaving Dachau, believed that there had been only two cars with seventy-five dead, However it has been found, in an incontrovertible manner, that there were three.

(2) The survivors believed that there was only one, or at the most two cars without deaths, while we have found that there were eight and possibly nine.

Total: 546 deaths.

This is the "maximum possible" total. In certain cases I

have eliminated the lower figure. For instance Liotier counted 32 dead, and I have chosen to accept the other estimates from the same car, raising the count to 36 in order to be sure that the count is not diminished, although Liotier's statement seems to me to be perfectly complete and objective.

* * *

In starting the effort at the reconstitution of the list of departure from Compiègne, it seemed to me that an acceptable spread in the death count could be expressed as 483 minimum and 546 maximum (the minimum based on the verification at Sarrebourg, and the maximum on the statements of the survivors). Both figures, 483 and 546 are very far from the 984 put forward at Dachau and at the Metz trial.

It was now necessary to establish a double file system:

(1) The departure file (July 2, at Compiègne).

(2) The arrival file (July 5, at Dachau).

The number of dead can be calculated by deducting file No. 2 from file No. 1.

Working from original documents has presented a number of problems.

(A) *Legibility:* The Register of Compiègne and the lists (roll call, barber, sick bay, etc.) are handwritten and a number of names are indecipherable or partially effaced. Successive photographs at a variety of f-stops have made it possible to establish most of these names.

The original enrollment register of Dachau is typed, and only one matriculation, No. 88,006, has disappeared. But the deportee-secretaries, Germans and Poles, have germanized or polonized the spelling, inversed family and first names, and made many misprints. In order to accord the lists of Compiègne and Dachau, the dates of birth must be compared.

(B) *Homonyms:* In more than ten cases, the given names were the same.

(C) *False names:* Many of the Resistant deportees were arrested under their "pseudos," and kept them at Compiègne (Rival's name was Rykner, etc.).

(D) *Particles:* Where are we to look for Père Bernard Letourneux de La Perraudière?, under L, T, D, P? Depending on the list, he can appear under any of these.

(E) *Statements:* Once the files have been established they must be verified and compared with the mass of statements which have been collected, and whether the deportee had been cited as present or absent at arrival, and finally referring to the study of Pierre Garban and the Ministry of Veterans, to make sure that our conclusions are the same, at least as to the 464 names already indexed.

It is possible that the published list of the dead is not entirely correct. There are surely some spelling errors, but these could be included in the "acceptable spread," and the list can be considered "true" with a margin of error of ten names, more or less.

I. — THE 536 DEAD
OF THE CONVOY OF JULY 2, 1944

Abadie Maurice-Pierre
Abvril Joseph
Allègre Pierre-Roger
Alliot Marcel-Adolphe
Amery Maurice
André Gilbert
André Rolland
Antemayou Georges
Arbaud André
Archambault Maurice
Arnaubec Pierre
Arroserre Bertrand
Asnard Angel
Aubry Albert
Aubuisson Maurice
Baan Bernard
Ballesdent Marcel
Balthazard Robert
Barbaria Albert
Barbazanges Albert
Bare Robert
Bargheon Paul
Barrat Louis
Barribaud Robert
Barrier Auguste
Barrois Marcel
Bartoli Désiré
Barusseau Paul
Basilio Pierre
Bastiat France
Batistini Jean
Baudiffier Marcel
Baudrant Lucien
Baumgartner Roger
Beaudonnat René
Beaupère Claude
Becart Maurice
Becaud Marcel
Becquin Edmond
Beguibistain Julien
Bellanger Maurice
Bellet or
    Bellot Charles
Benet Pierre
Benet Joseph
Bennin André
Berger René
Bernard Maurice
Bernard René
Bernouville René
Berruyer Paul
Bertrand René
    (born Sept. 22, 1913)
Bertrand René
    (born Sept. 2, 1906)
Besançon Bernard
Beucher René

Beynie or
    Beynel Julien
Bigot Jean
Billando Juste
Binet Marcel
Blanc Aimé
Blattes André
Boissier or
    Boissierre André
Bonnetet Georges
Bontemps Roger
Bonvin Marius
Bordet Henri
Borel Guy
Bouillaguet Jean
Boulanger Jean
Boulicault or
    Boulicourt Emile
Bourdeau André
Bourges Francis
Bourguignon Edmond
Bouscatel Robert
Boussard Emile
Bouvier-Paron Emmanuel
Boyer Louis
Brahier Claude
Brahier Jean-Pierre
Bras Jean-Pierre
Brigaldat Henri
Brink Gerardus
Brule André
Buch Auguste
Bulher Maurice
Bugfin des Essarts
    Georges
Busch André
Buissonnet Louis
Caille Pierre
Callame André
Calvo Francis-Louis
Cano Robert
Cappus Albert
Caron Jean
Carpentier Gaëtan
Carre Gérard
Carreau Charles
Cavigioli Lucien
Cesat Henri
Ceuprie Albert
Chalus Marius
Chadrin Michel
Challier Antonnin
Chalmet René
Chambon Louis
Chambonnière Robert
Chambras Jean
Chamrelan Raymond

Champenier Jean-
    Baptiste
Chaneil Jean
Chanel Maurice
Chanudet Raymond
Chapat François
Charpy Robert
Chardon Claudius-
    François
Chardon Gabriel
Charron Marcel
Chassain René
Chaumard Olivier
Chavineil Jean
Chevalier Arthur
Chiffre Pierre
Chosson Antoine
Chuller Denis
Chupin Louis
Claveau Jacques
Clere Claudius
Closset Achille
Closset Joseph
Closset Léon
Coeffic Jean
Cognet Albert
Cohn Léon
Colin Bernard
Collin Lucien
Commercon Joanny
Corbet Henri
Corsenbras Maurice
Coste Jean
Couprie Albert
Courbon Marius-Robert
Couturaud Camille
Crabbe Raoul
Craisset or
    Croizet Roland
Crotti Roméo
Daleme or Dalsme
    Bernard-Fernand
Dambin Emile
Dantheny François-
    Auguste
Dasilva Bernard
Dassaud or
    Daussaud Claude
Dassaud Claude-Vincent
Dauchet Arthur
Daubal Kléber
Debelle Wladimir
Decourcelle Raymond
Decagny Alfred
Délabranche Gaëtan
De Lacroix-Vaubais
    Bernard

Delange Jacques
Delarue or
  Delame Bernard
Delavie André
Delettre Jean
Deleuze Georges
Delorme Marcel
Deplanque Pierre
De Luce alias
  Sebere Pascal
Denegen Pierre (Jean)
Denhaene Paul-Henri
De Peich Raymond
Deplanque Pierre
Depré Jean
Depuy Georges
Derache François
Deschaumes Marcel
Destrieux Léopold
D'Hulst Maurice
Didelot Léon
Diest Pierre
Dintrinchs Charles
Dlang Vincent
Douchet Arthur
Domenech François
Domenech Laurent
Dore Manuel (Marcel)
Dourille Paul-Emile
Drille François
Dromas Raymond
Dubray Marcel
Dubuc Pierre-Marie-Paul
Duchateau Georges
Duchateau Pierre
Ducrot Jean
Ducrocq Alphonse
Duerot or
  Ducrot Gaëtan
Dufaure Léonard
Dufour Elie-René
Duhoux Jean
Dumas Raymond
Dumont Paul
Dupont Louis
Dupuis Gaston
Duro Joseph
Dury Jean
Dussolier or
  Dusselier André
Dutrion Frédéric
Dutestol René
Duverneix André
Duvigean Marcel
Dyonne Augustin
Ecker Pierre
Eloy Henri-René
Ensuque or
  Enauque Paul-Félix
Epelé René
Fabre Roger-Louis
Fanny Jules
Fargerel Daniel

Fauconnier Georges
Faucher Armand
Favre René
Faye Jacques-Pierre
Fischer Bernard
Foliot Robert
Forestier Joseph
Forestier Joseph-Emile
Fortoul Lucien
Fortunade Germain
Foucher Germain
Fournet Alfred
François Pierre
Gabart Julien
Gaillard Jean-Marius
Gaillard Robert
Gaizeau or
  Grizeau Louis
Galand Louis
Gallant Camille
Garnier Emmanuel
Garroux Marcel
Gateau Fernand
Gaubet Jacques
Gaud Marcel
Gauthier Michel
Genay Roger-Georges
Genevoix Marcel
Genez Jean
Gerlot Alfred
Gillot Maurice
Gillard Joseph
Gocres or
  Goeres Marcel
Godard Gilbert
Gonat Maurice
Gontelle Joseph
Gossioux Camille-Lucien
Gossieux Pierre
Goumy Louis
Gourdain Gaston
Graillault Alphonse
Guillam Louis
Guillaume Joseph-
  Edouard
Guillet René
Guillou Roger
Guillou Lucien
Guindet Henri
Guitard Laurent-Jean
Guy Henri
Guyamart André
Hardelin Edouard
Hamel René
Hassler Paul
Heckert Antoine
Hervo Victor
Hilaire Gustave
Hofmann Joseph
Hospital Antoine
Huet Georges
Huguet Louis
Huilier Georges

Hurtault Jean
Infarnet André
Jacobe Raoul
Jaffre Emmanuel
Jakubovicz Jacques
Jame Jacques
Jaouen Raymond
Jardinier André
Jasker Paul
Joffroy Lucien
Jolais Jean
Jonnard Marius
Joulet or
  Jolibet Louis
Jourdan Georges
Jouvenon Louis-Marius
Juillet Albert
Jusseau Jean
Judel Henri
Kicheder Lucien
Kidchlia or
  Kischka Victor
Kosprzyk André
Lacanal Antoine-Jean
Lacassagne Georges
Lagouche Marius-Pierre
Lamoureux Olivier
Landais Pierre
Lapalus Victor
Laporte Léon
Larnaud Georges
Laslier Albert
Lassalle Serge
Laurent Marcel
Lavel Jean
Laveissière Marcel
Lavergne Christophe
Laviolette René
Lavrut or
  Lavaut Georges
Lebec Jean
Leblanc Jean
Le Borgne Yves
Le Bris Jean
Lecointe André
Lecerf Gustave
Leclerc Marcel
Lecouturier Emile
Léon Jean
Le Ferret or
  Leferrec Georges
Lefevre Georges (Jean)
Le Floc André
Le Gac Gérard
Legeay Antoine
Léger Jean
Le Guennec Jacques
Leguillou Edouard
Le Henaff Yves-Henri-
  Léon
Lehou Armand
Lelandais Fernand
Lemacon Henri-Jacques

Henri Liotier, at the liberation of the camp of Allach, April 30, 1945. Placed in quarantine in Dachau in Blocks 17 and 19, with the survivors of the Death Train, he was transferred, on August 11, to the Allach camp. Henri Liotier was one of the 84 survivors in his car, in which there were 36 deaths.
Author's Archives

Lemartel Paul
Lemoigne Joseph
Le Roux Paul
Leroy Gaston
Lesport Marcel
Lestric Jean
Lete Rosa-Aimé
Levasseur Emile
Levialle Claude-Charles
Lombard René
Loth Victor
Louaze Louis
Lucas René-Nicolas
Lusson Robert
Magiard Robert
Maresse Claude
Malet Henri
Manuel Victor-Charles
Marc René
Marcaud Henri
Marquer Francis
Marquis Marius
Martin André
Martin Eugène
Martin Louis-Germain
Martin Roger
Martin-Dupont Jacques
Martin-Garcia Félix
Marre Jean-Marie
Marty Joseph
May Lucien
Massot Lucien-Emile
Massot Pierre
Masson Pierre
Mauren Louis
Mazurek Jean
Mechache Saïd
Meneyrol Henri
Mercier Robert-André
Meric Pierre
Mesnard Jean
Meunier Fernand
Michelon alias
    Marc Macelex
Michelot Roger
Migot Georges
Million Albert
Million Ferdinand
Miqueau or
    Migreau Pierre
Mirabel Maurice-
    Augustin
Moneger Jean
Monnier René
Mony Emile
Morel Henri
Morfouasse François
Moricaut André
Moulin Gilbert
Mouly Antoine
Nacowsky-Domarad
    Jean
Nadeau Jean-Jacques

Naszys-Kiewicz
    Wladyslaw
Navarra Armanos
Neplaz Alfred
Niel Gabriel-Elie
Nikis Mario
Noorlander Ares
Noury Michel-Marie
Oarreau Charles
Olivier Gilbert
Olivier Jean
Paccara Jean-Baptiste
Paquier Emilien
Partarrieu Laurent
Patrice Emile
Pebeyre Pierre
Peghoses or
    Peghabes Joseph
Pegliasco Joseph
Pellicer James
Pennel Robert
Perceau Maurice
Perrier Jean
Perrier Jean-Henri
Perrut Henri
Person Marcel
Pesanet or
    Pesquet Edouard-
    Edmond
Peuch Raymond
Peyriguen Gilbert
Phelippeau René
Philippe André-Jean
Philippe André-Julien
Picon Raymond
Pinetto-Pinette Corrado
Porte Pierre
Piquet Désiré
Poivremaud Lucien
Poncet Jean-Claude
Pontier Marius
Pougnale Césarin
Poujet Roger
Pourradier André
Prat Roger
Puy-Bonnet François
Quero Anselme
Rault or
    Raoult Jean-Pierre
Raynouard Serge
Reaubert Yves
Relare Marius
Reverdy Louis-Auguste
Renaud Marcel
Reze Jacques
Ricome Auguste
Richard Anselme
Richard-Kerken Marcel-
    Edouard
Richeter Marcel
Rideau Michel
Riffard Serge
Rigal Gaston

Ringuet Marcel-François
Rix Georges-Gabriel
Robert Adolphe
Roche Marcel
Rodetti Pierre
Rodriguez Adolphe
Rohre Marcel
Rolin Paul
Rollin Georges
Roty dit Ryal or
    Raty Armand
Rougier or
    Rouzier Joseph
Roussel Léopold
Rousselin Henri
Roux Jean
Roux Robert
Rovelli Albert
Roy Paul
Rozec Jean-Jules
Saffrey André
Saillard Jean
Salatie Robert
Sangoy Jean
Sanitas André
Santini Joseph
Sarron or
    Sareon Antonin
Schmidt Robert
Schroeder Heinrich
Schirmann Jan
Segeral Henri
Serrero Jean
Seytoux Charles
Sflug Joseph
Souchon Marcel
Starzoniski Edmond
Sulpice Pierre
Szablewski François
Tacher Marius
Tachon René-Paul
Taconnet André
Taillefer André
Taillefer Jean
Tailler Henri
Tardy Roger
Tartière Guy
Teissyere René
Templier Gabriel
Temporal Pierre
Teodosio Arribas
Thedié Maurice
Theron Xavier
Therond Jean-Philippe
Thevenet Louis-Emile
Thevenet Louis-Emile
Thevenot Robert
Toussain Paul
Toussain Pierre
Trahichet François
Tramel Léon
Trehin Ferdinand
Trintignac André

Trodet Joseph
Trousset Paul
Troya Joseph
Vacher Léon
Valentin Fernand
Valoni Jean
Varin Marcel
Vatrin Henri
Vaugel Jacques
Verdier Léon
Viala Gaston

Victor Roger
Vidal Charles
Villeneuve Jules
Vinchon Jules-Julien
Vion Marcel
Vion Michel-Edouard
Viricel Jean-Joseph
Virmoux or
   Voimoux Louis
Vlès Fred
Vivier Louis

Wadoux René
Walser Lucien-Pierre
Watering Cornélius
Werth alias
   Marius Richard
Wons Jean
Yhellou or
   Yhmellou Joseph
Zagaun Roger-Joseph

II. — THE 1,630 SURVIVORS
OF THE DEATH TRAIN

Abadie René
Achard Pierre
Agostini Vincent
Agranier Jean
Ahmed Ben Amara
Albagnac Gilbert
Albert Roger
Alexeline Emile
Alexia Paul
Algret Anselme
Alibert Armand
Alicot André
Allacouf Maurice
Allard Thomas-Ernest
Alligrini Pierre
Allogne Sylvain-Clément
Alphen (Van) Johannes
Amiens or
   Amiel Vincent
Anciand Albert
André Joseph
Andreiss André or
   Jean
Andreu Innocent
Angoste François
Arakelian Arakel
Arbaul Lucien
Arbin Louis
Arbinet André
Archippe André
Ardaillon Jean-Louis
Armand Lucien
Armangue Frédéric
Armengol Victor
Arnoux Gabriel
Arribas Théodosio
Arrieu Jean-Louis
Arveuf Félix
Asselin Gilbert
Atchadourian Agop
Aubergeon André
Aubert Edouard
Aubert Jean

Aubert Victor
Auboiron Jean
Audony Marius
Augagneur Jean
Auger Claude-Roger
Augière Fernand
Auguet Louis-Pierre
Auguste André
Auguste Marceau
Aujol Maurice
Auran Francis
Avora Angel
Aymar Charles
Aymard Robert
Azagra-Ansado Pascal
Azema Robert
Aznard Angel
Back André
Bacon Marcel
Bagarie André
Bagarie Pierre
Baille Robert
Baillot René
Balalud Robert
Balança Jules
Balderelli Louis
Balin André
Balaguer Michel
Ballet Simon
Balp Bruno
Balp Jean
Balp Pierre
Baltet Maurice
Banchelin Gaston
Bandel René
Bandois Florian
Bandras Claude
Baral Arsène
Baraona Louis
Barbazanges Jean-
   Martial
Barbazanges Pierre
Barbier Gabriel

Barbieri Gino
Barbe Emile
Barde François
Bardet Gilbert
Bardou Aimé
Barge Petrus
Bargos Albert
Barlot Joseph
Barrachin Georges
Barrau Jacques
Barre Louis
Barret Jean
Barry de Romanot Alain
Baseaules André
Bassaler Jean
Bastide Pierre
Bastin Pierre
Bateil Joseph
Baud Marius
Baudry Abel
Baudry Henri
Baumgartner Joseph
Bayet François
Bayet Henri
Bayska Wladislaw
Beardot Pascal
Beaufort Alexandre
Beguin René
Beigenger Albert
Bellarbre Robert
Bellier André-Louis
Bellier Paul
Bellot André
Bellot Roger
Ben Azouzi Miloud
Benard Paul
Bennasar Pedro
Benne Gabriel
Benneton Henri
Benoni Gabriel
Bent Philippe
Benthin Jacques
Berchard Laurent

Berger Emile
Bermejo Patrice
Bernachon Pierre-Louis
Bernardie Léonard
Bernado Georges
Bernanos Jean
Bernard Henri
Bernard Maurice
Bernard Pierre
Bernex Jean
Bernit Georges
Beroud Jean
Berrier Roger
Bert Joseph
Berthet Joseph
Bertino Louis
Besse Henri
Besson André
Besson Armand
Besson Roger
Besufeist Adolphe
Betrancourt Henri
Bettinger Charles
Beucler Fernand
Beuruay Clément
Bezia André
Beziau Léon
Biche Jean-Léon
Bidault René-Noël
Bidet Ernest
Billon Pierre
Billot Henri
Binet Pierre
Binger Louis
Bion Paul
Biosca Marius
Bismes Hubert
Biwer Henri
Bixel Georges
Blampain Jean
Blanc Robert
Blanchard Charles-
    Edmond
Blanchet Francisque
Blardone Mario
Bochaton Maurice
Boirier André
Boissat Paul
Boissier Jean
Boitrenaud Lucien
Bonardi Jacques
Bondoux Paul
Bongain Alphonse
Bonhomme Georges
Bonnaire Armand
Bonnard Jacques
Bonnaud Arthur
Bonneau René
Bonnefon Georges
Bonnet Emile
Bonnet Marcel
Bonnet Paul-Louis
Bonnetete Eugène

Bonneville Camille
Bonnot Henri
Bons Etienne
Bontemps Emile
Boquet Charles
Bordes Marcel
Bordus Noël
Bordeu Marius
Borely Pierre-René
Bories Jean
Bosch Raymond
Bost Eugène
Botte Fernand
Botte Raymond
Boucault Pierre
Bouchard Roger
Boucrat Edmond
Boueilh Didier
Bouland André
Bouland Robert
Boulant Jules
Bourdoiseau Marie
Bourgouin Fernand
Bourguet Roland
Bourguignon Louis-
    Maxime
Bourigault Fernand
Bournazel François
Boursier Robert
Boury Robert
Boussion Louis
Boutier Paul
Bouvier Jacques
Bouvier Maurice
Bouygues Jean-Auguste
Bouyssi André
Bouzid Robert
Bozonnet Robert
Bretou André
Breval Jean
Brahin Alexander
Bras André
Brechet Gilbert
Brack Jean ou Jacques
Brechet Raymond
Bredon Pierre
Bretin Maurice
Bretaut or
    Brice Raymond
Brigandat Henri
Brisse Auguste
Brivadier Marcel
Brivadier Maurice
Brochard Maximin
Broggi Victor
Bronchard Jacques
Brouard Georges-Félix
Brousse Jean
Brousse Louis
Bruat Antoine
Bruere Jean
Brumard Roger
Brun Adolphe

Brun Henri
Brun Jean
Brun René
Brunet Georges
Brunet Marcel
Brunet Pierre ou Emile
Brunet René-Gaston
Brunie Léon
Brutelle Maurice
Buatois Marcel
Buatois Roger
Buck Emile
Buiret Joseph
Buisson Marius
Bur Jacques
Buret Albert
Busca Guy
Burgos André
Bussier Lucien
Bussieres Jean
Bzik Jean
Cabocel Georges
Cabocel Louis
Cabocel Lucien
Cadet Honoré
Cadreau René
Callegari Pietro
Cambrun Jules
Camus René
Canac Albert
Cances Marius
Canon Lucien
Cantarzoglou Simon
Capelle Daniel
Capicaumont Roger or
    Claude
Carabajol François
Carbonaro Hugues
Carmagnac Roland
Carmille Léon-François
Carouge André
Carre Abel
Carrère Louis
Carrière Jean
Cartier Roger
Cassagnère Paul
Castagnoli Clément
Castets René
Castex Edouard
Catalano Henri
Catel Auguste
Caumières Raymond
Caussain Robert
Cavaille René-Louis
Cayo or
    Cayre Adrien
Cayre Jean
Cayrel Jacques
Cayrel Maurice
Cazala Roger
Cazes René
Celerier André
Celma Fernand

Cerandon Marcel
Cerveaux René
Cette Roger
Chabbert or
    Chabbart Georges
Chabert Roland
Chaigneau René
Chamouton Marcel
Champeau Paul
Champeaux Jean
Chandioux Jean
Changeat François
Chanourdie Julien
Chanson Albert
Chant Henri
Chantelauze Pierre
Chapalain Jean-Yves
Chapeau Jean-Marie
Chapuis René
Chapus Henri
Charbonneau André
Charbonneau Robert
Charbonnier Maurice
Chardenal Jean-Marie
Charité Maurice
Charlot Georges
Charlot or
    Charbot Lucien
Charmillon René-Léon
Charpentier Julien
Charpentier Albert
Chartier Jean
Chartier Edmond
Chartier Lucien
Chastel Antoine
Chatard Marcel
Chatelard-Toinet Félix
Chatelard-Toinet Henri
Chatelard-Toinet Honoré
Chaubart Henri-Jules
Chaumerliac Jean
Cheneval François
Cherbury Désiré
Chevalier Maurice
Chevrier Maxime
Chiavarini Charles
Chiffre Pierre
Chiron Max
Chocat Emile
Chosson Alfred
Chottin Jean
Citron Pierre
Clair Henri
Clapot François
Claude Jean
Claudel Georges
Clauzade André
Claverie Jean-Marie
Clunet-Coste Eugène
Cluzel Henri
Cluzel Roger
Codonatto Robert
Cochet Robert

Cohn Henri
Coirier Frédéric
Coirier Guy
Coissac Henri
Colbert Henri
Coldefy Henri (Lucien)
Colin Maurice
Collard Lucien
Collas Roger
Collot Désiré
Colognac Pierre
Colombani Gérard
Combaud Henri
Comba Paul
Cominio Amadio
Comino Mario
Comino Virginio
Compagnon Jean
Compagnon Louis
Compagnon Pierre
Condolf René-Marcel
Contesenne Emile
Contesenne Roger
Coquelle René
Corner William
Cornu André
Cosset or Cosse Oscar
Couchoud Claudius-
    Emile
Coudard Gérard
Coudere Raymond
Coudert Lucien
Couhé Henri
Coulaudon Gilbert
Courbon Marius
Couroyer Henri (Louis)
Courteau Lucien
Courtes André
Courtiel Lucien
Courtier Jean
Courtine Marcel
Couteaux Paul
Couvin Robert
Couvry Charles
Cova Santagrou Angel
Coynel Gaston
Cramoix Louis
Crantelle Albert
Craste Joseph
Crespeau Gustave
Crespeaux Amédée
Cristol Raymond
Croiset Louis
Croquet Martial (Marius)
Cros Lucien
Cros Maurice
Dalban Noël
Dallot Auguste
Damiani Jacques
Danguy Jean
Dartout Roger
Dasso Salvatore
Dath Guy

Dauguy Raymond
Daumas André
Dauquier Louis
Dauphin Marcel
David Paul-Pierre
Davies Michel
Dayat or
    Dayet Georges
Debreville Robert
Debrus Julien
Debuire Charles
Decortiat Gabriel
Dehouck Fernand
Deiss Joseph
Dejaeghere André
Dejone Georges
Delacroix Lucien
Delaire Victor
Delamare Joseph
Delampert François
Delauyna Alphonse
Delavert Paul
Delbecque Maurice
Delbeuf Joseph
Delbosse Eloi
Deldon François
Delescot Gilbert
Deligny Léon
Deligny Marcel
Delivet Auguste
Delovard Moise
Delpech André
Delpech Félix
Delpeyrou Louis
Delsol André
Deltrieu Jean
Delvile André
Demaegdt Raymond
Demartine Léon
Demazeau François
Demede François
Demeuse Pierre
Demontferrand Bernard
Denis Jean-Paul
Depraetere Jean
Dequay Aubin
Derdinger Léon
Derichaud Marcel
Deschuymer Henri
Desjardins Henri
Desson Alfred
Detraz Ulysse
Detrée Armand
Deumong or
    Doumenc Jean-Marie
Deumong or
    Doumenc Pierre
Dhaille René
Dhenain Pierre
Diana Cincenco
Diederichs Noël-Alfred
Dilme Amagat
    Gumersindo

Dirson Maurice
Doderer Roger
Dolignon René
Dominguez José
Dominici Joseph
Donche Louis
Doucet Henri
Doudar Henri
Dousson André-Joseph
Dousson Benoît
Doyen or
  Donyen Jean
Dragon René
Druon Jean
Dubreuil Bertrand
Dubreuil Georges
Drouhin Raymond
Drouin Guillaume
Dubarry Gilbert
Dubié Jean
Dubois Alexis
Dubois Louis
Dubois Paul
Duboys Jacques
Dubrenet Louis
Dubreuil Georges
Duchein Jean
Duclos Jean-Marie
Duclos Louis-Jean
Ducloux Simon
Ducrocq Maurice
Duflot Jean-Paul
Dugourgeot Louis
Duhaze Pierre
Dujardin Christian
Dulauroy André
Dulcier Marcel
Dulon Pierre
Dumait Roger
Dumas Jean
Dumas René
Dumont Jean
Dumont Lucien
Dupaza or Dufaza Jean
Dumur René
Dupont Henri-Jacques
Dupuyroux or
  Dupeyroux Simon
Duquesne Bernard
Durand Fernand
Durand René
Dussel Guillaume
Dussopt Pierre
Dussour Paul
Duto Jabat José
Duvivier Louis
Ecochani André
Egger Léon
Egger Paul
Egon Louis
Elouard Robert
Encrevé Pierre
  (born Dec. 8, 1894)

Encrevé Pierre
  (born May 18, 1926)
Engel Georges
Ernst Camille
Escobar Dearte Laurent
Espegel Edmond
Espino-Luengo Felipe
Espitallier Maurice
Estève Jean-Louis
Estforges Jean
Etie Paul
Evrard Eugène
Evrard or
  Euvrard Maurice
Eyssidieux Jean
E... or
  F... (No. 88,006). This
  registration number was
  given to Ernst and to
  another deportee.
  Number 88,005 does
  not exist.
Fabre Maurice
Fage Martial
Fagot Francis
Falgayrac Jacques
Fanni Angelin
Farelle Roger
Fargeot Alexandre
Farjot Jean
Farnaud Raymond
Farre Albert
Farrugia Jean
Fasquet Fernand
Fauchia Virgile
Faugere Raymond
Faugeroux Eugène
Fauriat Marcel
Favre Louis
Fayat Henri
Fayolle or
  Feyolle Louis
Fayt Albert
Febvre Louis
Feddi-Areski L.
Felzine René
Fernandez Ruiz
Ferodet Alain
Ferraton Antoine
Fety Jean
Feuermann Fernand
Feyel André
Fillatre Lucien
Filhol Jean
Filhol Raymond
Finet Claude
Flamant Théodore
Fleutret Jean
Fleynac Pierre
Foix Jean-Louis
Fondrat Roger
Fonfrède Marcel
Fons Justin

Fontaine Paul
Fontan Prosper
Fontbonne Pierre
Forestier Guy
Forestier Noël
Forissier Gaston
Forman Marcel
Fortier Paul
Fortoul Paul
Fouard Marcel
Fourcade Henri
Fourcade Marius-
  François
Fournier Clément
Fournier Roger
Fourreau Lucien
Fourt Raymond
Fraysse Jean
Fremion Roger
Frendenreich Pierre-
  Albert
Fery Pierre
Fretigny Jean
Frety Roger
Fritsch (alias Darry)
  Roger
Fromentin Georges
Fromentin Jean
Fromiou Roger
Fuchs Stéphane
Fully Georges
Furlan Louis
Fuste Hervé
Gagnoux Jean
Gaillard André
Gaillard Gilbert
Gaillard Marcel
Gaillet René
Galand Louis
Galimier Louis-Ernest
Gallet René
Galloy Klébert
Galy Jacques
Galy Léopold
Gamboni Antoine
Gamboni Emile
Gamboni Ermine-Frédéric
Ganière François
Ganivette Raymond
Ganster René
Garcia Francisco
Garcia François
Garcia Henri
Garcia-Morales Ignacio
Garcia Selafi
Gardon Jean
Garesse Gaëtan
Garnal Jacques
Garnier Georges
Garron Léon
Garrouste or
  Garroustex Pierre
Gasset Gabriel

Gaucher Marius
Gauthier Joseph
Gayton Maurice
Geliu André
Genay Roger
Genibredes Emile
Genot Roger
Gensac Jean
Gentel Albert
Genty Claudius
Geoffroy Henri
Georges Maurice
Georgeton Gaston
Gérard Louis
Gérard or
   Girard Roger
Geraudy or
   Geraudie Pierre
Germaine Pierre
Gervais Marc
Geze Charles
Ghisetti Joseph
Ghisgant Marcel
Gibeault Georges
Gibiat François
Gicquel Pierre
Gilbert Octave
Gilfiks Maurice
Gillard Jean (Jacques)
Gilles André
Ginies Albin
Ginoux Louis
Girard Elzear
Girard Henri
Girard Henri M.
Girardon Maurice
Giry Eugène
Gladieu or
   Gladoev Robert
Glass Pierre-René
Glory Ernest
Gloux Pierre
Gobenceaux Jean
Goesin Henri
Goigoux Félix
Golowin Yvan
Gomard René
Gombard Roger
Gomez Louis
Gonzalès André
Gonzales Vincent
Gorse Eugène
Gorse Louis
Gosselin Gaston
Goubert Marius
Goudour Pierre
Gouget Victor
Goulard Gaston
Goulard Georges
Goumard Jacques
Goumy Alexis
Goumy Gabriel
Gouraswski Wladislaw

Gourdin Léonidas
Gourg Pierre
Gourret Paul
Goutaudier Louis
Grandjean Marius
Grandowcz Herszek
Granger Louis
Gras Julien-Joseph
Graux Marcel
Grellier Hubert
Grellier Jean-Marie
Grenier Roger
Grégoire Albert
Groff René
Gros Daniel
Guedo Fernand
Guehenneg or
   Guennec Jean
Guemalmasian Vorak
Guenin Marcel
Guenzi René
Guéraud Claude
Guérin Gustave
Guérin Marcel
Guerlesquin André
Guerlesquin Yves
Guerzoni Jaurès
Guigonis Marcel
Guihard Jules
Guijarro Gregorio
Guilbon Marcel
Guillard Jacques
Guillot Camille
Guimera Jean-Victor
Guinet Georges
Guirandon Hippolyte
Gusse Michel
Guyonnet Claude
Guyonnet Roger
Haadj Raymond
Habermacher Maurice
Hachon André-Auguste
Hairos Louis
Hais Louis
Hardouin Alfred
Harkati Hocine
Harvey Roger
Haymard Gérard
Hazebrouck Robert
Hébert Emile
Hébrard Alfred
Hecht Charles
Hecht Didier
Helluy Joseph
Hennequin Louis
Henrion Henri
Henriot-Colin Marius
Heriot Gaston-Alfred
Héritier Roger
Hernandez-Lopez
   Télesforo
Hernandez Manuel
Heyde or Heyd Henri

Hickel François
Hirbec Henri
Hochedez Lucien
Hortion or Horion Louis
Houde Lucien
Houe André
Houlbregue André
Hoyoux Jean
Hoze Jean-Charles
Huc Ange
Hucq Henri
Huet Jean
Hulin Marcel
Husson Henri
Huyard Henri
Imbert Germain
Istria Simon
Ivars Marius
Izard André
Jacquemaud or
   Jacquemond Pierre
Jacques Jean
Jamain Auguste
Jamain Jean
Jamarin Joseph
Jamonneau Guy
Jane Antoine
Jardin Louis
Jardin René
Jarles Maxime
Jassaud or
   Jessaud Paul
Jaulertou Maurice
Jeandot Eugène
Jeanne Emile
Jeannin Charles
Jeckert Anton
Jessel Eugène
Job Louis
Joffet Robert
Jonquais Georges
Jordery Claude
Josefovits Albert
Joubaud Emile
Joubert Alain
Joubert Gaston-Désiré
Journani Marius
Journet Joseph
Jouvenin Raymond
Judon Félix
Juel François
Juhel Alphonse
Juliot Raymond
Jumeau Jules
Kania or
   Kenia Bernard
Karachi Mohamed
Kasprzay Jean
Kaufmann Albert
Kegel (de) Jean
Keiff Henri
Ker Marcel
Kienzler Alphonse

Klein André
Kozlica Damac
Kreb Alfred
Kuchler Auguste
Labesse Georges
Labolle Paul-Joseph
Labonne Antoine
Laboureur Jean
Labranle Max
Labroche René
Lacaille Georges
Lacaux Georges-Paul
Lacaze Michel-Baptiste
Lachaud Jean
Lacroix Pierre-André
Lafille Georges
Lafitte-Binagrov Frédéric-
  Pierre
Laffon Roger
Laforge Jean-Pierre
Lagaille Bernard
Lagarde Philippe
Lages Marcel
Lages Marcel-Léon
Laidet Marcel
Laigre Jean
Laillette Emile
Lajoix Charles
Lajoumard Jean
Lajudie Maurice
Laliemand Léopold
Lalut Henri
Lamada Auguste
Lamarque Maurice
Lambert Charles
Lambert Emile
Lambert Henri
Lambert Jacques
Lambert Lucien
Lamirault Claude
Landbeck René
Landou Abel
Langa-Louret Jean-
  Robert
Lanze Robert
Laporte Jean
Laporte Joseph
  (born July 6, 1910)
Laporte Joseph
  (born Feb. 2, 1922)
Laporte Robert
Larcher André
Lardy Lucien (Julien)
Larnac Etienne
Larnaud Georges
Lartigues Jean
Lasnet de Lanty Jean
Lassus Jean
Latour Jacques
Laurent Christian
Laurent Jean-Marc
Laurent Paul
  (born Sept. 30, 1921)

Laurent Paul
  (born Oct. 8, 1925)
Lautissier Jean
Laval Claude-Pierre
Lazard Gilbert
Lazcane Gia
Lebail Honoré
Le Bean Marcel
Le Botlan André
Lebrun Gustave
Le Caguie Albert
Lecamus Simon
Leccia Joseph
Leccia Laurent
Lecène Pierre
Lechevallier Philippe
Leclercq Bernard
Lecordon Louis
Le Coq Joseph
Le Diguerber Patrick
Lediouris Jacques
Ledouguet Alexis
Lefebre Emile
Lefile Maurice
Lefloch Louis
Le Français Louis
Le Gardic André-Marie
Leger Pierre
Leglien Albert
Le Goff Lucien
Legrange André
Legreve Léon-Eugène
Legros Robert
Le Guen Jean
Le Guern Yves
Leichman Eugène
Leidner Christian-Célestin
Lejeune Jacques
Le Lamer Martial
Lelench Mathurin
Lemaire Charles
Leman Henri
Le Marie Pierre
Lemoine René
Le Moullec Jean
Lempa Georges
Lenard Camille
Lenard Joseph
Lencou Roger
Le Névé César
Le Ny Yves
Leobal Jacques
Léonard Michel
Le Page Louis
Le Penant Christian
Lepert Edouard
Le Play Auguste
Le Pley Hugues
Leprettre Raoul
Lequeux Roger
Lequin Etienne
Leraille Camille
Le Roux Armand

Leroux or
  Larouex Emile
Leroux Louis-Marie
Lesaffre Emile
Lesage Ernest
Le Senn Louis
Le Sausse Jean
Lescop André
Lesevre Georges
Lemile Jean
Levasseur Marcel
Leveque or
  Levegue Gaston
Levicille Charles
Levillain Félix
Leygnac Marcel
Lhopitault Désiré
Limousin Henri
Liotier Henri
Lidust or
  Liust Henri
Lochv Maurice
Loire André
Loiseau Justin or
  Loisseau Juste
Lopez Joseph
Lormet or
  Lhermet Pascal
Loubet Marius
Louis Emile
Lousteau Cyprien
Luc Georges
Lucas Louis
Lukasiewicz Joseph
Lupart Fernand
Lupetit Jean-Louis
Lurier Albert
Lurol René
Lutz Jacques
Macheny Emile
Madaule Pierre
Madelmont Jean-Pierre
Maffre Clément-Henri
Mailly-Nesle (de) Jean
Mainetti Jacques
Maire André
Maire René
Maistre Joseph
Maksymio Jean
Malaquin René
Mallet Marcel
Malleucci Paul
Malmartel Marc
Malthet Gaston
Malzac Eugène
Mamon Pierre-Eugène
Mangematin Emile
Marcano Louis
Marceau Maurice
Marchand Igor
Marchive or
  Marcive Gaston
Marconnet André

Maréchal or
  Maréchel Paul
Marenbaud Georges
Margerit Robert
Marguin Georges
Mari Paul
Marijuan Louis
Mariermann or
  Marionneau Maurice
Marques Armand-Alfred
Marsille Alain
Marteau or
  Martenu Maurice
Martel Jean-Louis
Martin Albert
Martin Charles
Martin Louis
  (born Sept. 4, 1911)
Martin Louis
  (born Feb. 1, 1923)
Martin Paul
Martinel or
  Mertinel Georges-Louis
Martinot Pierre-Maurice
Martinez Avelino
Martinez Dilio
Martinez Jean (Johan)
Martz Paul-Charles
Marynis Charles
Mas André
Masajada Joseph
Massegasa or
  Masegosa Paul
Masset Louis-Robert
Massias Jean
Massias Lucien
Massip Germain
Masson Georges
Masson Gustave
Massoulle Pierre
Matayvage or
  Matayvege François-
  Victor
Mathieu Claude
Mathieu Marcel-François
Mattéo or
  Matéo Henri
Maupoil Bernard
Maurel Armand
Mazaud Lucien
Mazel André
Mazic or
  Mazie Victorin
Mazot Roger
Méant Louis
Mechin André
Meffre René
Meï Bengazi
Melesi Louis
Ménard Maurice
Méon Gilbert
Méquillet Michel
Mercier Charles

Mercier Marcel
Mérec Jean
Méric or
  Mévic Jean-Pierre
Merle Eugène-François
Mesle Roger
Metrat René
Mettey René
Meunier Albert
Meunier René-Lionel
Meyer André
Meyer Paul
Michaut Victor
Micheau Henri
Michel Marius
Michelot or
  Mechelod Jacques
Micheu Pierre-Roland
Miel Auguste
Migeat Jean
Miglionico Paul
Maignard or
  Mignard Auguste
Milani Joseph
Mile Nicolich
Milhau Henri
Mille Serge
Millet Jean-Charles
Millienne René
Minvielle Pierre-Joseph
Miquel François
Miro Jean
Modere or
  Modéro Emile
Mohrade or
  Mohorade Martin
Moine Lucien
Mokkfi Rabat
Molina Marcel
Mommessin Maurice
Monaihy or
  Monamy Louis
Monel or Morcel André
Monguillon Henri-Jean
Moniez François
Monneret Etienne
Mounen Nicolas
Montagne Maurice
Moutagne or
  Montagne Jean
Moutagné or
  Montagne Claudius
Monteil Raymond
Montjanel Léon
Montmory Marius
Montorsi Robert
Moral Jean
Moral or
  Morel Maurice
Morand Gustave
Mordziatek Casimir
Moreau André
Moreau Armand

Moreau Edouard
Moreau Marcel
Moreau Pierre
Morel André
Morello Jean-Joseph
Moreno Joseph
Morfet Jean-Baptiste
Morge Marcel
Morge Pierre
Morgon Georges
Morin Louis
Morisson Paul-François
Morlanne Louis-André
Morlet Jean
Morlot Louis
Mouchet François
Mouchot Paul
Moulin André
Moulis Henri
Mouret René
Mournetas François
Mouton Albert
Mules Victor
Mummolo Joseph
Munier Albert
Nantois Pierre
Napoléon Jacques-Marie
Navrot Henri
Nees Charles
Neron Pierre
Neyrat Henri
Nicolaie Raymond
Nicot Joseph
Nicourt Albert
Nivet Albert
Noblet André
Nodot René
Nouailhaguet Julien
Nouveau Albert
Nouveau André
Nouveau Georges
Nouzies Paul
Ny Raymond
Ochsenbein Jacques
Oleksiak François
Oria Victoriano
Orlic Pierre
Orloff Georges
Orvain Pierre
Ortu Robert
Osos Paul
Osti Eugène
Oury Jean
Ouvrieu Charles
Pade Aimé
Page André
Pages Jean
Pages Justin
Pagetti Gavroche
Pailhes Georges
Pajot Lucien
Palabost or
  Palabast Joseph

Palier Charles
Palumdo or
  Palumbo Cologuo
Panchetti Jean-Charles
Panicalli or
  Panicali Paul
Pannetiers Gilbert
Pardo Manuel
Parfait Raymond
Parhillat Emile
Paris Philippe
Parouty Marcel
Parrot Marcel
Parry Jean
Pascal Jean
Pascal Lucien
Pascal Roger
Passuto Guerino
Pastuier Jean
Paupy Henri
Pedron Alexis
Pegard Maurice
Peghaire Raymond
Pelatz Paul
Pelias Léon
Pelissier Félix-Roger
Pellat-Finet or
  Pellat-Binet Alphonse
Pellaut Constant
Pellegeais Lucien
Pelletier or
  Pellitier Simon
Pelot Albert
Peltzer François-Jean-
  Louis
Penelle Paul
Penfornis Jean
Perault Jean-Jacques
Perdreau Jacques
Péré Jean-Emilien
Perez François
Pérez Martinez-Pédro
Périaut Eugène
Perraca Philibert
Perraudière (de La)
  Bernard
Perreolaz Jean
Perrichon Georges
Perrier André
Perrier Aimé-Joseph
Perrin Marc
Perrisin Jean
Perrot France
Perrot Albert-Maurice
Perrot Marcel
Peters Ludovic
Petit André
Petit Charles
Petit Henri
Petit Jean
Petit Marceau
Petit Paul
Petitjean Alfred

Petitjean Marcel
Petitot André
Petonnet Henri
Petrov Ivan
Peuch Paul
Peupion Félix
Peyrateaud Joseph
Peyron Guy
Pezery Maurice
Philippe Achille
Picard Louis
Pichene Louis-Alfred
Pichot Roger
Picot de Pledran Olivier
Picote Georges
Picques or
  Piques Jules
Piedbout Gaston
Pieters Jean
Pietke François-Joseph
Pietric Stanislas
Pillian or
  Pillon Victor
Pillot Gérard
Pinaud Rémy
Pioline Auguste
Planchard Maurice
Planque Edouard
Planteligne Louis
Plantier Pierre-Lucien
Plantin Pierre-Paul
Plas Léon
Plas Léopold
Plé Bernard
Plique Raymond
Plumet Pierre
Pochon Henri-François
Poclet Bernard
Podevin Jean
Point Bernard
Poirier André
Pollet Léon
Pompily François
Poncy or
  Ponca Louis
Pontonnier Claude
Portales Miguel
Porte André
Portes Jean-Gabriel
Portier Roger
Posluszny Jean
Potreau Victor
Pouchet Raoul
Pougeon André
Pougheon Jean
Pouleriguen Yves
Poulet Roger
Poulin Georges
Pouly Marcel
Pourcignes Henri-Paul
Pouzeratte Ernest
Pouzioux Alexandre
Prapuolenis Joseph

Prat Jean-Félix
Prefale or
  Prefole Joseph
Pretto Guido
Prevel René
Prevost Alphonse
Priem Albert
Prieto Joseph
Priolon Paul
Priou Raymond
Proust André
Prugnard André
Pungnaud René
Puech Jean
Puyo René-Jean
Quemere Jean
Quémerais Jean
Quequiner or
  Queguiner Jean
Quinet Cyprien
Rabaté Lucien
Rabinovitsch Léon
Ramage Antoine
Ramond or
  Ramen Louis
Ratajezyk Stanislas
Rathberger Pierre
Rathonie Louis
Ratier André
Ratisbonne Jacques
Ravatin Jean
Raymond Jean
Raynaud Pierre
Rebiere Pierre
Regat Francis
Regis Jean
Reglan or
  Regla Martin
Remaury Jacques-Paul
Remond Louis
Remy Pierre
Renard Guillaume
Renaut Auguste
Renouard Joseph
Resseguier Léon
Rey Johanès
Reynaud Marcel-Joseph
Rheinhardt Emile-
  Alphonse
Riand Edmond-Jean
Richard Henri
Richard Joseph
Ricong Roger
Rieussec Théophile
Rigollot Etienne
Ringard Georges
Riol Pierre
Riot or
  Riost René
Rival or
  Rykner Gabriel
Rivero-Garcia Auguste
Rivoal Yves

Robert Pierre
Robidet René
Robin Louis
Roches-Bernariat
  François
Roche Pierre
Rocher Auguste
Rochet Charles
Rodet Louis
Rodriguez Vendrell
Roger Alphonse
Roger Henri
Roger Marcel
Rohmer Francis
Roland Maurice
Rolland Jean
Rolland Olivier
Rolle Georges
Rollot Raymond
Ronceray Georges
Ropars Pierre
Ropiquet Pierre
Roqueirol Marcel-
  Adolphe
Roman Alexandre
Rosier Georges
Rosier Jean
Rossetti Pietro
Rossi Jean
Rossignol André
Rospars Robert
Roudaut Armand
Rouillon Roger
Roule or
  Roure Jean
Rousseaux Jean
Roussel François
Roussel Roger
Roussette Victor
Roux Antoine
Roux Emile-Pierre
Roy Fernand
  (born March 19, 1922)
Roy Fernand
  (born July 16, 1896)
Roy Maurice
Rozan Camille
Rudeau Georges
Ruigblanque or
  Puigblanque Alexandre
Ruamps Eugène
Ruamps Henri
Rusciek Jean
Sabatier Robert
Sablé Marcel
Sadaune or
  Sadaume Maurice
Sagnet Paul
Sajoux Jean
Sallaud Yvon-Eugène
Salle André-René
Sala Gérard
Salasc or Salase Roger

Salin Marcel
Salitet Henri
Salomon René
Sanauc Aventin
Sanchez-Escriban
  Joachim
Santos-Gonzales Antonio
Sarrau or
  Sarran Pierre
Sarrault Pierre
Sauliere Jean-Louis
Sauret Alphonse
Sauteraud Lucien
Savary Célestin
Savary Joseph
Saves André
Savigny Jean-Gaston
Sayer or
  Soyer Henri
Scardac Aba or
  Aba Scerdace
Seidler Léon
Sénéchal Julien
Scoffier Louis-Jacques
Scotto di Rinaldi Louis
Schaumacker Achille
Schatz Joseph
Schelstraete Télesphore
Schenke Edmond
Scherrer Paul
Schlesser François
Schier Richard
Schier Robert
Schmerer Noël
Schneider Tadeuz
Schouchine Nicolas
Schoullier René
Schre Augustin
Schwad Henri
Schwartz Jean
Secretant Charles
Segelle Pierre
Seigneuret or
  Seingneuret Henri
Sellenet Fernand
Sellenet Pierre
Serre Armand
Serre Charles
Serre René
Sergent Pierre
Servant Etienne
Sevat Robert
Sicre Roger
Sidoli Antonio
Sibut Edouard-Joseph
Silvestri Narcisse
Simon André
Siret Bernard
Sirvent Eugène
Sivek Stanislas
Solladin Raymond
Slipko André
Sombstay Jean

Sordet or
  Sordot Jean
Sotton Alexandre
Sotton Jannes
Soucaze des Soucaze
  Firmin
Soucaze des Soucaze
  Sylvain
Soulange-Bodin Roger-
  Noël
Soulier Marie-Marc
Saullisse or
  Soulisse Maurice
Spriet Marcel
Spules Jan
Stankowitch Eugène
Steff Joseph-Jules
Stefanini or
  Stefani Alexandre
Stemler René
Stoppazo Pierre
Surdol Henri
Susini Jean
Tagnard Paul
Taillade Jean
Tajan Pierre
Talbordet or
  Talberdet Ernest
Talou Raymond
Tallet Pierre
Tangre Georges
Tapia or
  Tapin Michel
Tarbouriech Maurice
Tarillon Augustin
Tarrerias Marcel
Tastayre Paul
Tcherkachienne
  Constantin
Teichmuller Jacques
Teiler Roger
Terrasse Jean
Terrassier Léopold
Terrise Marius
Terry Michel
Tessier Marcel
Tessiot Paulin
Tesson André
Teysonnière (de La)
  Joseph-Henri
Thamie Claude
Thebaut Michel
Tely Georges
Therme Xavier
Thery Paul
Thevenet Jean
Theyssier Robert
Thiery Gérard
Thierry René
Thillot Auguste
Thillot Jules
Thomas Albert
Thomas Jean

Thomas Marcel
Thomas Roger
Thomelet Joseph
Thomet André
Tiercelin Fernand
Tiercelin Jacques
Tiollier Victor
Tixier André
Togni Jean
Toucard Aimé
Tougard Maurice
Touré Etienne
Tourier Jean-Jacques
Tournarie Jean
Tournois Jean
Tourvielle Auguste
Trajan Guy
Troyka Jean
Tresallet Louis
Trincal Gaston
Troncin Guillaume
Trousseau Michel
Truchard Jean
Uber Maurice
Urzhy Thomas
Usnarski Joseph
Vacher Arsène
Vadot Ludovic-Arnold
Vaissie Cyrille
Vaissie René
Valade Henri
Vales Germain
Valette Georges
Vallon Robert
Valiton Yves
Valours Jean

Vauclin André
Vautey Louis
Vera-Mariano Michel
Verchuren André
Verdier Paul
Verdier Pierre
Vergne Marcel
Vessières André
Verlhac Albert
Vésir Antoine
Vésir Jacques
Viacroze Jean-Auguste
Viani Charles
Viard Charles
Vidal Antonio
Vidal Michel
Vidalie Raymond
Vigne Jean-Martial
Vignon Georges-Michel
Vigour Marcel
Vigouroux Georges
Vigouroux Louis
Vigouroux Maurice
Vigouroux Roger
Villedieu François
Villeneuve Aimé
Villette Bernard
Villevieille Julien
Villiers Georges
Vinaty Noël
Vincent Jacques
Vincent Louis
Vincent Roger
Vindret Gilbert
Viola Georges
Vivet Marc

Vogel Jacob
Voutey Maurice
Vurgnoux Manos
Walker Jacques
Wayant Emile
Wawryszkiewicz
    Wladyslaw
Wecknmann Pierre
Weil Paul
Weiss Georges
Wesse Robert
Wetta André-Louis
Wetta René-Léon
Weyne Marcel
Wicker François
Willieme Roger
Winter Louis
Woloszynowsky Stéphan
Wons or
    Edouard (Konrad)
Wroz or
    Wros André
Wyzsocki or
    Wysocki Félix
Wyntg or
    Wyntz Edouard
Yan Yves
Ybert Désiré
Ysabella Emile
Zakrejvski Yefime
Zielinski Victor
Zelek Edouard-Jean
Zebrit Saïd
Zabinski Tadeuz
Zo Georges

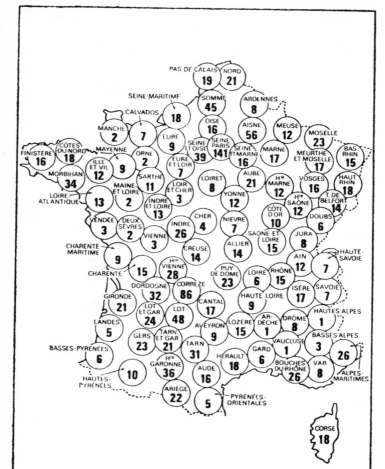

The deportees of the Death Train
by department of origin

(This diagram covers only 1,486 names)

Nationalities

The nationalities of the 1,630 survivors of the Death Train were as follows:

American	2
Austrian	3
Belgian	7
Dutch	1
English	2
French	1,511
German	1
Greek	3
Hungarian	2
Italian	16
Polish	24
Romanian	1
Russian	5
Spanish	40
Swiss	7
Turk	1
Yugoslav	4

Phenomena which appear in a confined atmosphere, due to the crowding of human beings in a restricted space: Guillaume TRONCIN, pharmacist.

(1) *Deficiency of oxygen.* Privation of oxygen leads to torpor which ends in death without psychic disturbances. This is not what occurred in a large number of the cars.

(2) *Elevation of partial pressure by carbonic anhydride (CO_2), not to be confused with carbon monoxyde.*

We are convinced that this gas was responsible for the symptoms. The very long stops of the train in the midst of the heat, and without the least current of air, made air renewal impossible.

The carbonic anhydride was produced by:

(a) the exhalation of the confined men; and

(b) the fermentation of the straw.

Carbonic anhydride, or carbon dioxide, being heavier than air, an atmosphere, constantly poorer in oxygen and richer in CO_2 formed immediately above the flooring of the car. Furthermore, in many cars, arguments, gesticulations and fights aggravated this process. When the men imitated the technique of submarine crews in difficulty, i.e., not moving, not speaking, and breathing the least possible, there were practically no deaths.

In my own case, my intoxication must have brought me very close to the point of no return. As a matter of fact, I was affected by hallucinatory disturbances which the other survivors do not seem to have experienced.

I was fully conscious of being in a train of deportees, taking me to Germany, but I was watching a very violent and lengthy battle, with weapons, between two clans. Yet, I learned later that, during the night of July 2-3, there had been no fighting in our car.

(3) The presence of carbon monoxide, if any combustion occurs, which was not the case for us.

(4) Presence of toxic amines and amides.

(5) Presence of urea which is transformed into ammonia. However, I do not recall any ammoniated odor.

(6) Increase in temperature augments the phenomena of pulmonary ventilation, hence of perspiration which also provokes cardiac disorders.

(7) Several deportees spoke of abundant sweating. In such cases an imbalance of the hydro-mineral system is produced and what the English term "heat exhaustion" appears. This imbalance is accelerated in the dark.

(8) It is found that heat at ground level modifies the oxygen and makes it less assimilable, in this way increasing the disorders due to its lack. And, in our case, almost all of us were lying down.

(9) It has been ascertained that crowding provokes syndromes of anguish and psychic disorders. By reason of the agitation they stimulate, these in turn, increase the consumption of oxygen and the level of CO_2 in the air.

To give you an example: if the material deposited on a cold wall in a confined atmosphere is collected, the product thereof, injected into an animal, will bring about its immediate death.

To summarize, a number of separate factors were at work and it is difficult to determine which of them was predominant.[1]

1.   Guillaume Troncin lives near Compiègne, and every morning he waits for the train that will take him to Paris, in front of the platform where, on a certain July 2, 1944, he embarked for Dachau.

ACKNOWLEDGMENTS

On October 1, 1970 the list of survivors of the Death Train that I had been able to reconstitute contained 347 names. Out of these 347 deportees, 161 agreed to draft an account of their voyage, specifically for this book. These are cited in footnotes as "unpublished manuscript" I thank them in particular. This book is their book.

Agranier Jean (Arpajon)
Arakelian Arakel (Bollène)
Aubert Edouard (Paris)
Auganeur Jean (Vienne)
Bagarie André (Farges-en-Septaine)
Balp Bruno (Paris)
Balp Jean (Créteil)
Balp Pierre (Paris)
Baltet Maurice (Marseilles)
Barbazanges Jean (Tulle)
Barlot Joseph (Saint-Ours-lès-Roch)
Bellot Roger (Noyon)
Berger Emile (Beaumont-de-Périgord)
Bernado Georges (Pavie)
Bernard Pierre (Aire-sur-la-Lys)
Bert Joseph (Lachaux)
Beziau Léon (Angers)
Bidault Noël (Tours)
Billot Henri (Le Puy)
Biosca Marius (Nîmes)
Bixel Georges (Saint-Gaudens)
Bondois Florian (Le Tignet)
Bonneau René (Tulle)
Bozonnet Robert (Ambérieux-en-Dombes)
BronchardJacques(Reims)

Canac Albert (Toulouse)
Carrère Louis (Salles-sur-Adour)
Catalano Henri (Nice)
Cayrel Jacques (Figeac)
Cette Roger (Le Puy)
Chanourdie Lucien (Tulle)
Chapalain Jean-Yves (Le Mans)
Charpentier Albert (Neufchâtel-sur-Aisne)
Chaubart Henri (Vaux-sur-Seine)
Chosson Alfred (Cournon d'Auvergne)
    Manuscript arrived too late.
Clunet-Coste Eugène (Grenoble)
Cluzel Henri (Saint-Etienne)
Coirier Frédéric (Foussais)
Cornu André (Lignères)
Coulaudon Gilbert (Châteauroux)
Couvin Robert (Sedan)
Dartout Roger (Limoges)
Delescot Gilbert (Loivre)
Deltrieu Jean (Angoulême)
Desjardin Henri (Poulainville)
Dessimond Paul (Mably)

Dhenain Pierre (Grand-
  Quevilly)
Drelon Pierre (Tulle)
Engrève Pierre (Foussais)
Espino-Luengo Felipe
  (Saint-Paul-de-Jarrat)
Espitallier Maurice
  (Antibes)
Evrard Eugène (Cahors)
Fabre Maurice (Nîmes)
Fagot Francis (Rouen)
Farjot Jean (Le Coteau)
Favre Louis (Caussade)
Foix Jean-Louis
  (Lannemezan)
Fonfrède Marcel (Grenoble)
Forestier Guy (Paris)
Fourcade Henri (Toulon)
Fuchs Stéphane (Paris)
Fully Georges (Paris)
Gaillard Marcel
  (Bonnatrait-Sciez)
Garcia Henri
  (Castelmaurou)
Garcia-Santos Antoine
  (Saint-Paul-de-Jarrat)
Garnal Jacques (Cahors)
Gasset Gabriel (Clermont-
  l'Hérault)
Glory Ernest (Verlhac-
  Tescou)
Gonzalès André
  (Toulouse)
Gorawski Wladislaw
  (Toulon)
Gourg Pierre (Semalens)
Grenier Roger (Chambon-
  Feugerolles)
Gros Daniel (Volvic)
Guéraud Claude (Mâcon)
Guérin Marcel (Margny-
  lès-Compiègne)

Habermacher Maurice
  (Vénissieux)
Hamburger Gilbert (Paris)
Helluy Joseph (Nancy)
Hoyoux Jean (Marrakech,
  Maroc)
Huyard Henri (Poitiers)
Journet Marius (Pressiat-
  Treffort)
Kienzler Alphonse
  (Mulhouse)
Klein André (Marseilles)
Labolle Paul (Montauban)
Lacaze Michel
  (Villebrumier)
Lambert Henri (Niort)
Larnac Etienne (Arles)
Lartigues Jean (Tulle)
Laslier Albert (Peymenade)
Laval Claude (Castres)
Lecène Pierre (Caen)
Lefrançois Luis
  (Combourg)
Lepenant Christian
  (Fougères)
Liotier Henri (Nevers)
Louis Emile (Amiens)
Lutz Jacques (Voiron)
Madaule Pierre (Castres)
Maire René (Grenoble)
Mamon Pierre (Castres)
Marteau Maurice (Magne)
Martinez Jean (Cahors)
Mas André (Montauban)
Masset Robert (Tours)
Mechin André (Neuilly-
  sur-Seine)
Mercier Marcel (Paris)
Michaut Victor (Clamart)
Migeat Jean (Reims)
Monneret Etienne
  (Thoissey)

Moreau Marcel (Mornex)
Mourmetas François (Tulle)
Oria Victoriano (L'Union)
Orvain Pierre (Paris)
Parrot Marcel (Chinon)
   Manuscript arrived too late.
Pascal Lucien (Clermont-Ferrand)
Pelet Pierre (Vire)
Pelot Albert (Oiselay)
Perraudière (de La) B. (Limoges)
Perreolaz Jean (Aulnay-sous-Bois)
Perrin Marc (Lyons)
Petit André (Montpezat-de-Quercy)
Poclet Bernard (Le Cannet)
Praetere (de) Jean (Rosières-Saint-André, Belgique)
Prapuolenis Joseph (Crosnes)
   Manuscript arrived too late.
Préfole Joseph (Roanne)
Prungnaud René (Bron)
Puyo René (Bordeaux)
Remaury Jacques (Saverdun)
Renouard Joseph (Saint-Brieuc)
Richaud (de) Marcel (Cormeilles-en-Parisis)
Rohmer Francis (Strasbourg)
Ropiquet Pierre (Niort)
Rouillon Roger (Saint-Maur)

Roux Pierre (Champagnac-le-Vieux)
Rovan Joseph (Meudon)
Rozan Camille (Calais)
Rykner Gabriel (Ozoir-la-Ferrière)
Salle André (Annonay)
Samuel Jean (Rouen)
Serre Armand (Alès)
Sirvent Eugène (Paris)
Solladié Raymond (Tarbes)
Soules Jean (Pont-de-la-Maye)
Tastayre Paul (Decines)
Tessiot Paulin (Saint-Michel-sur-Orge)
Thely Georges (Imphy)
Thomas Albert (Penhars)
Thomas Jean (Rouen)
Tixier André (Dijon)
Troncin G. (Compiègne)
Vauclin André (Martainville-Epreville)
Verchuren André (Chantilly)
Vésir Antoine (Cahors)
Viacroze Jean (Tulle)
Viard Charles (Grand-Couronne)
Villedieu Jean (Beaumont)
Villevieille Julien (Aix-en-Provence)
Villiers Georges (Paris)
Voutey Maurice (Dijon)
Weil Paul (Paris)
Wicher François (Saint-Benoît-de-Carmaux)
Zielinski Victor (Commentry)

I ALSO THANK:

Monsieur Michel Debré, Minister of State for National Defense; Monsieur André Fanton, Secretary of State; Monsieur Perier, Director of Police and Military Justice; Monsieur Berger, on detached service, who gave me access to the files of the Procedure of the Permanent Tribunal of Metz, assigned to the "Dietrich affaire."

Monsieur Pierre Garban, in charge of installations in the Ministry for Veterans' Affairs, who has built up, since 1945, many detailed studies of classification covering all the concentration camps and who allowed me to consult his voluminous archives (see Annex IV).

Herr Karl Sauer of the *Vereinigung der Verfolgten des Naziregimes* (Frankfurt-am-Main).

Monsieur Jean-Marie Fassina, for Arolsen.

Monsieur Paul Durand, Honorary General Inspector of the S.N.C.F., historian of the Iron Resistance, and also the press services of the S.N.C.F.

Monsieur Edmond Michelet, President of the *Anciens de Dachau* (former prisoners of Dachau), and Doctor Georges Fully, its General Secretary, both of whom gave me valuable advice on the preparation of this book.

*   *   *

But this effort to reconstitute the voyage which started July 2, 1944, could never have been accomplished without the additional help of very many witnesses who were not part of the convoy, and agreed to meet me or to prepare special "unpublished manuscripts" as the travelers in the train had done.

FOR COMPIÈGNE

Boissonnat Odile (Paris)
Charpentier Paul (Pau)
Cremel Raymond (Saint-Jouy)
Dorgny Martial (Compiègne)

Dumas M. (Saint-Quentin)
Forré Yvette (Compiègne)
Frizon Cyriaque (Compiègne)
Gervais Philippe (Paris)
Jacquet Raymond (La

Tour-du-Pin)
Lecoq Emile (Compiègne)
Merlin Raoul (Compiègne)
Pâques Alfred
  (Compiègne)
Poiret Roland (Clairoix)

Monseigneur Théas Pierre-
  Marie (Tarbes)
Agency of the *Parisien
  Libéré.*
Station Chief
Red Cross Committee

Monsieur André Poirmeur, the first historian of the Camp of Compiègne gave me the benefit of his vast experience and made his archives available to me. As for Monsieur Marcel Guérin, a deportee on the Death Train, he was tireless in his search at Compiègne, for the S.N.C.F. personnel who had participated in the formation and the conducting of the train.

FOR SOISSONS

Dessongins Louis
  (Venizel)
Mme Frot J. (Soissons)
Legros François alias
  "Paul" (Crouy)
Mangotte M. (Couloisy)
Obrier Cady (Soissons)

Obrier Paul (Soissons)
Mme Pennard (de) (Paris)
Seudron M. (Chief of
  Soissons Station)
Countess Olivier de La
  Rochefoucauld
Red Cross Committee

FOR SAINT-BRICE

Antoine Georgette (Saint-
  Brice)
Aubert Pierre (Reims)
Bardin Jules (Reims)
Barthélémy René
  (Reims)
Billaudelle Jean (Saint-
  Brice)
Chenet Marcel (Reims)
Florenz Raymond (Reims)
Gérard Claude (Reims)
Lapierre Julienne (Saint-
  Brice)

Maujean Laurent (Saint-
  Brice)
Maujean Pierre (Saint-
  Brice)
Mme Morizet (Reims)
Pasquier Réjane (Reims)
Pinel J. (Saint-Brice)
Tisseur Denise
  (Châteauroux)
Tisseur Robert
  (Châteauroux)
Viret Marthe (Châteauroux)
Viret Raymond (Reims)

Most of these witnesses were found thanks to the efforts of Daniel Pellu, information chief of the newspaper *L'Union* (Reims).

FOR REIMS

Baveret Andrée (Reims)
Gérard Claude (Reims)
Mulette Pierre (Reims)
Nicolas Marceau
  (Reims)
Pélican Lucien (Reims)
Perraux Gaston (Reims)

Mme Pierre Fernande
  (Reims)
Renard Paul Emile (Reims)
Rousset Jean (Reims)
Station Chief
Red Cross Committee
Newspaper *L'Union*

FOR CHÂLONS-SUR-MARNE

Adalbert Louis (Châlons)
Bertrand Noël (Châlons)
Sister Gasnier, Daughter of
  Charity

Station Chief
Red Cross Committee

FOR FISMES, BAR-LE-DUC

Durand Henri
Louis (Station Chief)
Nickelaus James

Bardin Ernest
Bellier J.
Cochenet M.

FOR FRONTIGNY, LEMUD, PELTRE

Boime Andrée
Boime Edouard
Boime Eugénie

Morainville Charles
Mme Vogein J.
Schneider Jules

FOR NOVÉANT

Falala Bernard
Petitcolas Maurice

Schnaebele Antoine
Teyssères Marcel

FOR SARREBOURG

Bauman Julien
Mme Boulier F.
Dillenschneider Joseph
Dreidemy Eugène
Friant Michel
Genevé Charles
Gérardin A. (Main Station Chief)
Hiebel Charles
Kitta Bernard
Koestler Alice
Koestler Jean
Mme Konanz S.
Martin Jules
Mulherr Roderich (Heidelberg)

Muller René (Doctor)
Oliger Auguste
Mme Rohfritsch
Rouschmeyer Auguste
Schaefer Cyril
Schnepf René (Assistant Station Chief)
Schnitzer Albert
Spitz Marie
Ulm Georges
Paul Benz (Assistant Chief Editor of the *Républicain Lorrain*)
R. Schoeser (Agency of *Républicain Lorrain,* at Sarrebourg)

FOR HAGUENAU

Gerber M. (Station Chief)   Reichmann Ernest

FOR DACHAU (ARRIVAL)

Berthelemy Jean   Fabing Léon

Documents collected by the *Amicale de Dachau*: Prosper Fontan; Pierre Bernachon; Marcel Chamouton; Constand Tcherkachine; Lieutenant Colonel Portes.

* * *

And finally, my special thanks go to: Jean-Baptiste Mahaut; Georges Montefusco; Jacques Salvarini; Alain and Janine Tubiana, who patiently and efficiently established the index file of the deportees of July 2, of the convoy dead, of the survivors (see Annex IV).

* * *

TABLE OF CONTENTS

Printed in Spain
Published by Ferni
Distributed by Friends of History

Printer industria gráfica sa   Tuset, 19   Barcelona
Sant Vicenç dels Horts   1978
Depósito legal B. 12535-1978
Printed in Spain